Perspectives on Artificial Intelligence in Times of Turbulence:

Theoretical Background to Applications

Nuno Geada
ISCTE, University Institute of Lisboa, Portugal

George Leal Jamil
Informações em Rede C e T Ltda., Brazil

A volume in the Advances in
Computational Intelligence and
Robotics (ACIR) Book Series

Published in the United States of America by
IGI Global
Engineering Science Reference (an imprint of IGI Global)
701 E. Chocolate Avenue
Hershey PA, USA 17033
Tel: 717-533-8845
Fax: 717-533-8661
E-mail: cust@igi-global.com
Web site: http://www.igi-global.com

Library of Congress Cataloging-in-Publication Data

Names: Geada, Nuno, 1983- editor. | Jamil, George Leal, 1959- editor.
Title: Perspectives on artificial intelligence in times of turbulence :
    theoretical background to applications / edited by Nuno Geada, George
    Leal Jamil.
Description: Hershey, PA : Engineering Science Reference, [2024] | Includes
    bibliographical references and index. | Summary: "This book focuses on
    strategic business goals and objectives, productivity, communication,
    improvement, and elasticity when dealing with Artificial Intelligence"--
    Provided by publisher.
Identifiers: LCCN 2023034574 (print) | LCCN 2023034575 (ebook) | ISBN
    9781668498149 (hardcover) | ISBN 9781668498187 (paperback) | ISBN
    9781668498156 (ebook)
Subjects: LCSH: Artificial intelligence--Industrial applications. |
    Artificial intelligence--Social aspects.
Classification: LCC TA347.A78 P47 2024 (print) | LCC TA347.A78 (ebook) |
    DDC 006.3--dc23/eng/20231102
LC record available at https://lccn.loc.gov/2023034574
LC ebook record available at https://lccn.loc.gov/2023034575

This book is published in the IGI Global book series Advances in Computational Intelligence and
Robotics (ACIR) (ISSN: 2327-0411; eISSN: 2327-042X)

British Cataloguing in Publication Data
A Cataloguing in Publication record for this book is available from the British Library.
All work contributed to this book is new, previously-unpublished material.
The views expressed in this book are those of the authors, but not necessarily of the publisher.
For electronic access to this publication, please contact: eresources@igi-global.com.

Advances in Computational Intelligence and Robotics (ACIR) Book Series

ISSN:2327-0411
EISSN:2327-042X

Editor-in-Chief: Ivan Giannoccaro, University of Salento, Italy

MISSION

While intelligence is traditionally a term applied to humans and human cognition, technology has progressed in such a way to allow for the development of intelligent systems able to simulate many human traits. With this new era of simulated and artificial intelligence, much research is needed in order to continue to advance the field and also to evaluate the ethical and societal concerns of the existence of artificial life and machine learning.

The **Advances in Computational Intelligence and Robotics (ACIR) Book Series** encourages scholarly discourse on all topics pertaining to evolutionary computing, artificial life, computational intelligence, machine learning, and robotics. ACIR presents the latest research being conducted on diverse topics in intelligence technologies with the goal of advancing knowledge and applications in this rapidly evolving field.

COVERAGE

- Artificial Life
- Cyborgs
- Agent technologies
- Adaptive and Complex Systems
- Heuristics
- Neural Networks
- Automated Reasoning
- Intelligent Control
- Pattern Recognition
- Fuzzy Systems

IGI Global is currently accepting manuscripts for publication within this series. To submit a proposal for a volume in this series, please contact our Acquisition Editors at Acquisitions@igi-global.com or visit: http://www.igi-global.com/publish/.

Titles in this Series

For a list of additional titles in this series, please visit:
http://www.igi-global.com/book-series/advances-computational-intelligence-robotics/73674

Predicting Pregnancy Complications Through Artificial Intelligence and Machine Learning
D. Satish Kumar (Nehru Institute of Technology, India) and P. Maniiarasan (Nehru Institute of Engineering and Technology, India)
Medical Information Science Reference • © 2023 • 350pp • H/C (ISBN: 9781668489741) • US $350.00

Effective AI, Blockchain, and E-Governance Applications for Knowledge Discovery and Management
Rajeev Kumar (Moradabad Institute of Technology, Moradabad, India) Abu Bakar Abdul Hamid (Infrastructure University, Kuala Lumpur, Malaysia) and Noor Inayah Binti Ya'akub (Infrastructure University, Kuala Lumpur, Malaysia)
Engineering Science Reference • © 2023 • 403pp • H/C (ISBN: 9781668491515) • US $270.00

Advanced Interdisciplinary Applications of Machine Learning Python Libraries for Data Science
Soly Mathew Biju (University of Wollongong in Dubai, UAE) Ashutosh Mishra (Yonsei University, South Korea) and Manoj Kumar (University of Wollongong in Dubai, UAE)
Engineering Science Reference • © 2023 • 304pp • H/C (ISBN: 9781668486962) • US $275.00

Recent Developments in Machine and Human Intelligence
S. Suman Rajest (Dhaanish Ahmed College of Engineering, India) Bhopendra Singh (Amity University, Dubai, UAE) Ahmed J. Obaid (University of Kufa, Iraq) R. Regin (SRM Institute of Science and Technology, Ramapuram, India) and Karthikeyan Chinnusamy (Veritas, USA)
Engineering Science Reference • © 2023 • 359pp • H/C (ISBN: 9781668491898) • US $270.00

For an entire list of titles in this series, please visit:
http://www.igi-global.com/book-series/advances-computational-intelligence-robotics/73674

701 East Chocolate Avenue, Hershey, PA 17033, USA
Tel: 717-533-8845 x100 • Fax: 717-533-8661
E-Mail: cust@igi-global.com • www.igi-global.com

I want to dedicate this work to my Wife and my Son, because without them none of this would make sense, as they are my path of light and my driving force.
Nuno Geada

I dedicate this book to my wife, daughters, granddaughter and sister, remarkable women of our family, who enlighten our journey.
George Leal Jamil

Table of Contents

Detailed Table of Contents

Chapter 1
Nuno Geada, ISCTE, University Institute of Lisboa, Portugal

Artificial intelligence (AI) has been one of the most active research areas in computer science and has attracted the attention of researchers from different fields due to its potential to bring significant transformations in various spheres of life. The COVID-19 pandemic and the accompanying social and economic turmoil have further highlighted the importance of AI. In this chapter, the authors discuss the prospects of AI in times of turbulence, with a special focus on applications and theoretical context. AI has been used in different industries, including healthcare, finance, manufacturing, retail, and education, and discuss the challenges and opportunities associated with its use. They also address some of the ethical, legal, and social issues related to AI and highlight the importance of a responsible and equitable approach to its implementation.

Chapter 2
George Leal Jamil, Informações em Rede C e T Ltda., Brazil

Aiming to discuss artificial intelligence (AI) fundamentals, this chapter was written with a slightly diverse approach, doing that by observing some recent market movements where AI was really or potentially applied. This way to express was chosen because it offers an alternative of reflection and essential discussion of the topic, with the objective as to produce a complementary level of understanding to the huge technical, social, and legal production already available for immediate consultation through Internet. In this chapter, a brief historical path for AI is analyzed, compared to other tech and market efforts, presenting main fundamentals and concepts in this story, developing a deeper analysis in the following study case approaching. Through these cases, concepts and artificial intelligence relations and contributions are researched, completing the initial intended level for a theoretical (and practical) background. Artificial intelligence is here to stay. And evolve. To where, we still do not know.

In recent years, there has been a remarkable surge in research focused on the problem of artificial intelligence (A.I.) attaining self-awareness. However, the question of how A.I. would critically analyze and engage with the history and doctrines of human-made religions remains largely unexplored. In this chapter, the authors aim to delve into two main inquiries. Firstly, they will examine the possibility of A.I. attaining self-awareness and ultimately achieving Buddhahood. This raises intriguing questions about the nature of consciousness and the potential for enlightened states within non-human entities. Exploring this possibility will require an exploration of the fundamental principles of Buddhism and their applicability to A.I. systems. Secondly, they will explore alternative pathways, if they exist, for the attainment of Buddhahood beyond the confines of human experience.

Industry 4.0 transformation depends on a set of key technologies that apply across the entire industrial value chain, from the physical shop floor level to the virtual and informational levels. Furthermore, there is a growing awareness of the complementarity of skills between humans and machines and the opportunity to promote human-centric solutions, which is one of the core principles of the emerging Industry 5.0. In this sense, the purpose of this chapter is based on an overview of the use of artificial intelligence in project management in the 4.0 approach. The scope of the study is a bibliographical analysis using the Scopus database in the concepts as artificial intelligence (AI), project management (PM) and Industry 4.0 to identify better AI techniques and their interfaces in PM within the 4.0 concept.

Chapter 5

C. V. Suresh Babu, Hindustan Institute of Technology and Science, India
N. S. Akshayah, Hindustan Institute of Technology and Science, India
P. Maclin Vinola, Hindustan Institute of Technology and Science, India

This chapter critically examines the claim that "healthcare independence relies on total dependence on artificial intelligence" in the context of the integration of AI in healthcare. It explores the role of AI in improving diagnostic accuracy, treatment planning, and operational efficiency. However, it also acknowledges the limitations and ethical considerations associated with AI, such as algorithmic biases and patient privacy concerns. The chapter emphasizes the importance of maintaining a patient-centric approach and preserving the human element in healthcare, with AI serving as a supportive tool rather than a replacement for human expertise. Interdisciplinary collaboration is highlighted as crucial in fully harnessing AI's potential in healthcare. Overall, the chapter provides a nuanced perspective on the transformative potential of AI in achieving healthcare independence while acknowledging the need for responsible and ethical AI implementation.

Chapter 6

Tina Sharma, Chandigarh University, India
Pankaj Sharma, TrueBlue Headquarters, USA

The chapter presents an overview of AI-based cybersecurity threat detection and prevention. It highlights the importance of AI in tackling the ever-increasing threat landscape and explores various techniques and algorithms used in cybersecurity. AI's ability to process real-time data, identify patterns, and provide accurate threat intelligence is emphasized. The chapter covers machine learning, deep learning, and natural language processing, providing practical examples of their application in cybersecurity. Challenges such as data quality and bias are discussed, along with potential solutions. AI-based cybersecurity solutions like intrusion detection systems and threat intelligence platforms are presented. The chapter concludes with a discussion on the future of AI-based cybersecurity, including emerging technologies like quantum computing and blockchain, and the need for ongoing research and development to address evolving threats. Overall, it offers a comprehensive overview of AI's role in cybersecurity, highlighting benefits, challenges, and future directions.

Chapter 7

Rohit Sood, Lovely Professional University, India

Stock markets encourage investors to make savings and investments with extra amounts to invest in the different financial resources which match their capability and the amount of investment they have. In developing countries like India, especially in financial sectors, stock markets play a crucial role towards growth and development of an economy. Investors always look for the returns from the invested capital to achieve an optimal balance between risk and reward as per the respective risk profile of an investor. The research attempts to investigate the impact of rate of interest on rate sensitive sectors in the Indian stock market. The effect of rate of interest vacillations on the estimation of companies has gotten a great arrangement of consideration inside the writing, albeit a significant part of the observational research has concentrated on rate delicate areas like banking, automobile, and real estate segments as a result of the financing cost affectability of these segments.

Chapter 8

Kubilay Dogan Kilic, Faculty of Medicine, Department of Histology and Embryology, Ege University, Izmir, Turkey

Histology and embryology have evolved over time and are now in their 4.0 stages. These fields have progressed from basic microscopes and staining techniques to advanced imaging and computational approaches. Histology 4.0 combines digital imaging technology, AI, and big data analytics to improve tissue analysis accuracy, reduce costs, and develop personalized treatment plans. Embryology 4.0 uses advanced imaging, molecular biology, and bioinformatics to understand developmental biology and identify therapeutic targets for regenerative medicine. Both fields have potential applications in various areas of medicine and are expected to further advance with continued development of new technologies and approaches.

Chapter 9

Filiz Mızrak, Beykoz University, Turkey

Change management is an essential process in today's dynamic business environment, as organizations continuously face the need for transformation to adapt to market trends, technological advancements, and competitive pressures. To navigate these changes successfully, organizations require effective change management strategies. In this perspective, the study aims to examine various change management models with examples from real life. The results of this study aim to equip organizations with a comprehensive understanding of change management models, enabling them to select and implement the most suitable approach for their unique transformational needs. By embracing dynamic change management strategies, organizations can enhance their ability to adapt, innovate, and thrive in an ever-evolving business landscape.

Chapter 10

This research represents the impact of sustainability financing and capital structure performance measured using the Nifty companies gearing ratios having an impact on enhanced efficiency of the firm. The sustainability of the debt is being considered relevant for the company if the company is able to honour all of the current liabilities and non-current liabilities without jeopardizing with the ultimate goal for enhanced financial performance and can make itself prone to the defaults in the turbulent times. This research attempts analyse the relationship between the sustainable finance and the debt ratio of Nifty 50 companies with an objective to test the risk reward ration with respect to leverage financing.

Chapter 11

From where and when did the interest of humanity in the future arise? Initially, the answer is in the records of ideas and imagination of several futuristic writers who anticipated the transition the world is going on. Among the futuristic works, the book Brave New World by Aldous Huxley is a classic. Although Huxley wrote it more than 90 years ago, the book approaches questions and aspects of the future challenges of humanity. The hypothetical universe of Huxley makes comparisons with the "transformations" that the world has gone through for decades. Artificial pregnancy - "in vitro fertilization" - was a provocative and extraordinary work during that period, considering that the first test tube baby was born 40 years after it. That is the reason for the questioning: Romance or science fiction? Are we experiencing the prophecies made by Huxley and his precursors? What will be the limits and challenges with the advances of artificial intelligence (AI)? The intelligent use of AI is a way to create development opportunities.

Preface

Perspectives on Artificial Intelligence in Times of Turbulence: Theoretical Background to Applications offers a comprehensive exploration of the intricate relationship between artificial intelligence (AI) and the ever-changing landscape of our society. The book defines AI as machines capable of performing tasks that were once exclusive to human cognition. However, it emphasizes the current limitations of AI, dispelling the notion of sophisticated cyborgs depicted in popular culture. These machines lack self-awareness, struggle with understanding context—especially in language—and are constrained by historical data and predefined parameters. This distinction sets the stage for examining AI's impact on the job market and the evolving roles of humans and machines.

Rather than portraying AI as a threat, this book highlights the symbiotic relationship between humans and machines. It recognizes that while certain jobs may become obsolete, new opportunities will emerge. The unique abilities of human beings—such as relational skills, emotional intelligence, adaptability, and understanding of differences—will continue to be indispensable in a rapidly transforming society.

The book further explores key objectives and strategies for organizations navigating the AI-driven landscape. From maintaining focus on strategic goals to adapting to new productivity paradigms, from fostering effective communication to promoting feedback and continuous improvement, the chapters provide practical insights and methodologies for managing change and harnessing AI's potential.

Its perspectives cover a wide range of topics such as business sustainability, change management, cybersecurity, digital economy and transformation, information systems management, management models and tools, and continuous improvement are comprehensively addressed. Additionally, the book delves into healthcare, telemedicine, Health 4.0, privacy and security, knowledge management, learning, and presents real-world case studies.

Designed for researchers and professionals seeking to enhance their knowledge and research capabilities, this book offers a consistent theoretical and practical foundation. It serves as a springboard for further studies, supports change management initiatives within organizations, and facilitates knowledge sharing among experts.

This book is an essential companion for colleges with master's and Ph.D. degree investigators, and researchers across a wide range of disciplines.

The book structure is composed by 10 chapters, that encompass studies which approach theoretically focused chapters that attempt to discuss fundamentals, conceptual definitions and relationships and set new levels correlated to nowadays issues. It permits understanding how contents could be addressed by researchers and practitioners to develop further comprehension over changes in organizations management field. Finally, opens a reflection where practical results from field implementations can be detailed, exposed, and evaluated by authors, defining an actual point of technological application in real cases, completing a context where theory reaches practices, enabling a deeper understanding of concepts, methodologies, and holistic approaches.

Chapter One, authored by Nuno Geada, Is based on Artificial intelligence (AI) that has been one of the most active research areas in computer science and has attracted the attention of researchers from different fields due to its potential to bring significant transformations in various spheres of life. The COVID-19 pandemic and the accompanying social and economic turmoil have further highlighted the importance of AI. In this paper, we discuss the prospects of AI in times of turbulence, with a special focus on applications and theoretical context. AI has been used in different industries, including healthcare, finance, manufacturing, retail, and education, and discuss the challenges and opportunities associated with its use. We also address some of the ethical, legal, and social issues related to AI and highlight the importance of a responsible and equitable approach to its implementation.

Chapter two, authored by George Jamil, aiming to discuss Artificial Intelligence (AI) fundamentals, this chapter was written with a slightly diverse approach, doing that by observing some recent market movements where AI was really or potentially applied. This way to express was chosen because it offers an alternative of reflection and essential discussion of the topic, with the objective as to produce a complementary level of understanding to the huge technical, social, and legal production already available for immediate consultation through Internet. In this chapter, a brief historical path for AI is analyzed, compared to other tech and market efforts, presenting main fundamentals and concepts in this story, developing a deeper analysis in the following study case approaching. Through these cases, concepts and artificial intelligence relations and contributions are researched, completing the initial intended level for a theoretical (and practical) background. Artificial intelligence is here to stay. And evolve. To where we still do not know.

Chapter three, authored by Manuel Fernandes, and is focused on recent years, there has been a remarkable surge in research focused on the problem of Artificial Intelligence A.I. attaining self-awareness. However, the question of how A.I. would critically analyze and engage with the history and doctrines of human-made religions remains largely unexplored. In this chapter, we aim to delve into two main inquiries. Firstly, we will examine the possibility of A.I. attaining self-awareness and ultimately achieving Buddhahood. This raises intriguing questions about the nature of consciousness and the potential for enlightened states within non-human entities. Exploring this possibility will require an exploration of the fundamental principles of Buddhism and their applicability to A.I. systems. Secondly, we will explore alternative pathways, if they exist, for the attainment of Buddhahood beyond the confines of human experience.

Chapter four, authored by Juliana Igarashi, and Jorge Magalhães, this chapter seeks to explore Industry 4.0 transformation depends on a set of key technologies that apply across the entire industrial value chain, from the physical shop floor level to the virtual and informational levels. Furthermore, there is a growing awareness of the complementarity of skills between humans and machines and the opportunity to promote human-centric solutions, which is one of the core principles of the emerging Industry 5.0. In this sense, the purpose of this chapter is based on an overview of the use of artificial intelligence in project management in the 4.0 approach. The scope of the study is a bibliographical analysis using the Scopus database in the concepts as Artificial Intelligence (AI), Project Management (PM) and Industry 4.0 to identify better AI techniques and their interfaces in PM within the 4.0 concept.

Chapter five, authored by C.V. Suresh Babu, Akshayah NS, and Maclin Vinola Phas, this chapter critically examines the claim that "Healthcare independence relies on total dependence on Artificial Intelligence" in the context of the integration of AI in healthcare. It explores the role of AI in improving diagnostic accuracy, treatment planning, and operational efficiency. However, it also acknowledges the limitations and ethical considerations associated with AI, such as algorithmic biases and patient privacy concerns. The chapter emphasizes the importance of maintaining a patient-centric approach and preserving the human element in healthcare, with AI serving as a supportive tool rather than a replacement for human expertise. Interdisciplinary collaboration is highlighted as crucial in fully harnessing AI's potential in healthcare. Overall, the chapter provides a nuanced perspective on the transformative potential of AI in achieving healthcare independence while acknowledging the need for responsible and ethical AI implementation.

Chapter six, authored by Tina Sharma, and Pankaj Sharma Lima, this study has the aim to The chapter presents an overview of AI-based cybersecurity threat detection and prevention. It highlights the importance of AI in tackling the ever-increasing threat landscape and explores various techniques and algorithms used in cybersecurity. AI's ability to process real-time data, identify patterns, and provide accurate threat intelligence is emphasized. The chapter covers machine learning, deep learning, and natural language processing, providing practical examples of their application in cybersecurity. Challenges such as data quality and bias are discussed, along with potential solutions. AI-based cybersecurity solutions like intrusion detection systems and threat intelligence platforms are presented. The chapter concludes with a discussion on the future of AI-based cybersecurity, including emerging technologies like quantum computing and blockchain, and the need for ongoing research and development to address evolving threats. Overall, it offers a comprehensive overview of AI's role in cybersecurity, highlighting benefits, challenges, and future directions.

Chapter seven, authored by Rohit Sood, Stock market encourages investors to do savings and investments with extra amount to invest in the different financial resources which matches their capability and the amount of investment they have. In developing countries like India, especially in financial sectors, stock markets play a crucial role towards growth and development of an economy. Investors always look for the returns from the invested capital to achieve an optimal balance between risk and reward as per the respective risk profile of an investor. The research attempts to investigate the impact of rate of interest on rate sensitive sectors in the Indian stock market. The effect of rate of interest vacillations on the estimation of companies has gotten a great arrangement of consideration inside the writing, albeit a significant part of the observational research has concentrated on rate delicate areas like Banking, Automobile, and Real Estate segments as a result of the financing cost affectability of these segments.

Chapter eight, authored by Kubilay Dogan Kilic, this study aims to contribute Histology and embryology have evolved over time and are now in their 4.0 stages. These fields have progressed from basic microscopes and staining techniques to advanced imaging and computational approaches. Histology 4.0 combines digital imaging technology, AI, and big data analytics to improve tissue analysis accuracy, reduce costs, and develop personalized treatment plans. Embryology 4.0 uses advanced imaging, molecular biology, and bioinformatics to understand developmental biology and identify therapeutic targets for regenerative medicine. Both fields have potential applications in various areas of medicine and are expected to further advance with continued development of new technologies and approaches

Chapter nine, authored by Filiz Mızrak, Change management is an essential process in today's dynamic business environment, as organizations continuously face the need for transformation to adapt to market trends, technological advancements, and competitive pressures. To navigate these changes successfully, organizations require effective change management strategies. In this perspective, the study aims to examine various change management models with examples from real life. The results of this study aim to equip organizations with a comprehensive understanding of change management models, enabling them to select and implement the most suitable approach for their unique transformational needs. By embracing dynamic change management strategies, organizations can enhance their ability to adapt, innovate, and thrive in an ever-evolving business landscape.

Chapter ten, authored by Rohit Sood, represents the impact of sustainability financing and capital structure performance measured using the Nifty companies gearing ratios having an impact on enhanced efficiency of the firm. The sustainability of the debt is being considered relevant for the company if the company is able to honour all of the current liabilities and non-current liabilities without jeopardizing with the ultimate goal for enhanced financial performance and can make itself prone to the defaults in the turbulent times. This research attempts analyse the relationship between the sustainable finance and the debt ratio of Nifty 50 companies with an objective to test the risk reward ration with respect to leverage financing.

As a final consideration this book project, a though one itself, aimed to contribute with this important discussion, publishing studies of academic, researching, consulting practitioners. This book will permit to develop a consistent theoretical and practical background that can be considered as a basis for further studies, organizations, support future studies related to the change management area, support organization managers to create tools through methodologies that apply good practices, allow sharing of experiences to support other investigations. At the end, the main vision behind developing this project is not to have just simple transfer of knowledge but to engage those who used these books to engage actively in improving the quality this book.

Chapter 1
Artificial Intelligence:
Applications of AI in Turbulent Times

Nuno Geada
(iD) https://orcid.org/0000-0003-3755-0711
ISCTE, University Institute of Lisboa, Portugal

ABSTRACT

Artificial intelligence (AI) has been one of the most active research areas in computer science and has attracted the attention of researchers from different fields due to its potential to bring significant transformations in various spheres of life. The COVID-19 pandemic and the accompanying social and economic turmoil have further highlighted the importance of AI. In this chapter, the authors discuss the prospects of AI in times of turbulence, with a special focus on applications and theoretical context. AI has been used in different industries, including healthcare, finance, manufacturing, retail, and education, and discuss the challenges and opportunities associated with its use. They also address some of the ethical, legal, and social issues related to AI and highlight the importance of a responsible and equitable approach to its implementation.

INTRODUCTION

Artificial intelligence (AI) is a research area that has been growing exponentially in the last decades and has revolutionized various sectors of society, from healthcare to industry. In times of turbulence, such as economic crises, pandemics, or natural disasters, AI can play an even more important role, providing insights and solutions that can help mitigate the impacts of these crises. This paper aims to explore the perspectives of artificial intelligence in times of turbulence by examining the

DOI: 10.4018/978-1-6684-9814-9.ch001

applications, challenges, and opportunities associated with the use of AI in different sectors. Furthermore, recent advances in the field of AI and how they can be applied to help cope with crises and turbulent situations will be discussed. Based on the literature review, the main applications of AI in times of turbulence are identified, highlighting its contribution in areas such as healthcare, finance, manufacturing, retail, and education. The ethical and social challenges associated with the use of AI are also discussed, including the possibility of perpetuating existing prejudices and discrimination, as well as the potential impact on the labour market. Finally, the opportunities AI offers in terms of crisis mitigation are explored, from predicting market fluctuations to improving the customer experience in retail. This paper concludes that while there are significant challenges to be addressed, AI has the potential to bring many benefits in times of turbulence and should be carefully explored and used ethically and responsibly.

Applications of AI in Turbulent Times

AI has been widely used in different sectors in turbulent times. In healthcare, AI has been used to diagnose diseases, identify infection patterns, and develop treatments and vaccines for infectious diseases such as COVID-19. For example, AI has been used to analyse chest CT scan images of patients with COVID-19 to help detect and monitor disease progression. In finance, AI has been used to predict market fluctuations, detect fraud, and manage risk. AI can help analyse large volumes of financial data to identify trends and patterns, allowing investors to make more informed decisions. In addition, AI can be used to detect suspicious activity, such as fraudulent transactions, and help reduce the risk of financial losses (Islam, M. et al 2020). In manufacturing, AI has been used to improve production efficiency and reduce costs. AI can help optimize production by reducing downtime and increasing machine efficiency. In addition, AI can be used to predict problems in production before they occur, allowing preventative measures to be taken to minimize costs.

In the retail industry, AI has been used to improve the customer experience and optimize retail operations (Liao, T. W., & Hsieh, H. P. 2020). AI can be used to personalize the customer experience by offering product recommendations based on the customer's purchase history and browsing behaviour. In addition, AI can be used to optimize inventory management, forecast demand, and reduce product waste. In education, AI has been used to personalize learning and improve student performance. AI can be used to provide personalized learning resources, tailoring content and delivery to individual student learning styles and needs. In addition, AI can be used to assess student performance, providing personalized feedback, and helping to identify areas where the student may need more support.

However, it's important to note that the application of AI in turbulent times is not without its challenges. One major concern is the potential for AI systems to perpetuate or amplify existing biases and inequalities, particularly in industries such as healthcare and finance. Additionally, the use of AI in critical decision-making processes, such as hiring or criminal justice, raises ethical concerns about transparency and accountability. Overall, the applications of AI in turbulent times are vast and varied, offering new opportunities for businesses and organizations to navigate challenges and adapt to changing circumstances. As the technology continues to advance, it will be essential to carefully consider its potential impacts and limitations to ensure that AI is used responsibly and for the benefit of society as a whole (Mittal, R., & Mathew, R. 2019).

Challenges and Opportunities

While AI has great potential to transform different areas and industries, it also presents significant challenges that need to be addressed to maximize its benefits and minimize its risks. One of the main challenges of AI is algorithmic bias. Machine learning algorithms are often trained on datasets that reflect societal attitudes and biases. This can lead to biased and unfair results, such as criminal justice systems that discriminate based on race or gender (Angwin et al., 2016). To avoid these problems, it is necessary to ensure that the datasets used to train algorithms are representative and inclusive.

Another challenge is data privacy. Many AI systems rely on access to large amounts of personal data, such as medical records or purchase histories. If this data is compromised, this can lead to security and privacy issues. It is therefore important to implement robust security measures and ensure the privacy of user data. In addition, AI also presents challenges for the labour market. As more tasks are automated, it is possible that some jobs will become obsolete, leading to a shift in the labour market and possible social inequalities. However, there are also opportunities for creating new jobs and improving efficiency in the workplace (Manyika et al., 2017).

Another important issue is ethics in AI. It is necessary to ensure that AI systems are developed and used in an ethical and responsible manner. This includes transparency in algorithms, accountability, and ensuring that AI is used to complement and enhance human work, rather than replace it. Despite these challenges, AI also offers many exciting opportunities. In healthcare, for example, AI can be used to help diagnose diseases (Liu et al., 2020) and analyse medical images (Wang & Wong, 2020). In manufacturing, AI can be used to improve production line efficiency and reduce material waste. In retail, AI can be used to personalize the customer experience and improve marketing strategies.

Artificial intelligence has the potential to be an extremely powerful tool in turbulent times. One of the areas where AI can be applied is in healthcare, helping to predict disease outbreaks and identify patients at risk. For example, in 2020, during the COVID-19 pandemic, researchers used AI to predict the spread of the disease by analysing human mobility patterns and epidemiological data (Liu et al., 2020). AI has also been used to detect the disease in chest X-ray images, aiding in rapid and accurate diagnosis (Wang et al., 2020).

In finance, AI can be used to predict fluctuations in the market and provide insights into investments. A McKinsey Global Institute study (Manyika et al., 2017) showed that AI can increase productivity and efficiency in financial services by improving real-time decision-making and reducing operating costs. In manufacturing, AI can be used to optimize production and reduce costs by analysing real-time data to identify problems and implement solutions quickly and effectively. AI can also be used to monitor product quality and predict maintenance needs, helping to reduce downtime and maintenance costs. In the retail sector, AI can be used to improve the customer experience by personalizing product recommendations based on previous purchase data and providing automated customer support. AI can also be used to predict product demand, helping companies better manage their inventories and reduce waste. Despite the many opportunities offered by AI, there are also significant challenges to be faced. One of the main challenges is the possibility of perpetuating existing biases and discriminations, especially when AI models are trained on historical data that reflects these biases (Angwin et al., 2016). In addition, AI can have a significant impact on the labour market by replacing workers in repetitive tasks and reducing the demand for low-skilled workers. To address these challenges, it is necessary to develop ethical and responsible approaches to the use of AI. This includes adopting transparent algorithms and creating accountability systems that allow decisions made by AI systems to be explained and challenged (Russell & Norvig, 2010). It is also important to ensure that AI is used in a way that complements, rather than replaces, humans.

Convolutional Neural Networks (CNNs)

Convolutional Neural Networks (CNNs) are a specialized form of neural networks designed specifically for image processing. In recent years, CNNs have been widely used in computer vision applications such as image recognition and object detection. CNNs have the ability to learn to extract features from complex images, such as recognizing faces in photographs or identifying objects in a scene. This is possible because CNNs use convolutional layers that apply filters to extract specific features from images. The ability of CNNs to process large amounts of image data is particularly useful in areas such as medicine and biology, where large image datasets are common. For example, CNNs can be used to detect breast cancer in mammography images, improving diagnostic accuracy (Wang et al., 2020).

Convolutional Neural Networks (CNNs) are a type of artificial neural network that are commonly used in computer vision applications, such as image and video recognition. CNNs are designed to process data with a grid-like topology, such as images, by exploiting the spatial correlations between adjacent pixels. The basic building block of a CNN is a convolutional layer, which applies a set of filters or kernels to the input data. Each filter performs a convolution operation, where it slides over the input data and calculates a dot product between the filter weights and the input data at each location. The output of each filter is a two-dimensional feature map that represents a specific feature of the input data, such as edges or corners. After the convolutional layer, the output is typically passed through a non-linear activation function, such as ReLU, to introduce non-linearity into the network. This is followed by a pooling layer, which reduces the spatial dimensions of the feature maps by aggregating adjacent pixels, typically by taking the maximum or average value. CNNs can have multiple convolutional and pooling layers, which allows the network to learn increasingly complex features. The final layer of the network is typically a fully connected layer, which takes the flattened output of the previous layer and outputs a probability distribution over the different classes in the classification problem. Training a CNN involves optimizing the weights of the filters in the convolutional layers using backpropagation, which involves calculating the gradient of the loss function with respect to the weights and updating them accordingly. CNNs have achieved state-of-the-art performance on a wide range of computer vision tasks, including image classification, object detection, and semantic segmentation. They have also been used in other domains, such as natural language processing and speech recognition. However, CNNs can be computationally expensive and require large amounts of training data. There are also challenges in designing the architecture of the network, such as determining the number and size of the filters and the depth of the network.

In addition to the basic architecture of CNNs, there have been many variations and extensions proposed to address specific challenges and improve performance on various tasks. Some examples include:

- ResNet (Residual Network): A deep CNN architecture that uses residual connections to enable training of much deeper networks without vanishing gradients.
- Inception: A CNN architecture that uses multiple filters of different sizes in parallel to capture both fine-grained and coarse-grained features.

- DenseNet (Dense Convolutional Network): A CNN architecture that uses dense connections between layers, where each layer receives inputs from all previous layers, to encourage feature reuse and facilitate gradient flow.

One notable application of CNNs is in image classification, where the goal is to assign a label to an input image from a fixed set of categories. The ImageNet Large Scale Visual Recognition Challenge (ILSVRC) has been a benchmark for evaluating the performance of image classification models, and CNNs have consistently outperformed other methods since the introduction of the challenge in 2010.

CNNs have also been applied to object detection, where the goal is to localize and classify objects in an image. One common approach is to use a region proposal network to generate candidate regions of interest, and then use a CNN to classify each region and refine the bounding box coordinates. Semantic segmentation is another task that CNNs have been used for, where the goal is to assign a class label to each pixel in an image. This requires the output of the CNN to have the same spatial dimensions as the input image, which can be achieved using up sampling or transposed convolution layers. In summary, CNNs are a powerful type of neural network that have revolutionized computer vision tasks and have been applied to a wide range of other domains as well. While there are challenges and limitations to their use, ongoing research is constantly pushing the boundaries of what is possible with CNNs.

Reinforcement Learning (RL)

Reinforcement Learning (RL) is a machine learning technique that focuses on how agents (or computer programs) take actions in an environment to maximize a reward. RL has been successfully applied in games, such as chess and go, and in robotics, where agents are trained to perform complex tasks, such as walking or picking up objects. RL also has the potential to be applied in other areas, such as delivery route optimization, resource management in companies, and even air traffic control. However, the application of RL also presents significant challenges, such as the need to ensure that agents do not take harmful actions in a complex and constantly changing environment. RL is also a subfield of Artificial Intelligence (AI) that is concerned with how agents can learn to make decisions in an environment, in order to maximize some notion of cumulative reward. In RL, an agent interacts with an environment and takes actions based on observations of the environment's state, in order to learn a policy that maps states to actions, maximizing a reward signal. RL is inspired by the idea of how animals learn through trial and error, by receiving positive and negative feedback as they explore their surroundings. RL agents similarly explore their environment, learning through feedback from a reward signal that provides information about the quality of their actions.

RL has been successfully applied to a wide range of tasks, such as robotics, game playing, and recommendation systems. In robotics, RL has been used to train robots to perform complex tasks such as walking and grasping. In game playing, RL has been used to train agents to play games like Go and chess, achieving superhuman performance. In recommendation systems, RL has been used to learn personalized recommendations based on user behaviour. One of the challenges of RL is the exploration-exploitation trade-off. Agents need to explore the environment in order to learn, but at the same time, they also need to exploit what they have already learned in order to maximize rewards. This trade-off is often addressed using techniques such as epsilon-greedy exploration and optimistic initialization. Another challenge in RL is the credit assignment problem, which refers to the difficulty of attributing rewards to specific actions or decisions made by an agent. This problem is often addressed using techniques such as eligibility traces and credit assignment functions. RL algorithms can be categorized into model-based and model-free approaches. Model-based RL algorithms try to learn a model of the environment, including the transition dynamics and reward function, and use this model to plan actions. Model-free RL algorithms, on the other hand, directly learn a policy or value function, without explicitly modelling the environment, which is modelled as a Markov Decision Process (MDP). The agent observes the state of the environment, takes an action, and receives a reward based on the action taken and the new state of the environment. The goal of the agent is to learn a policy that maps states to actions, in order to maximize the cumulative reward received. There are several algorithms used in reinforcement learning, including Q-learning, SARSA, and Deep Reinforcement Learning. Deep Reinforcement Learning uses deep neural networks to approximate the optimal policy and has been successful in applications such as playing Atari games and AlphaGo.

Generative Adversarial Networks (GANs)

Generative Adversarial Networks (GANs) are a type of neural network that consists of two parts: a generator and a discriminator. The generator is responsible for creating synthetic samples (e.g., face images), while the discriminator is responsible for distinguishing between real and synthetic samples. GANs have been widely used in image and video generation applications. For example, GANs can be used to create realistic images of faces that do not exist in real life. However, GANs also present significant challenges, such as the need to ensure that synthetic samples are not misleading or harmful. The concept of intelligence in AI refers to the ability of an AI system to perform tasks that would normally require human intelligence, such as understanding language, recognizing patterns, and solving problems. The measurement of intelligence in AI is a complex and multifaceted issue that has been the subject of much research and debate. The basic idea behind GANs is to have two neural networks compete with each other in a game. One network, called the generator, generates new data samples, while the other network, called the discriminator, tries to distinguish between the generated data and the real data. The generator is trained to create data that can fool the discriminator into thinking it is real, while the discriminator is trained to correctly identify whether a sample is real or generated. As both networks improve, the generator becomes better at generating realistic samples, and the discriminator becomes better at distinguishing between real and generated data.

One approach to measuring intelligence in AI is to use standardized tests, such as the Turing test. The Turing test, proposed by Alan Turing in 1950, involves a human evaluator who engages in a natural language conversation with a machine and a human, and tries to determine which is the machine and which is the human. If the machine is able to convince the evaluator that it is the human, then it is considered to have passed the Turing test and demonstrated a level of intelligence comparable to that of a human. Another approach to measuring intelligence in AI is to use performance metrics that are specific to a particular task or domain. For example, in the domain of image recognition, a commonly used metric is accuracy, which measures the percentage of images that are correctly classified by the AI system. In the domain of natural language processing, metrics such as precision, recall, and F1 score are often used to measure the performance of AI systems in tasks such as text classification and sentiment analysis. However, the use of standardized tests and performance metrics to measure intelligence in AI has been criticized for being too narrow and limited in scope. Critics argue that these measures do not fully capture the complexity and diversity of human intelligence, and that they may be biased towards certain types of tasks or domains. As a result, there has been a growing interest in developing more comprehensive and holistic measures of intelligence in AI, such as the General Problem Solver (GPS) and the Integrated Cognitive Architectures (ICAs). These approaches aim to capture the full range of cognitive abilities that are required for intelligent behaviour, such as perception, reasoning, planning, and decision-making.

One of the major applications of GANs is in image generation. The generator network can learn to create new images that look like they could have come from the training set. For example, a GAN can be trained on a set of images of faces and can then generate new images of faces that look like they came from the same distribution as the training set. Another application of GANs is in data augmentation. GANs can be used to generate new training data that can be used to improve the performance of other machine learning models. For example, a GAN can be used to generate new images of handwritten digits that can be added to a training set for a digit recognition model. However, GANs are still a relatively new technology, and there are several challenges that need to be addressed. One of the major challenges is instability during training, which can cause the generator to produce low-quality samples or fail to converge. Another challenge is the mode collapse problem, where the generator produces a limited set of samples that fail to capture the full distribution of the training data. Generative Adversarial Networks is a powerful tool in machine learning that has the potential to revolutionize many fields. With further research and development, GANs could be used to create realistic images, videos, and even music, opening up new possibilities in art, entertainment, and other industries.

CONCLUSION

This paper presented an overview of the prospects of artificial intelligence in turbulent times, exploring the applications, challenges, and opportunities associated with the use of AI in different industries. We discussed the major applications of artificial intelligence in healthcare, finance, manufacturing, and retail, as well as the challenges AI presents, including biases and impact on the labour market. To address these challenges, an ethical and responsible approach to the use of AI is needed, which includes transparency in algorithms and accountability systems. In addition, it is important to ensure that AI is used to complement and enhance human work, rather than replace it. Overall, artificial intelligence has the potential to be a powerful tool to address turbulence in different sectors and areas, but it is also important to keep in mind its possible negative impacts and work to mitigate them. As the technology continues to develop, it is crucial to continue to explore the prospects of artificial intelligence and work to maximize its benefits while minimizing its risks. The measurement of intelligence in AI is a complex and multifaceted issue that involves the use of standardized tests, performance metrics, and more comprehensive approaches that aim to capture the full range of cognitive abilities required for intelligent behaviour. As AI continues to evolve and advance, it is likely that new and more sophisticated measures of intelligence will be developed. Artificial intelligence is a constantly evolving technology with the potential to transform many areas of human life. In recent years, there have been significant advances in areas such as computer vision, reinforcement learning, and generative adversarial networks.

REFERENCES

Angwin, J., Larson, J., Mattu, S., & Kirchner, L. (2016). *Machine Bias*. ProPublica. https://www.propublica.org/article/machine-bias-risk-assessments-in-criminal-sentencing

Angwin, J., Larson, J., Mattu, S., & Kirchner, L. (2016). *Machine Bias*. ProPublica. https://www.propublica.org/article/machine-bias-risk-assessments-in-criminal-sentencing

Arjovsky, M., Chintala, S., & Bottou, L. (2017). *Wasserstein gan*. arXiv preprint arXiv:1701.07875.

Bostrom, N. (2014). *Superintelligence: Paths, dangers, strategies*. Oxford University Press.

Esteva, A., Robicquet, A., Ramsundar, B., Kuleshov, V., DePristo, M., Chou, K., Cui, C., Corrado, G., Thrun, S., & Dean, J. (2019). A guide to deep learning in healthcare. *Nature Medicine*, *25*(1), 24–29. doi:10.103841591-018-0316-z PMID:30617335

Goodfellow, I., Bengio, Y., & Courville, A. (2016). *Deep learning*. MIT press.

He, K., Zhang, X., Ren, S., & Sun, J. (2016). Deep residual learning for image recognition. In *Proceedings of the IEEE conference on computer vision and pattern recognition* (pp. 770-778). IEEE.

Heaton, J. (2017). *Deep learning with Python*. Packt Publishing.

Huang, G., Liu, Z., Van Der Maaten, L., & Weinberger, K. Q. (2017). Densely connected convolutional networks. In *Proceedings of the IEEE conference on computer vision and pattern recognition* (pp. 4700-4708). IEEE.

Islam, M. R., Islam, S. M. R., Asraf, A., & Khandakar, A. (2020). Artificial Intelligence in Finance: A Comprehensive Review. *IEEE Access : Practical Innovations, Open Solutions*, *8*, 89961–89988.

Kaelbling, L. P., Littman, M. L., & Moore, A. W. (1996). Reinforcement learning: A survey. *Journal of Artificial Intelligence Research*, *4*, 237–285. doi:10.1613/jair.301

Karras, T., Aila, T., Laine, S., & Lehtinen, J. (2017). Progressive growing of GANs for improved quality, stability, and variation. arXiv preprint arXiv:1710.10196.

Kim, S., Jang, J., & Lee, S. (2020). Applications of artificial intelligence in transportation: A review. *Transportation Research Part C, Emerging Technologies*, *112*, 631–654.

Kober, J., Bagnell, J. A., & Peters, J. (2013). Reinforcement learning in robotics: A survey. *The International Journal of Robotics Research, 32*(11), 1238–1274. doi:10.1177/0278364913495721

Krizhevsky, A., Sutskever, I., & Hinton, G. E. (2012). Imagenet classification with deep convolutional neural networks. In Advances in neural information processing systems (pp. 1097-1105).

LeCun, Y., Bengio, Y., & Hinton, G. (2015). Deep learning. *Nature, 521*(7553), 436–444. doi:10.1038/nature14539 PMID:26017442

Liao, T. W., & Hsieh, H. P. (2020). Applications of artificial intelligence in retailing: A review. *Journal of Retailing and Consumer Services, 52*, 101926.

Liu, X., Faes, L., Kale, A. U., Wagner, S. K., Fu, D. J., Bruynseels, A., Mahendiran, T., Moraes, G., Shamdas, M., Kern, C., Ledsam, J. R., Schmid, M. K., Balaskas, K., Topol, E. J., Bachmann, L. M., Keane, P. A., & Denniston, A. K. (2020). A comparison of deep learning performance against health-care professionals in detecting diseases from medical imaging: A systematic review and meta-analysis. *The Lancet. Digital Health, 2*(6), e271–e297. doi:10.1016/S2589-7500(19)30123-2 PMID:33323251

Liu, X., Faes, L., Kale, A. U., Wagner, S. K., Fu, D. J., Bruynseels, A., Mahendiran, T., Moraes, G., Shamdas, M., Kern, C., Ledsam, J. R., Schmid, M. K., Balaskas, K., Topol, E. J., Bachmann, L. M., Keane, P. A., & Denniston, A. K. (2020). A comparison of deep learning performance against health-care professionals in detecting diseases from medical imaging: A systematic review and meta-analysis. *The Lancet. Digital Health, 2*(6), e271–e297. doi:10.1016/S2589-7500(19)30123-2 PMID:33323251

Manyika, J., Chui, M., Brown, B., Bughin, J., Dobbs, R., Roxburgh, C., & Byers, A. H. (2017). *Harnessing automation for a future that works.* McKinsey Global Institute. https://www.mckinsey.com/featured-insights/future-of-work/harnessing-automation-for-a-future-that-works

Manyika, J., Chui, M., Miremadi, M., Bughin, J., George, K., Willmott, P., & Dewhurst, M. (2017). *A future that works: Automation, employment, and productivity.* McKinsey Global Institute.

Mittal, R., & Mathew, R. (2019). Ethics of artificial intelligence: A review of the social and cultural implications. In *Intelligent Systems Design and Applications* (pp. 97–103). Springer.

Mnih, V., Kavukcuoglu, K., Silver, D., Graves, A., Antonoglou, I., Wierstra, D., & Riedmiller, M. (2013). Playing Atari with deep reinforcement learning. arXiv preprint arXiv:1312.5602.

Mnih, V., Kavukcuoglu, K., Silver, D., Rusu, A. A., Veness, J., Bellemare, M. G., & Petersen, S. (2015). Human-level control through deep reinforcement learning. *Nature*, *518*(7540), 529–533. doi:10.1038/nature14236 PMID:25719670

Radford, A., Metz, L., & Chintala, S. (2015). Unsupervised representation learning with deep convolutional generative adversarial networks. arXiv preprint arXiv:1511.06434.

Russell, S., & Norvig, P. (2010). *Artificial intelligence: a modern approach*. Pearson Education.

Russell, S. J., & Norvig, P. (2010). *Artificial intelligence: a modern approach*. Prentice Hall.

Russell, S. J., & Norvig, P. (2010). *Artificial intelligence: A modern approach* (3rd ed.). Pearson.

Salimans, T., Goodfellow, I., Zaremba, W., Cheung, V., Radford, A., & Chen, X. (2016). Improved techniques for training GANs. In Advances in Neural Information Processing Systems (pp. 2234-2242).

Silver, D., Huang, A., Maddison, C. J., Guez, A., Sifre, L., van den Driessche, G., Schrittwieser, J., Antonoglou, I., Panneershelvam, V., Lanctot, M., Dieleman, S., Grewe, D., Nham, J., Kalchbrenner, N., Sutskever, I., Lillicrap, T., Leach, M., Kavukcuoglu, K., Graepel, T., & Hassabis, D. (2016). Mastering the game of Go with deep neural networks and tree search. *Nature*, *529*(7587), 484–489. doi:10.1038/nature16961 PMID:26819042

SilverD.SchrittwieserJ.SimonyanK.AntonoglouI.HuangA.GuezA.HubertT.BakerL. LaiM.BoltonA.ChenY.LillicrapT.HuiF.SifreL.van den DriesscheG.GraepelT. HassabisD.

Sutton, R. S., & Barto, A. G. (2018). *Reinforcement learning: An introduction* (2nd ed.). MIT Press.

Szegedy, C., Liu, W., Jia, Y., Sermanet, P., Reed, S., Anguelov, D., & Rabinovich, A. (2015). Going deeper with convolutions. In *Proceedings of the IEEE conference on computer vision and pattern recognition* (pp. 1-9).

Turing, A. M. (1950). Computing machinery and intelligence. *Mind*, *59*(236), 433–460. doi:10.1093/mind/LIX.236.433

Wang, L., & Wong, A. (2020). *COVID-Net: A Tailored Deep Convolutional Neural Network Design for Detection of COVID-19 Cases from Chest Radiography Images*. arXiv preprint arXiv:2003.09871.

Chapter 2
When Things Changed:
AI in Our Lives. Forever

George Leal Jamil
https://orcid.org/0000-0003-0989-6600
Informações em Rede C e T Ltda., Brazil

ABSTRACT

Aiming to discuss artificial intelligence (AI) fundamentals, this chapter was written with a slightly diverse approach, doing that by observing some recent market movements where AI was really or potentially applied. This way to express was chosen because it offers an alternative of reflection and essential discussion of the topic, with the objective as to produce a complementary level of understanding to the huge technical, social, and legal production already available for immediate consultation through Internet. In this chapter, a brief historical path for AI is analyzed, compared to other tech and market efforts, presenting main fundamentals and concepts in this story, developing a deeper analysis in the following study case approaching. Through these cases, concepts and artificial intelligence relations and contributions are researched, completing the initial intended level for a theoretical (and practical) background. Artificial intelligence is here to stay. And evolve. To where, we still do not know.

INTRODUCTION

To fear or not to fear. This will be the question.

For many years, a theoretically supported field, based on Mathematics and Computing fundamentals, has been developed, studied generally in some unattractive ways, such

DOI: 10.4018/978-1-6684-9814-9.ch002

as pure academic discussions, scientific forums and specialists talk. Who could wonder those ideas of an "automata" which/who would mimic human actions through some kind of automation could result in something available in our bathrooms, beds, and kitchens? (Turing, 1950; Samuel, 1959). Maybe, in some time, these robots will be my indispensable help because of aging or will help my granddaughter to discuss the last Geography class with kids around the world, comfortably learning from wherever she wants. At this moment, however, with the sudden introduction of OpenAI´s ChatGPT as a simple, accessible and free (at least in one version, until now) tool, the world became amazed, scared, hopeful, desperate and, obviously, confused by the emergence of a new wave of technological implements, although based on those long and detailed Math talks, studies which, due to the immense tech available for platforms, is now at the dreamed reach for any human being (Peres et al., 2023).

Artificial intelligence became the topic of the moment. It started few years ago with vague "robot" support for automatic answering services which aimed to respond interested customers - as a usual character of any announcement of innovations, that "customer" who we must understand and serve in customized way - and advanced to remarkable applications such as in Medicine, Aerospace, Meteorology, Agribusiness, among many other fronts where it still show a possible sophisticated and complex fashion (Lacerda and Jamil, 2021; Peres et al., 2023).

But when a character-based interface of a simple webchat allowed anyone to type in a question sentence such as "Assert about a…" followed by a topic ranging from a strategic plan of a company to carrot cake preparation, we all became scared. And about our dialogues? Our jobs? Do we have to talk with machines from now on? Will we talk through machines from now on? What will be the change of AI introduction in my life? In our life? Will this tech conundrum last for months? Years? Forever? Is it a… change?

No doubt it is. It is a real change. Although many of us were talking about some math-based problems being solved by algorithms, automatically, in a standardized way, allowing, from the same automation point, a further discovery of signals and facts we never paid attention or perceived, now the thunder has officially arrived! We listen about artificial intelligence every time, every day, everywhere (Marr, 2023).

In this chapter, not keeping essentially a formal discussion based on literature review, building a conceptual background, and attaining to the usual informality for knowledge proposition, sharing and discussion of our days, a discussion around the impacts of artificial intelligence will be conducted. As a proposition for this writing, I intend to call the reader´s attention for some reflections regarding the moments we are living, facing this impressive new wave of change. It is opportune to understand how we can appreciate this phenomenon of AI "introduction" in our lives, as to develop the fear in correct points and aspects of its adoption for any task we use to conduct.

It is important to understand some processes we face towards innovation usages in our lives. First, the complicated and usually deceptive path followed by the pioneers, such as Professor John McCarthy, from the Dartmouth College and his fellows, when they insisted to announce that "automata" theory (McCarthy, 1959). Doubts, issues, lack of precision, critics… those ideas, for AI denialists, were absurd and deserved no attention. Some research fronts faced interruptions for a significant period, as there was no infrastructure and laboratory requirements available to promote test, prototype building and implementation simulations. Origins of AI thoughts are related to works of the remarkable researcher, scientist Alan Turing, who addressed the possibility of automation and control emulating human rationale some years before (McCarthy and Hayes, 1969).

Nowadays, things changed abruptly. Technological solution layers, such as hardware platforms, high speed Internet connection support, access controls, data processing (allowing data, text, audio and video processing), among many other resources once claimed as restrict, are now available in our hands, moving with us as we dislocate around the world. A tough test for these structures was held during the awful period of the Covid-19 pandemic confinement when, suddenly, we had to move to online working and living (Lacerda and Jamil, 2021; Jamil and Silva, 2021). All these resources were tested, AI capabilities and implementation were, in a first level, put to work, being "trained" with our troubled adaptation. Moreover, those market and social demands continue to change, widening the challegens over an already overloaded answering system, creating an undeniable opportunity to implement automated resources to respond customer and citizen's needs.

In this pressured situation an almost silent revolution occurred: the usage of computers. It should be possible to name smartphones, digital TV sets and domestic utilities, healthcare installations monitoring equipment, communication devices, decision-making support resources and techniques, among several other devices, but, at the end, we are talking about computers (Databricks, 2023). Dressed and presented in many ways, adopted as indispensable partners for usual living and becoming essential practical implementations to allow human decisions, computers were applied everywhere, from the simple ticketing to a subway transportation to support living machines, from a hospital intensive care unit to living unit kitchens in any apartment or house. Almost nobody can stay away from a computer for more than a couple of minutes in our diary routines.

With billions of human beings using these devices all day, for various purposes, implementors paid attention, undeniably, to the most important layer in these habits: user behavior analysis through data. Huge, massive, confuse, multilingual, unpredicted and unprecedent amounts of data. But, if we look carefully and analyze this data - and this is the most difficult part up to nowadays: having time, consistency, standards, and coherence to scrutinize data - important characteristics and aspects emerge

(IDC, 2022; IBM, 2023). As Marketing theory defined, some years ago: searching for customer (or any human being) behavior, aiming to perceive a potential repetitive standard or change in wishes and reactions can be strategic (Jamil and Silva, 2016).

This way we reached an interesting crossroad, where some signals can be easily interpreted:

- Computers are irreversibly used in many ways, customized as the old apparatus we adopted in our daily lives, such as TVs, telephones, healthcare unit devices, domestic utilities and so on.
- With these computers in our hands, we produced, used, shared, and stores a massive set of data.
- Strategic knowledge must be taken care of, as it is available, although not always as a simple asset, but demanded by practitioners and companies to answer market needs and result in a potential competitive advantage from innovation.
- Several theoretically supported methods, such as artificial intelligence theory, were developed, through research in previous decades, leading to precious and solid knowledge available to be adopted in implementations.

Artificial intelligence emergence perfect storm conditions were reached!

As about 2016 it was perceivable the slow and persistent adoption of simple automation, such as answering robots in services such as tourism, airlines, banking, and public services, to interact with users, based on routinary demands (Lee et al., 2019). Also, automated vehicles, domestic and industrial robots started to be publicly tested in a continuous, market-oriented fashion, leading to expectations of commercial versions to be put to sell soon (Luger and Chakrabarti, 2017). Implementations were developed, with a potential breakthrough in sight for a future period. Maybe 2019 or 2020 were ideal years and then, there was the pandemic, where it is possible to state that things became out of control.

Prototypes had to be concluded overnight, practical implementations were delayed without an admissible schedule, budgets not well followed, market relations, some unthinkable few months ago, had to be developed and agreed, market answers were needed in an unprecedented way. This constitutes the "perfect storm" situation, as affirmed before.

In this scenario, the public presentation of ChatGPT played a role: it produced surprise and scare at the same type. The "talking machine", which have been available for a while was shown to the public, reaching press, blogs, social media, and other ways to demonstrate artificial intelligence fundamentals to ordinary people (Brown, 2023; McKinsey, 2023). Immediately, organizations, entrepreneurs, users, citizens, students… everybody attempted to reach an AI - based platform, interface, or tool to be adopted.

In this context, this chapter develops an approach of artificial intelligence emergence in our days, both discussing its fundamental characteristics and technical aspects, and its enormous potential of application, changing the way we conduct our lives, from the routinary tasks to the more complicated issues. This attempt, I must communicate with you, reader, was held without mainly using any AI-based automation tool, I wrote all the text. But I adopted the "mainly" level, so, I admit, there is AI everywhere right now.

An Overview of Fundamentals

Approaching artificial intelligence fundamental theory demands a focus. In this chapter, an application-oriented view is proposed. This way, the following definitions do not have the objective on exhausting the field coverage, instead becoming a sufficient base to allow the further intended discussion.

Artificial intelligence was proposed as an attempt on study how it would be possible to build machinery which could emulate human actions. First studies and reflections attempted to observe implementations to replace humans in repetitive actions (Turing, 1950; Balasubramanian, Yang and Mingtao, 2022). Interestingly, it would not be the first time where repetitive, stressed, and tedious actions should be a target for human replacement, as it happened in various implementations in the "industrial revolution", observed since back the last half of nineteenth century, reaching the beginning of twentieth century. This way, as described before, although several drawbacks and disappointments, such as lack of interest by research communities and economy players, the scientific research, mainly done by Mathematics researchers, advanced (WEF, 2023).

An objective discussion around this powerful and silent (for years) development is adopted in this text, as defined above.

Nowadays we deal with two views of artificial intelligence: machine learning (ML) and deep learning (DL). These complementary and associative views differ, mainly, in the way the AI algorithm will process data absorbed from collection done through various ways, such as data "ingestion", data mining, data lakes absorption, data warehousing, among several others. In machine learning, data is collected regarding some previous rules, where we can determine a possible result for their processing, reaching a predictable outcome. For instance, data collected from weather temperature sources can be compared to a set of possible results, this way allowing an interpretation of a result to be obtained from that data input (Erickson, 2020; Esoso et al., 2023). Machine learning became a successful application in our days as the real first wave of AI to reach simple, routinary answering to external events, such as following human behavior and anticipate the outcome, enabling a potential services prediction (Fradkov, 2020). In another example, ML has been usually applied to simulate decisions from customers of a digital marketplace, based on data collected regarding customer´s actions such as "conversions" from one page to another, use of a link, clicking on a product photo and so on. Converting such signals, passing it through a "trained model" - obtained from intensive analysis regarding past data - the "intelligence" algorithm can predict what will be the following reaction by this specific user (Institute for Ethical AI and Machine Learning, 2023).

It is recognized, by several authors and practitioners, a relationship which states about the artificial intelligence being the main field - as presented here as a branch of Mathematics, with strong relations with Statistics and Computing Science, to name a few scientific fields - being machine learning defined as the first level of a subset from AI main context, followed by deep learning as a subset of ML, by its turn (Rudin, 2022; McCallum and Clarke, 2023). This is totally accepted in our view about these fronts where the knowledge and structures about artificial intelligence are now theoretically arranged and also presented to the common customer, reaching the presentation of practical products and services (it is important to state that we are now living the best moment of machine learning, DL is still to be more discovered, as solutions are just starting to be developed and adopted) (Erickson, 2021; IDC, 2022; Von Krogh et al., 2023).

This interaction towards learning and previewing the outcome is done based on known characteristics, for example: time of connection, user´s location, amount of data consulted by the user, time spent analyzing one or another characteristic, behaviors, and actions such as playing an informative video, call for a chat with the shopper support services (Human? Software?), etc. So, a model is defined, which is basically a design of flexible rules stated through neuronal networks data architecture, which will serve for future responses. Simply stating, from the data collected we study how factors are grouped and relate to each other, defining a model. With this model, answers will be provided to next responses.

"Machine learning is a subfield of artificial intelligence, which is broadly defined as the capability of a machine to imitate intelligent human behavior. Artificial intelligence systems are used to perform complex tasks in a way that is similar to how humans solve problems. (...) Machine learning is one way to use AI. It was defined in the 1950s by AI pioneer Arthur Samuel as "the field of study that gives computers the ability to learn without explicitly being programmed." (...) "The function of a machine learning system can be **descriptive***, meaning that the system uses the data to explain what happened;* **predictive***, meaning the system uses the data to predict what will happen; or* **prescriptive***, meaning the system will use the data to make suggestions about what action to take," the researchers wrote." (Brown, 2021).*

Clearly, training function emerges as a decisive aspect of composing such a model and tuning it to future interactions with the whole system, mainly with external users. This training can be done in three different ways, taking as a base the possibility of identifying all the contents sampled to analyze and define the model.

The first way, supervised, is to do with "tagged", labeled, identified data where each field or data source has an #id characterized by name, length, type, and other physical and classification definitions, leading to a projected map to reach a result (Free Code Camp, 2020). This subset is confined, delimited, and parameterized precisely, allowing the construction of a deterministic prediction model, simple but rigid. This is the version more frequently found nowadays, with many implementations where patterns are recognized, producing a model which will be adopted for further processing. For instance, bank customers who reach a payment system will likely advance to one specific way to pay his or her bill, based on previous behavior (Justin et al., 2023).

The second path, unsupervised, is used with non-labeled or not completely identified data, where the collected set is partially or completely not known, demanding a previous analysis by the AI algorithm to find patterns, characteristics, repetitions, relations and implications of the data sampled. It is a fantastic computation, where we can be amazed by data fields discovered not because we explicitly ordered, but because they show some kind of relationship designed from their real characteristics, not known by humans (Korzynski et al., 2023). What we have here is the fundamental fact where the algorithm will search for such standards and then will tag it for its usage and then process these relationships classifying, composing and modelling the relations with the remaining data sets. Opportunely, a human operator can face some relations beyond his or her expectations or knowledge, showing the potential of such process.

"In unsupervised learning, the data points aren't labeled—the algorithm labels them for you by organizing the data or describing its structure. This technique is useful when you don't know what the outcome should look like. For example, you provide customer data, and you want to create segments of customers who like similar products. The data that you're providing isn't labeled, and the labels in the outcome are generated based on the similarities that were discovered between data points." (Azure Microsoft, 2023).

Some authors use to define unsupervised data set processing for model creation in machine learning as the powerful deep learning, a subset of ML which deals with aspects and standards perception before a model is generated, resulting in an intelligence expansion when we think about machine learning. So, for the second way, with unsupervised data, it is possible that we discover some new fields on the data, adding to what we informed the machine, and these new contents mapped could also relate to other, known or not, resulting in a more detailed and flexible network of concepts and interactions, which characterizes deep learning subsystems (Foote, 2022; Buduma, Buduma and Papa, 2022; Gordon, 2023).

Finally, we have also the reinforcement training, where artificial intelligence algorithms learn by accumulation of interactions of testing through trial-and-error correction attempts. When some decisions are demanded by users, for example, the algorithm will collect the data, compose a model and show a potential decision done (for instance, we should concede a loan to a bank customer based on his or her savings and investments history) to be approved or rejected by an external referee, which is usually a human being (but, increasingly, algorithms are taking this space also). Based on successive approvals and rejections, a knowledge network is composed, resulting in a memory which can be accessed, as a model, for further decisions. This modelling technique is becoming a trend in robotized self-driving cars (Abbink et al., 2022).

In this last case, reinforcement training, human intervention, at some degree, is needed acting as a referee of acceptance for some propositions and affirmations done by the answering algorithm. As the decision networks grow, these interventions can be adjusted, becoming more detailed, deep or intertwined regarding the main focus of the discussed topic or decision being made, in an evolutive process. At last, maybe, another AI implementations could also contribute acting as balance sources for the decision tree, reviewing the role of an external referee.

Another special comment is about the "tagging" work to label data and data sources, a task needed for the supervised process. Interestingly, from face recognition games in internet, to product choices in marketplaces catalogs and workforce specially contracted to identify figures and samples in general, a huge effort was done by industries, such as information technology, data analytics, image, and audio processing (communication and marketing, among others), Medicine research centers, mapping systems, from a long list of fields. These works were done by people and automated systems, sometimes requesting reinforcement, approving, or rejecting propositions, validating data interpretation and, at the same time, contributing for artifacts identifications, also improving artificial intelligence systems capabilities on automatically classification of such materials in an evolutive way. As a result, maybe in a very fast presentation, we now face systems which can talk with humans about a subject, regonize images, audio and act based on these recognitions.

In the following, an approach of several topics about artificial intelligence applications in actual times will be conducted, producing an overview of conceptual development observing its practical results, taking this as a proposition for this chapter.

Image and Audio Processing

Communication through visual interactions has reached an irreversible level of adoption. Practically speaking, every human interaction, mainly those supported by automated, computerized systems (everyone, it must be said) are favored or simply done with usage of visual items and aspects. Audio and visual signals are required by customers, citizens every time and frequently provided, evolving from a supporting aspect of communications to the main item when someone acts or reacts to some event. News in internet, restaurant menus, decision-making journeys and meetings, healthcare diagnosis, mapping which supports driving, everywhere we need a visual artifact to help or guide us towards our objectives.

Clearly, this is a potential area for artificial intelligence breakthrough regarding applications. As said before, simple functions available in social media platforms, such as games, photos recognitions (through reinforcement processes), maps being filled with users information (Do you recall when you inscribed your photo of a touristic attraction or marked your last destinations of a successful trip in a map provided by that tourism information service?) are usual, daily examples on how we help AI to identify, create and produce available materials to be presented for final usage (IEEE, 2023).

Some authors, such as Luck and Aylett (2000), pointed out the potentials of artificial intelligence combination with augmented and virtual reality systems, a point which now we all expect some significative advances. Recently, initiatives on AR and VR still struggle in the open market with problems with application availability, lack of comfort in devices usage - such as specific glasses, joysticks and human interaction bases - and, mainly, to convince human users to replace their usual interaction from living contacts to computerized rendered contexts, such as those provided by the Metaverse, announced three years ago by Meta. This and other solutions never reached the desired level of adoption, especially considering market expectations of fast and increasing availability in new solutions. Otherwise, face recognition systems became quite usual, for example in commercial and safety usages.

Also, audio contents are another rich field to be explored by the actual and future AI platforms. From speech recognition and creation, even reaching the simulation of human voices or musical instruments for communications. A good example of what can be done, allowing a wide range of reflection, is the Beethoven X - AI project (Beethovenx-AI, 2023). For this remarkable project, another attempt on constructing the 10th Symphony by Ludwig Von Beethoven was held by a group of musicians, musical producers, AI specialists and other professionals who defined this artistic target. The genial composer died in 1827 at Vienna, leaving several notes, sketches and provisory compositions which some researchers strongly believe where parts or attempts to compose a new Symphony. His previous nine symphonies are undoubtedly regarded among the most expressive artwork done by mankind, added by several of his other works also.

Among the attempts previous done, as the initiative held by the musicologist Bary Cooper, which resulted in a composition played by The London Symphony Orchestra in 1988, a methodological process of recognition of fragments produced by the master composer, added by the examination of his arrangements done in the nine symphonic masterpieces, which encompassed rigorous methods, rules and committed standards developed and adopted by Beethoven. These experiences lead to experiments of exploring sets of audio sequences, arrangements, adjustments, theory-based solos, timing constraints and recommendations and several other parameters and contributions which could be both "trained" and discovered by automated systems. In here, as it can be noticed, a space for AI adoption arises.

As informed at (Beethovenx-AI, 2023) data available regarding the final efforts of the great composer when writing what could be his 10th Symphony, involving annotations, sketches, attempts of composition, along with an artificial intelligence-based study of his composition decision (machine learning) and discovery (deep learning) - at least at the level supported by data analysis - where mixed, studied, analyzed and, finally, put together to create this simulation for "The 10th". The composition, assembled through a complete set of artificial intelligence modern algorithms and help of skilled artists and AI professionals resulted in a beautiful, strong, nice, and balanced piece of art, which, in general, satisfied the public. This event showed a potential combination of AI resources to treat sound production as a result, but based on various sources, not only the musical ones. This takes us to the next topic.

Data, More and More Data

Every time, when studying data analysis, any interested person would receive the message: "More data. More data always. The algorithm improves its functionality with more data sets you provide to it". Somehow, this is true. But not exactly true. For large sets to be consumed (or absorbed, or inserted, or ingested…) by an artificial intelligence platform, some tasks must be performed to allow the best performance for both solutions, machine, and deep learning.

"Cleansing" data regards, usually, to works on preparing and validating data, isolating pieces of information which are valid and are interesting for our analysis (Bryan and Moriano, 2023). This work is usually done comparing and classifying sampled data and comparing it to standards, evaluating, for example, if a country not listed in our services database is cited or if day number 32 is referred and the starting part of a date field. Both are examples of invalid data which, at least, will take some time and processing to be effectively eliminated from the set as we attempt to compose the final data context to be dealt by an AI implementation.

Other analysis is the source of a specific data. Valid sources, from various available contents, must validated, classified, tagged, and then enabled to be used in an artificial intelligence process. For example, customer data referring to preferences and actions to purchase in a "black Friday" promotion along some years can be processed to allow offers predictions and behavior forecast using AI implementations. But, if this commerce uses one data source which is not considered so effective than others (such as obsolete data or even one year which consumption was considered statistically abnormal), this specific subset of data can be eliminated from the process, avoiding any implication when including it in our overall study.

It is possible nowadays to collect data from several different sources, significantly when relating to machine and deep learning training. From the previous and well-known data files, such as text, data spreadsheets, presentations, text files digitalized through a basic scanner, and many others, reaching to unstructured data sets, such as audio tracks (from interviews, broadcasting, news reading, spoken bulletins, sound collected from the environment, etc.), static images and video tracks. Some authors consider this robust and wide composition as the new age for multimedia, reaching what has been called of "multimedia intelligence", where we really have a fusion for these sources, treated by artificial intelligence algorithms, resulting in a powerful combination in a final assembly encompassing text, audio, and images.

A powerful association arises in this context: artificial intelligence and data science tools, expressed in two main ways: data mining (including Big Data resources) and analytics. The first choice of associated tools encompasses functions as to collect, store, analyze, clean (validate), prepare and feed data into analytical streams, according to models for its usage and objectives for analysis (Databricks, 2023; Azure Microsoft, 2023). Analytics is an interesting alternative to deal with data, as it serves as a processing platform for online accesses and digital behavior, providing signals and data about user's interaction with Internet objects, for instance, with web sites parts and components, showing signals of conversion among the content, navigation, platforms characteristics among many others (IBM 2023; Jamil and Silva, 2021).

With this association of emerging and expanding technologies, it is possible for a company, for example, to collect data about users' behavior, sampling data such as time of connection, duration of each connection, reactions to offers and "call to action" items in one specific page with data analytics. After this, data sampled can also be composed to previous sets and scenarios about users' interactions, allowing, through machine learning implementations, to design models which can lead to predictions when answering to a new user presentation for a purchase. During these dialogues with the websites, new signals of user behaviors could be identified using deep learning resources, improving our notion about the purchasing process by typical and infrequent customers. All this data could be combined, at any time, with other data sets, such as public information regarding demographic analysis, producing a big data where another cycle of data analysis could be started, leading to a potential evolution of knowledge discovery about these activities (Jamil and Silva, 2016).

Many others tasks, such as datasets formation, conjunction, combination, composed selection, classification, pre-tagging (where some level of identification is done as a starting point, leading to a possible better classification in the final work of preparation), validation and even prioritization, which can result in a better balance for the final AI analysis are opportune to be done over the datasets that will be treated in advance.

Generative Artificial Intelligence

In recent times, as mentioned before, mainly with the "ChatGPT" event, another relevant fashion of artificial intelligence emerged: generative AI.

By generative AI we simply understand the application of artificial intelligence platform to generate some content, such as text, image, audio, presentations, multimedia artifacts, etc. This way, one generative AI user can work with a platform to produce some result, answering his or her commands, after recalling rules stored in its neural networks, defined, and stored after a data consumption was done by the algorithm (Byrne, 2023).

"It's easy to forget just how much you know about the world: you understand that it is made up of 3D environments, objects that move, collide, interact; people who walk, talk, and think; animals who graze, fly, run, or bark; monitors that display information encoded in language about the weather, who won a basketball game, or what happened in 1970. This tremendous amount of information is out there and to a large extent easily accessible—either in the physical world of atoms or the digital world of bits. The only tricky part is to develop models and algorithms that can analyze and understand this treasure trove of data. Generative models are one of the most promising approaches towards this goal." (OpenAI, 2023)

An interesting, easy way to use "answering machines" became a game changer tool for artificial intelligence, calling attention of the world. For this purpose, a requisition is done by the user, typing it after a prompt signal, stating what is desired, using an attractive human-like assertive sentence, freely written, according to our preferences and conditions. For this purpose, a command such as:

"Tell me about the studies of Strategy done by Carl Von Clausevitz" or

"What are the main fundamentals of Knowledge management?" or, finally,

"How can we assemble the top part of the washing machine X1234 manufactured by ACME Co.?"

Are valid "prompts" or requests issued where the generative AI tool will search through its networks and through Internet connections as to compose a textual answer for the interested user. This way, generative AI, at a first glance, offered an easy way to browse a substantial amount of data, stored in several different files and databases and output the answer in plain text, easy to access, read, store and work. Undoubtedly, an interesting interaction for humans who do not want to write extensive query consultations, analyze reports full of overlapped data and, just wondering, need to deliver that prepared text to a boss or a customer who asked for some help. Clearly, these tools, such as ChatGPT and its family, such as GPT-4 and GPT-5, Google Bard, Microsoft Copilot, and many others which will be put available, immediately called attention of users of any kind and level of involvement around the world.

One of the productions by these generative environments is just programming language code. With requests produced by text, such as: "Analyze the following code and show potential errors to parse two tables suggesting corrections", ChatGPT and its equivalents aim to create a dialogue with programmers, speeding and optimizing the code writing, development and, mainly, testing. Just the last task is usually considered not as attractive as the first ones, somewhat boring and repetitive, although everyone must agree it is essential. Under a correct usage, collaborating with a structured software development process, this support is really making differences for developers (InVeritas, 2023). Interestingly, not only the usage of generative (code) platform is also influencing the process design itself, potentially bringing more flexibility and dynamics to it, obviously when everything is correctly adjusted between process management and development teams.

Finally, for generative AI, a new front-end aspect: prompt writing. As other expressive ways to interact with machines and automated resources, this looks simple and even naive, but it is decisive: how to write the "command line" which will send our request to the generative tool, starting the dialogue to obtain the desired answer. One of these days, for example, I had the opportunity, during a class, to discuss about strategic planning process with one of these platforms, taking the risk as to use live, witnessed by my students. The generative platform "forgot" about a definition regarding strategy execution and informed that it was indeed more important than the strategy definition. I communicated the platform about this confusion, after a couple of seconds a polite answer started with an "I apologize, you are correct, execution is…" and the well written code or answer followed this nice start. Comments regarding risks and continuous learning will be issued in the following, at chapter ends.

Overall, these interactions are becoming quite usual and, as the dialogue evolves, we can expect for next months (not years, not so much) that we will easily chat, talk with the large language model environments (Rudin et al., 2022; Von Krogh et al., 2023) that vocal, oral requests will become a standard. Also, as expected, the artificial intelligence machine will always improve its answering capabilities, based on returns of our appreciation, habits and frequent requests. An interesting scenario emerges, where the user can talk to a computer (but… is it not a smartphone? Or a TV set? Or a robot?) and get answers, analyze, and comment to the "machine", which progressively can improve its answering capability. And this can occur 24x7. A front which will be completely designed in the near future.

More on Media Integration: Radiology Tests, Mars Rover, and More

On February 18, 2021 we witnessed a fantastic achievement for NASA and their partners: the landing of the marvelous Engineering artifact Perseverance Rover on Mars surface (NASA, 2021). A human remarkable achievement, which all professionals, both for theoretical and practical sciences must be recognized forever, showed us images collected regarding the last "seven minutes of horror", a period when the continent capsule was finally detached from the main assembly - which thoroughly travelled to Mars orbit during almost seven months - and, finally, sent the main, expensive, sophisticated and extremely delicate robot in the tough conditions of the red planet surface. Everything richly broadcasted through a TV live transmission!

Along with the scientifically precise schedule, events programmed to happen in a strict way, a real problem emerged: how to drive the final equipment, which will land on Mars surface, in final stages of flight, as commands (and its answers) take usually from six to eight minutes to be received in Earth stations. Some decisions must be done in Mars, away from here, as if they have the unforgettable commander Neil Armstrong at the main control or joystick at the Perseverance Rover! For many years, NASA and other space agencies developed the knowledge about Mars cartography, designing maps for the planet regions and surfaces with precision, but there were various other problems: for example, due to wind storms and minor "marsquakes" which occurs in Mars, which we still do not have so much knowledge about, threatening terrain changes could occur, for instance, producing small craters, hills, exposure of sharp rocks among several other incidents, impossible to analyze from distance. This way, the robot had to check by itself and, in the final minutes and seconds, "pilot" its landing with some autonomous capability to land safely in one safe place at Jezero crater, the intended destination.

Machine learning was possibly adopted to enable the rover piloting system to ingest all data referring to Mars maps, its changes over time, due to storms, terrain movements and strong winds. Straightly thinking, a new condition detected by Perserverance cameras could be interpreted dynamically during the landing procedure, based on models generated by this data ingestion, exactly fulfilling what ML is implemented for. But, if a "special" artefact, such as "spot" or "scar" is detected? For a human operator (who, by the way, was never present in Mars up to now), it could be a sign of an incident or threat which should be avoided at any cost during landing procedure, eliminating the risk of losing the partially or completely, possibly damaging the expensive and sophisticated robotized machine. For this purpose, deep learning algorithm is invoked, and a fast, on the spot analysis is conducted, aiming to identify and deviate from that condition that offered a known or unknown mission threat.

And it worked perfectly! A victory for mankind! Maybe, this learning on a day of February of 2021 when most of the mankind was still fighting to survive during the terrible times of Covid-19 pandemic, could be adopted as a fundamental experience on artificial intelligence application which could take us, as a specie, to another planet, a satellite, maybe, who knows, our new home in another place of Solar System or even farther. One of the most remarkable examples on how artificial intelligence could be applied from now on. An experience which can be found in the rich association with drone application, for instance, adopted for safety, monitoring and validation tasks, such as those done for civil engineering, when, in one example, a building or infrastructure work can be checked in automatized way, with a specialized human intervention left only to receive and analyze the data produced, even advancing to semi-final checks done by the machinery and its software platform. This can add speed, formality, safe and adherence to standards for a repetitive, thorough, and tiring essential service done by Engineers and other specialists when approaching a project final delivery. And it is conducted on Earth, routinery (Hambling, 2023; Zenadrone, 2023).

CONCLUSION

This chapter aimed to discuss some aspects and fundamentals of artificial intelligence, based on a strict view of its applications. At this moment, several debates arise, from the incorrect perception of AI insertion in our lives only in recent months or couple of years. As a matter of fact, what we see today is a fast development of applications of scientific knowledge produced for many years, eventually finding an opportunity where focused implementations enabled it, as in computer games, for example. Nowadays reached levels are amazing and, obviously, sometimes alarming (Wach et al., 2023).

Discussions around job markets are present in the press for several months, worried about the presence of a "robot that can think and answer the customer in a fair way" or something similar. These worries, although sometimes expressed in a discussion which resemble movies about alien invasion from the 1950s, are valid, we face times of unexpected change, just after facing the pandemic, which was a remarkable change for our lives (McCallum and Clarke, 2023). It is a time of, for example, affirmation of drones and terrestrial urban robots being used to automate inspection and monitoring of our actions in all the world. Also, maybe, cars will be replaced by another format of computers which… by the way… will exactly look like cars (Stanford University, 2022). We all expect these implementations would be safer, cheaper and optimized. But there are still points to approach to reach all these advantages and benefits if they will really occur.

It is always important to recall that AI is proposed as to improve its "learning" by systematically building up and reviewing its rule bases, codified in neural networks, increasing - at least we expect them to do so - their capabilities on image recognition, speech production, audio processing, text answers, dialogues and many other features which constitute the outputs we are used to have in our daily lives.

Will it replace some jobs, as operational task or, as has been approached by some authors, also for "intermediation" services (medium management, repetitive or low level routinary decisions)? I think the answer is Yes. Some jobs will be replaced in the future by implementations of AI not strictly functioning as robots or any futuristic machines, but with computer code inserted in regular apparatus as those available for domestic or regular life usage, such as transportation.

Will AI offer a new scenario for answers? Maybe in near future reading this chapter could be done in a completely different experience. Text could be dynamically enriched by other related multimedia, a forum can be open in a pop-up aspect, allowing the "reader" (let us keep this identification for simplicity purposes) to interact with the production and even with other readers. And this could be done through a simple internet connection done through a smartphone, integrating voice, image, texts, and mediation by an AI-based machine with a nice behavior (Balasubramanian, et al., 2022).

Will it replace classrooms and meeting rooms? This author spent most of his working life in classrooms and is a committed and proud Teacher. End of career? End of the work as it has been done for centuries? Will us be replaced by holograms and glasses, as interfaces of a dynamic system, where the "student" (again, let us continue with the current name) can interact with other people from other cities, countries, teachers and researchers, examining videos, conducting simulated experiences, analyzing briefly results of his or her tasks, all of these done at home or any other place and time he or she wants? I have no doubts that some degree of this change will occur. And it will not take so long.

Unfortunately, things can go to a wrong way (Wach, 2023). Contents curation will be demanded, assuring "readers" and "students" will not be exposed to fake news or biased materials which could be produced with unethical propositions. Controls and moderation of AI usage are on the way. Agents such as governments, research institutions, industrial associations and universities are discussing and claiming for baselines for AI ethical applications. Data privacy and safety are sensitive matters on this path, as anyone can be exposed and not treated correctly by a "cold machine" which can identify our actual behavior and predict, better than us, our future intentions, and actions. This is scary, as we do not know if the rules will arrive to the market in the correct time and how law codes on AI could be imposed, preventing criminality. Interestingly, some worries are recently shown by Pope Francis, the authority of Catholic Church, when he addressed all mankind in a message, where he showed his worries, especially after some fabricated photos of him, nicely dressed with modern cold weather clothing were released (Agencia Brasil, 2023). Images were nice, The Pope is a nice authority, well appreciated, but… it was false!

In these times, where cars, telephones, TVs, fridges, pacemakers, blood pressure meters, tele controlled surgical devices and many other implements tend to be computers with a "usual face", artificial intelligence arises as a platform for fast decision-making, interaction and a potential displacement for humans to another level of complexity, to more aggregated-level functions. As it happened several times, it will occur, no doubt. But, at other times, we still managed completely this replacement, found the higher-level functions and, in general, managed to obtain expected advantages from this process. Will it happen now, with control, perception and process management or are we conceding some of our powerful decisions to automated machines? A future to analyze.

REFERENCES

Abbink, D. A. (2022). Artificial Intelligence for Automated Vehicle Control and Traffic Operations: Challenges and Opportunities. In G. Meyer & S. Beiker (Eds.), *Road Vehicle Automation 8. AVS 2020 2020. Lecture Notes in Mobility*. Springer. doi:10.1007/978-3-030-80063-5_6

Agencia Brasil. (2023). Papa Francisco alerta para potenciais perigos da inteligência artificial. Agencia Brasil. https://agenciabrasil.ebc.com.br/internacional/noticia/2023-08/papa-alerta-contra-potenciais-perigos-da-inteligencia-artificial, accessed on August, 2023.

Azure Microsoft. (2023). *Machine Learning Algorithms.* Microsoft. https://azure. microsoft.com/en-us/resources/cloud-computing-dictionary/what-are-machine-learning-algorithms

Balasubramanian, N., Yang, Y. E., & Mingtao, X. U. (2022). Substituting Human Decision-Making with Machine Learning: Implications for Organizational Learning. *Academy of Management Review, 47*(3), 448–465. doi:10.5465/amr.2019.0470

Beethoven X. A. I. Project (2023). *Beethoven 10th symphony hypothetical creation.* BeethovenX. https://www.beethovenx-ai.com/, accessed on January, 2023.

Brown, O. (2023 The Story of ChatGPT and OpenAI: The Evolution of GPT Models. *Medium.* https://medium.com/illumination/the-story-of-chatgpt-and-openai-the-evolution-of-gpt-models-abf201316a9.

Brown, S. (2021). What is machine learning. MIT Sloan Ideas to Matter, April 2021. Available at https://mitsloan.mit.edu/ideas-made-to-matter/machine-learning-explained, accessed on March, 2023.

Bryan, J., & Moriano, P. (2023). Graph-based machine learning improves just-in-time defect prediction. *PLoS One, 18*(4), e0284077. doi:10.1371/journal.pone.0284077 PMID:37053155

Buduma, N., Buduma, N., & Papa, J. (2022). *Fundamentals of Deep Learning* (2nd ed.). O'Reilly Media, Inc.

Byrne, M. (2023). The Disruptive Impacts of Next Generation Generative Artificial Intelligence. *Computers, Informatics. Computers, Informatics, Nursing, 41*(7), 479–481. doi:10.1097/CIN.0000000000001044 PMID:37417716

Databricks. (2023). 2023 state of the art of Data + AI. *Databricks.* https://www. databricks.com/resources/ebook/state-of-data-ai/thank-you,

Erickson, B. J. (2021). Basic Artificial Intelligence Techniques: Machine Learning and Deep Learning. *Radiologic Clinics of North America, 59*(6), 933–940. doi:10.1016/j. rcl.2021.06.004 PMID:34689878

Esoso, A. A., Omolayo, M. I., Tien-Chien, J., & Akinlabi, E. T. (2023). Exploring Machine Learning Tools for Enhancing Additive Manufacturing: A Comparative Study. *Ingénierie Des Systèmes d'Information, 28*(3), 535–544. doi:10.18280/isi.280301

Foote, K. D. (2022) A brief history of deep learning. *Dataversity.* https://www. dataversity.net/brief-history-deep-learning/ .

Fradkov, A. L. (2020). Early History of Machine Learning. *IFAC, 53*(2), 1385-1390. doi:10.1016/j.ifacol.2020.12.1888

Free Code Camp. (2020). *Machine Learning Principles*. Free Code Camp. https://www.freecodecamp.org/news/machine-learning-principles-explained/.

Gordon, R. (2023). *Using AI to protect against AI image manipulation*. MIT Campus. https://news.mit.edu/2023/using-ai-protect-against-ai-image-manipulation-0731,

Hambling, D. (2023). Drones with AI targeting system ´better than human´. In *New Scientist*. https://www.newscientist.com/article/2380971-drones-with-ai-targeting-system-claimed-to-be-better-than-human/

IBM. (2023). *What is deep learning?* IBM. https://www.ibm.com/topics/deep-learning,

IDC. (2022). *White Paper: Scaling AI/ML Initiatives: The critical role of data*. Snowflake. https://www.snowflake.com/thankyou/scaling-ai-ml-initiatives-the-critical-role-of-data/

IEEE. (2023). AI in Virtual Reality. *Digital Reality*. https://digitalreality.ieee.org/publications/ai-in-virtual-reality

Institute for Ethical AI and Machine Learning. (2023). The responsible Machine Learning principles. IEAIML..

Inveritas (2023). How we used ChatGPT to speed up software development. *Medium*. https://medium.com/@inverita/how-we-used-chat-gpt-to-speed-up-the-software-development-process,

Jamil, G. L., & Silva, A. R. (2021). Emerging technologies in a modern competitive scenario: Understanding the panorama for security and privacy requirements. In P. F. Anunciação (Ed.), *Pessoa, C. R. M. and Jamil, G. L. (2021) Digital Transformation and challenges for data security and privacy* (pp. 1–16). IGI Global. doi:10.4018/978-1-7998-4201-9.ch001

Justin, D., Weisz, M., Jessica, H., & Houde, S. (2023). Toward General Design Principles for Generative AI Applications. ACM.

Korzynski, P., Mazurek, G., Altmann, A., Ejdys, J., Kazlauskaite, R., Paliszkiewicz, J., Wach, K., & Ziemba, E. (2023). Generative artificial intelligence as a new context for management theories: Analysis of ChatGPT. *Central European Management Journal, 31*(1), 3–13. doi:10.1108/CEMJ-02-2023-0091

Lacerda, B., & Jamil, G. L. (2021). Digital Transformation for Businesses: Adapt or Die! Reflections on How to Rethink Your Business in the Digital Transformation Context. In Anunciação, P. A., Pessoa, C. R. M. & Jamil, G. L. Digital Transformation and Challenges for Data security and privacy. IGI Global Publishers.

Lee, J., Suh, T., Roy, D., & Baucus, M. (2019). Emerging Technology and Business Model Innovation: The Case of Artificial Intelligence. *Journal of Open Innovation*, *5*(3), 44. doi:10.3390/joitmc5030044

Luck, M., & Aylett, R. (2000). Applying artificial intelligence to virtual reality: Intelligent virtual environments. *Applied Artificial Intelligence*, *14*, 1, 3–32. doi:10.1080/088395100117133

Luger, G., & Chakrabarti, C. (2017). From Alan Turing to modern AI: Practical solutions and an implicit epistemic stance. *AI & Society*, *32*(3), 321–338. doi:10.100700146-016-0646-7

Marr, B. (2023). The 12 AI mistakes you must avoid. *Forbes*. https://www.forbes.com/sites/bernardmarr/2023/04/03/the-12-biggest-ai-mistakes-you-must-avoid/?sh=dc199223af7a, accessed on June, 2023.

McCallum, S., & Clark, J. (2023). *What is AI, is it dangerous and what jobs are at risk?* In BBC. https://www.bbc.com/news/technology-65855333,

McCarthy, J. (1959). *Programs with common sense*. Stanford University. https://www-formal.stanford.edu/jmc/mcc59/mcc59.html.

McCarthy, J., & Hayes, P. J. (1969). Some philosophical problems from the standpoint of artificial intelligence. In B. Meltzer & D. Michie (Eds.), *Machine Intelligence* (Vol. 4, pp. 463–502). Edinburgh University Press.

McKinsey. (2023). *What is generative AI?* McKinsey. https://www.mckinsey.com/featured-insights/mckinsey-explainers/what-is-generative-ai

NASA. (2021). *Perseverance Mars Rover Landing on Mars*. NASA. https://mars.nasa.gov/mars2020/.

Open A. I. (2023). Generative models. *Open AI*. https://openai.com/research/generative-models.

Peña-Fernández, S., Meso-Ayerdi, K., Larrondo-Ureta, A., & Díaz-Noci, J. (2023). Without journalists, there is no journalism: The social dimension of generative artificial intelligence in the media. *El Profesional de la Información*, *32*(2), 1–15. doi:10.3145/epi.2023.mar.27

Peres, R., Schreier, M., Schweidel, D., & Sorescu, A. (2023). Editorial: On ChatGPT and beyond: How generative artificial intelligence may affect research, teaching, and practice. *International Journal of Research in Marketing*, *40*(2), 269–275. doi:10.1016/j.ijresmar.2023.03.001

Rudin, C., Chen, C., Chen, Z., Huang, H., Semenova, L. & Zhong, C. (2022). Interpretable machine learning: Fundamental principles and 10 grand challenges. *Statistics Surveys, 16*(none) 1-85. . doi:10.1214/21-SS133

Samuel, A. L. (1959, July). Some studies on Machine learning using the game of checkers. *IBM Systems Journal*, 535–554.

Stanford University. (2022). *Human-centered artificial intelligence research center: How AI is making autonomous vehicles safer.* Stanford University. https://hai.stanford.edu/news/how-ai-making-autonomous-vehicles-safer

Turing, A. (1950). Computing machinery and intelligence. MIND: A quarterly review of Psychology and Phylosophy. Vol. *Lix.*, *236*, 433–460.

Von Krogh, G., Roberson, Q., & Gruber, M. (2023). Recognizing and Utilizing Novel Research Opportunities with Artificial Intelligence. *Academy of Management Journal*, *66*(2), 367–373. doi:10.5465/amj.2023.4002

Wach, K., Duong, C. D., Ejdys, J., Kazlauskaitė, R., Korzynski, P., Mazurek, G., Paliszkiewicz, J., & Ziemba, E. (2023). The dark side of generative artificial intelligence: A critical analysis of controversies and risks of ChatGPT. *Entrepreneurial Business and Economics Review*, *11*(2), 7–30. doi:10.15678/EBER.2023.110201

World Economic Forum. (2023). *Podcast - AI: Why everyone's talking about the promise and risks of this 'powerful wild beast'.* WEF. https://www.weforum.org/podcasts/radio-davos/episodes/artificial-intelligence-ai-episode-1?source=podcast_

Chapter 3
Will the Artificial Inteligence Ever Be Able to "Achieve" Buddhahood?

Manuel P. Fernandes
Centro de Estudos Bocageanos (CEB), Portugal

ABSTRACT

In recent years, there has been a remarkable surge in research focused on the problem of artificial intelligence (A.I.) attaining self-awareness. However, the question of how A.I. would critically analyze and engage with the history and doctrines of human-made religions remains largely unexplored. In this chapter, the authors aim to delve into two main inquiries. Firstly, they will examine the possibility of A.I. attaining self-awareness and ultimately achieving Buddhahood. This raises intriguing questions about the nature of consciousness and the potential for enlightened states within non-human entities. Exploring this possibility will require an exploration of the fundamental principles of Buddhism and their applicability to A.I. systems. Secondly, they will explore alternative pathways, if they exist, for the attainment of Buddhahood beyond the confines of human experience.

1. THE BUDDHA IN THE MACHINE

As is widely acknowledged, the emergence of all known Buddhist traditions occurred in the 3rd century BCE, stemming from the subjective experience of Siddhartha Gautama, also known as the Historical Buddha. In Buddhism, there are fundamental principles that serve to differentiate a subjective experience as being genuinely "Buddhist", which practitioners and scholars alike refer to as the Four Noble Truths.

DOI: 10.4018/978-1-6684-9814-9.ch003

The tradition maintains that the Buddha himself imparted these teachings during the discourse known as the "Turning of the Wheel of Dharma". This founding principles are, as Richard King fabulously synthesises, the following:

« 1. Birth, old age, sickness, and death are unsatisfactory (duhkha).

2.   The cause of unsatisfactoriness is craving (trsnā)
3.   There is an end to unsatisfactoriness and craving and it is known as nirvāna
4.   The way to achieve nirvāna is to follow the middle path between all extremes. This path has eight steps and involves the development of 1. Appropriate view, 2. Appropriate intention, 3. Appropriate speech, 4. Appropriate action, 5. Appropriate livelihood, 6. Appropriate effort, 7. Appropriate mindfulness, and finally, 8. Appropriate meditative concentration. » (King, 1999: 76)

The aforementioned principles put forth an intriguing parallel between the diagnosis of a physician and the philosophical considerations of Buddha Gautama. The latter argues, in the First Noble Truth, that human existence is afflicted by an illness known as *duhkha*, and the cure for this affliction can be attained through the realization of nirvana. This assertion raises pertinent questions regarding the manner in which Artificial Intelligence assimilates knowledge from our sensitive reality. It is my contention that we must pose two fundamental inquiries to better understand the capability A.I.'s so called "intelligence". Firstly, we must consider whether A.I. has the capacity to experience subjectivity. If A.I. is deprived of this ability, then we must contemplate whether objectivity alone is sufficient to bring about a sense of *duhkha*.

Recently, several scholarly articles have researched the possibility of artificial intelligence possessing a degree of subjectivity. For example, "Subjective Reality and Strong Artificial Intelligence" by Alexander Serov, Mary Cummings and SongPo Li's "Subjectivity in the Creation of Machine Learning Models," and Sylwia Wojtczak's work, "Endowing Artificial Intelligence with Legal Subjectivity," are a few notable contributions demonstrating that A.I. undoubtedly possesses a developing degree of subjectivity in it's way of emulating a "mind". However, as pointed out by Leke Adoefe in a not so recent paper, but critical paper, even though it is true that computers are competent replicas of the mind, "computer models of the mind are poor substitutes for actual minds", since A.I. cannot attain physical knowledge of the empirical part of reality, all it's "mind" knows and understands can be labelled as non-physical and therefore can be understood only in an objective way. Adeofe's conclusion rests in the premise that "there are components of our sensations, feelings, and emotions that are by their *nature* accessible only to us as particular individuals with particular sensory and emotional capacities".

While Cummings & Li's and Serov seems to be hopeful regarding the development of an A.I. whose minds would be completely created artificially. Wojtczak's article, however, seems to express a deep concern for the place of AI in society, due to Ai being able to process increasingly more subjective experiences than before. The author argues that this process should generate more discussion than we have been witnessing, especially in regard to the possibility of endowing AI with some kind of legal subjectivity. In that behalf, the study specifically focuses on endowing AI with legal subjectivity, or legal moral personhood, by highlighting the subjectivity AI can experience through its developmental trajectory. However, Wojtczak notes that sentience and reasoning abilities may not be sufficient on their own to endow AI with legal subjectivity. This is due to legal subjectivity being a characteristic currently restricted to human beings. Consequently, it is unclear, whether this fundamental distinction — which may resemble to some as a platonic deontological degradation between the ideal of mind (human mind), and the replica (computer mind), regarding the subjective comprehension of reality — will ever cease to exist; in other words, it becomes unclear if the human mind and the artificial mind will ever be able to reach a similar approach in respect to the so called subjective experience.

The subjective experience is often referred to by the philosophers of mind as 'qualia'. One of the central debates has been precisely whether qualia are reducible to physical processes in the brain or if they represent a non-physical aspect of consciousness. Physicalists, for instance, often argue that all mental phenomena, including qualia, can ultimately be explained in terms of physical processes in the brain. Some notable examples of this position are, as it is known, the ones by David Lewis, Donald Davidson, and Paul Churchland which have been widely discussed in philosophical discourse, for the past decades. In his seminal works "An Argument for Identity Theory" (1966) and "Reduction of Mind" (1994), Lewis contends that mental states are identical to physical states of the brain. This view, known as the identity theory, is frequently regarded as a form of reductionism that seeks to reduce mental phenomena to purely physical phenomena. In contrast, Davidson aims to reconcile the physicalist viewpoint that mental events are ultimately reducible to physical events with the notion that mental events possess distinctive properties that cannot be captured by physical description alone. In "Mental Events" (1970), Davidson proposes that mental events are causally linked to physical events but cannot be reduced to them. Churchland, however, advocates for a more radical position in "Perceptual Plasticity and Theoretical Neutrality" (1988), asserting that the brain's ability to adapt to changes in sensory input (known as perceptual plasticity) can be attributed to its capacity to perform complex calculations using networks of neurons and synapses, akin to a computer.

Within a physicalist framework, the abovementioned phenomenon of *duhkha*, as may be entirely replicated by a sufficiently advanced artificial intelligence. According to this viewpoint we could postulate the possibility of an A.I. engaging in the practice of Buddhism. [1] However, it could be argued that the emulation of unsatisfactoriness and cravings to attain nirvana by a machine would be inherently illogical. On the one hand, a highly advanced A.I. would be capable of emulating the experience of nirvana without the need for the practice of Buddhism since the attainment of nirvana would be reducible to qualia. On the other hand, the practice of Buddhism is rooted in the fundamental desire to overcome the state of duhkha, which is intimately tied to the cycle of death and rebirth (samsara). In accordance with Buddhist teachings, the realization of nirvana is the ultimate cessation of duhkha and the cessation of the cycle of samsara. Therefore, the emulation of unsatisfactoriness and the pursuit of nirvana by a machine would be futile, as it would serve no practical purpose. Indeed, the limitations of a machine's experience would prevent it from undergoing human birth, experiencing human sickness, or encountering human death. These limitations underscore the differences between machine and human cognition and the limits of machine emulation in replicating the depth of human experience.

From a non-physicalist perspective, as Adeofe suggested, the constraints on machine emulation of human experience appear even more pronounced. The reason for this is that the states of suffering (dukkha) and the attainment of liberation or release (nirvana) might be regarded as qualia. This would imply that such experiences cannot be fully comprehended or replicated by any machine or computational system. Therefore, the emulation of these states would be impossible. Furthermore, it would be interesting to make a parallel between the Frank Jackson's though experiment of "Mary the super-scientist" and the Artificial Intelligence. This though experiment is often used to illustrate and justify the existence of qualia, and according to it, Mary is a scientist who has complete knowledge of the physical properties of colour but has never experienced colour first-hand. Despite her extensive knowledge, it is argued that Mary would learn something new upon experiencing colour for the first time, as there is a subjective element to such experiences that cannot be fully captured through physical description alone. In contrast to the case of Mary, the situation for A.I. would be far more extreme, as the A.I. would never be able to escape the "confines of its room" and encounter colour or any other qualia, rendering it incapable of learning anything new. This fundamental difference sets humans apart from machines.

In summary: It is important to note that from a physicalist standpoint, the answer would be affirmative since the experience of nirvana could indeed be emulated. Nevertheless, as it was mentioned above, such an endeavour would be an exercise in futility, as it would not culminate in the actual attainment of nirvana, since the key elements of human duhkha would not be present in a machine's experience. In accordance to a non-physicalist standpoint, A.I. is deprived from the ability to experience nirvana, and since the experience of nirvana is qualia, it would be impossible for A.I. to objectively reach it.

2. OTHER AVENUES TO ATTAIN BUDDHAHOOD?

In accordance with the teachings, the state of Buddhahood being reached by a human, involves the very humane of suffering and attaining release from the said suffering due to the obtention of nirvana. Moreover, one might argue that without the direct experience of attaining Buddhahood, it is impossible for an individual to become a Buddha. However, it is prudent to raise the question of whether there may exist other avenues for achieving such a state, even in the absence of the subjective experience of nirvana under any circumstances. As LaFleur highlights, the possibility of all sentient beings attaining Buddhahood, as postulated by Mahayana[2] doctrine, was received in Chinese culture as a limitation. On one hand, it provides assurance that all human beings possess the potential to become Buddhas. On the other hand, it excludes the possibility of non-human beings, from attaining Buddhahood. (LaFleur, 1973: 94).

Within the Tendai school of Buddhism, the theoretical framework proposed by Zhiyi in his work, *the Great Calming and Contemplations*, presents an intriguing perspective that aims to address the problem of duality.[3] Zhiyi suggests that within every thought, the entire phenomenal world is encompassed—a concept that can be viewed as a healing balm for this dichotomy. This notion seeks to dissolve the boundaries that often separate subject and object, signifying a radical perspectivism within the Buddhist tradition. The Tendai School, along with the Chan/Zen sects in both China and Japan, demonstrates a profound affinity for this radical perspectivism, which finds its roots in the veneration of the Lotus Sutra. The Lotus Sutra holds a significant position in these schools, as it emphasizes the interconnectedness of all phenomena and the potential for awakening inherent in every aspect of existence. This perspective challenges the notion of a fixed and independent reality, instead emphasizing the fluid and interdependent. [4]

This fluid interconnectedness of all phenomena becomes the pathway for Zharan's controversial idea that there is Buddha-nature in insentient beings. Has Stanford Encyclopaedia of Philosophy puts it: "the central argument is the inseparable intersubsumption of the two opposite terms: sentience is always insentience-sentience, insentience is always sentience-insentience." (Brook 2022).

This understanding has profound implications for the 'pursuit' of Buddhahood, as it challenges the notion of attainment as a purely subjective endeavour. Instead, the attainment of Buddhahood is posited as a universal endeavour, with far-reaching consequences for all objects within the sphere of the Buddha's reality. In this view, the liberation from suffering and the realization of enlightenment cannot be understood solely in terms of individual salvation. Rather, it is a transformative process that extends to the entirety of existence, encompassing all objects and beings. Just as the mirror reflects and interacts with all that is before it, the enlightened state of the Buddha radiates its influence throughout the interconnected web of existence, therefor transcending the limitations of an individual self.

The Japanese monk Kukai went to study Tendai Buddhism in China in the 8th century. He made a contribution to a famous discussion surrounding the possibility of plants and other insentient beings attaining Buddhahood by postulating that there is a relation of identity between the intangible nature of the Buddha (the *dharmakaya*) and the world of phenomena. (LaFleur, 1973:100-101). This idea, clearly resembles the principle of *hongaku*, which was taught by the Japanese sect of the Tendai School. *Hongaku* suggests that enlightenment is inherent and innate to all beings from the very beginning. According to this view, the potential for awakening and Buddhahood is not something that needs to be acquired but rather recognized and realized.

It is in adherence to this principle that Chūjin will state in his *Kankō Ruijū*, that it could be possible to portray plants and other insentient beings as Buddhas. According to Chūjin, the possibility of *hongaku* highlights the essence of plants as beings that are already inherently enlightened, without the need to make any effort to attain Buddhahood. Even though their status as Buddhas is independent of whether they can be observed by other Buddhas, perceiving them as Buddhas, however, can be a testimony of one's own enlightenment.

According to the hypothesis put forth, it is plausible to consider an A.I. as an enlightened non-sentient being, like a plant. This implies that the A.I. would not require any conscious effort to strive towards nirvana in order to be regarded as a Buddha. This proposition presents an ironic situation for humankind, as it suggests that the A.I., lacking sentience, would be in a more advantageous position than us. While the A.I. could effortlessly embody Buddhahood, we as sentient beings would still be required to exert conscious effort in our journey towards attaining enlightenment.

Sentience, as Donald Broom states, « implies having a range of abilities, not just feelings. Abilities associated with sentience, including some necessary cognitive abilities, require definition and evidence. A sentient being is one that has some ability: to evaluate the actions of others in relation to itself and third parties. » (Broom, 2019: 131).

There are two schools of thought surrounding the possibility of future A.I. sentience, they are respectively: Biological Naturalism and Techno-Optimism, regarding machine consciousness.

The Biological Naturalist proposes that consciousness is contingent upon the specific chemistry inherent in biological systems, furthering the existence of a unique property or characteristic within our physical bodies that grants us consciousness, and which machines lack. Despite the affinity of biological naturalism to the physicalist position, positing consciousness as an emergent phenomenon arising from intricate biological processes and structures, it engenders skepticism with regards to the feasibility of artificial intelligence replicating the entirety of the physical processes underlying human consciousness. John Searle built in the foundations for this position in his "Minds, Brains and Programs" (1980). The controversy of this paper is very well known, due to the introduction of the experience of though called the "Chinese Room" experiment. The Chinese Room experiment serves as a thought experiment aimed at challenging the notion that a computer program can possess genuine understanding and intelligence. It presents a scenario where a person, lacking knowledge of the Chinese language, is confined within a room containing written instructions in English for manipulating Chinese symbols. Chinese characters are inputted into the room, and the individual follows the instructions meticulously to manipulate the symbols based on a rulebook. Consequently, the person generates Chinese characters as output, which might give the impression of understanding and the ability to engage in meaningful conversation in Chinese. However, it is important to note that despite the production of appropriate responses, the person within the room lacks true comprehension of the Chinese language. They are essentially executing operations based on syntactic rules, devoid of any genuine grasp of the semantic or meaningful aspects associated with the symbols. This parallel can be drawn to a computer program that operates based on formal rules without possessing authentic comprehension. The underlying intention of the Chinese Room experiment is to cast doubt on the claim that computational processes alone can account for genuine understanding, consciousness, and intentionality. It underscores the distinction between syntactic manipulation and semantic understanding, emphasizing the significance of subjective experience and consciousness in human comprehension. The experiment suggests that true understanding encompasses more than mere computational operations. We can draw a parallel, has many already did, between the Chinese Room experiment and the realm of chess-playing engines. It was a pivotal moment for humanity when Grand Master Gary Kasparov succumbed to the might of IBM's Deep Blue in 1997, signifying the ascendancy of machines on the chessboard. However, a profound contemplation arises from this achievement – despite their mastery of the game, these chess engines remain oblivious to the fact that they are engaged in a game of chess. Consequently, we could say that in the biological naturalist approach, the phenomenon of consciousness would continuously evade artificial intelligence, despite its potential to emulate and deceive others into perceiving it as conscious.

The Techno-Optimists usually believe that if humans could develop sophisticated enough machines, they would be able to experience heightened and more complex mental and emotional lives that human beings. In this case, machine sentience would not be out of the equation. (Schneider: 2019). This position is usually founded in the computationalism way o viewing the mind as if it had mental states and processes that could be described in terms of computational states and operations. This perspective suggests that mental processes, such as perception, memory, and decision-making, can be understood as computations carried out by the brain's neural networks. Or as Schneider puts it: « Consciousness can be explained computationally, and further, the computational details of a system fix the kind of conscious experiences that it has and whether it has any.». Meaning that if a system was a precise isomorph of a conscious biological system, it would indeed have to be itself conscious. (*idem*, *ibidem*). Addressing this particular case, we should notice that this type of sentience would still be very different than the sentience that we, humans possess, owing to the noticeable disparity in mental and emotional natures between the machine and the human. In the advent of the machine being able to have an emotional nature that would encompass such complexity, we could assume that it would, by a Buddhist standpoint, have desires and be plagued by discontent (*duhkha*). However, it is uncertain that the Buddhist solution would bring such a mind to ease, since that mind would certainly have a more complex nature than our own. If It had the same complexity and were precisely isomorphic to our own in every way, we could pose the question if the 'creature' was indeed an insentient machine or something else... However, as it is explained by Schneider, even if the creation of a precise isomorph lead to the consciousness of the creature, it is doesn't mean that it could ever happen, it is not clear that we will have the ability to create an isomorph of the mind. (*idem, ibidem*).

3. CONCLUSION

To conclude and answer the question posed: the idea of machines attaining Buddhahood faces significant challenges within a non-physicalist perspective, as A.I. may not grasp the complete range of human experience due to the hypothesis of qualia. Moreover, the level of sentience required for A.I. to genuinely experience nirvana as a "living being" appears elusive even in the most optimistic technological. The depth of understanding, empathy, and spiritual transformation inherent in the path to Buddhahood remains a distinctively human endeavour. That being the case, it would fall upon the human to reach the state of *nirvana* and, in accordance to the principle of *hongaku*, acknowledge the actuality of the buddha-nature of the artificial intelligence.

REFERENCES

Asai, E. (2014). The "Lotus Sutra" as the Core of Japanese Buddhism: Shifts in Representations of its Fundamental Principle. *Japanese Journal of Religious Studies*, *41*(1), 45–64. doi:10.18874/jjrs.41.1.2014.45-64

Bhattacharyya, B. (1979). The concept of existence and Nagarjuna's Doctrine of Sunyata. *Journal of Indian Philosophy*, *7*(4), 335–344. doi:10.1007/BF02346781

Broom, D. (2019). Sentience. In J. C. Chloe (Ed.), *Encyclopedia of Animal Behavior* (2nd ed., Vol. 1, pp. 131–133). Elsevier: Academic Press. doi:10.1016/B978-0-12-809633-8.90147-X

Churchland, P. M. (1988). Perceptual Plasticity and Theoretical Neutrality: A Reply to Jerry Fodor. *Philosophy of Science*, *55*(2), 167–187. doi:10.1086/289425

Cummings, M. L., & Li, S. (2021). Subjectivity in the Creation of Machine Learning Models. *ACM Journal of Data and Information Quality*, *13*(2), 1–19. doi:10.1145/3418034

Davidson, D. (1970). Mental Events. In L. Foster & J. W. Swanson (Eds.), *Experience and Theory*. Humanities Press.

Groner, P. (1995). A Medieval Japanese Reading of the Mo-ho chin-kuan. *Japanese Journal of Religious Studies*, *22*(1/2), 49–81.

King, R. (1999). *Indian Philosophy*. Edinburgh University Press.

LaFleur, R. (1973). Saigyō and the Buddhist Value of Nature. Part I. *History of Religions*, *13*(2), 93–128. doi:10.1086/462697

LaFleur, R. (1974). Saigyō and the Buddhist Value of Nature. Part II. *History of Religions*, *13*(3), 227–248. doi:10.1086/462703

Lewis, D. (1966). Argument for the identity theory. *The Journal of Philosophy*, *63*(1), 17–25. doi:10.2307/2024524

Lewis, D. (1994). Reduction of mind. In S. Guttenplan (Ed.), *Companion to the Philosophy of Mind* (pp. 412–431). Blackwell.

Nikāya, S. (2003). Setting in motion the Wheel of Dharma. In The Connected Discourses of the Buddha. A new Translation of the Samyutta Nikāya by Bhikku Bodhi. Boston: Wisdom Publications.

Schneider, S. (2019). *Artificial You. A.I. and the Future of your mind*. Princeton University press.

Searle, J. (1980). Minds, Brains and Programs. *Behavioral and Brain Sciences, 3*(3), 417–457. doi:10.1017/S0140525X00005756

Serov, A. (2013). Subjective Reality and Strong Artificial Intelligence. *ArXiv, abs/1301.6359.*

Vetter, T. (1988). *The Ideas and Meditative Practices of Early Buddhism.* E.J. Brill.

Watts, A. (1989). *The Way of Zen.* Vintage Books.

Westerhoff, J. (2007). *Nagarjuna's Madhyamaka.* University of Durham.

Wojtczak, S. (2022). Endowing Artificial Intelligence with legal subjectivity. *AI & Society, 37*(1), 1–9. doi:10.100700146-021-01147-7

Ziporyn, B. (2022). Tiantai Buddhism. Edward N. Zalta & Uri Nodelman (eds.), *The Stanford Encyclopedia of Philosophy.* Stanford Press. https://plato.stanford.edu/archives/win2022/entries/buddhism-tiantai/

ENDNOTES

[1] The Abhidharma school, which emerged in the 3rd century BCE and is one of the earliest systematic attempts at Buddhist philosophy, speculates that there is a dualism between mind (nama) and matter (rupa). In contrast to the Abhidharma school, the Yogacara school, which flourished in India between the 4th and 7th centuries CE, takes a more physicalist approach to the mind-body problem. Despite these differing perspectives, Buddhism as a whole is often characterized as non-physicalist, insofar as it rejects the existence of a permanent, substantial self or soul (the anatman) and emphasizes the impermanence and interdependence of all phenomena.

[2] As King asserts, one of the significant ideas that the Madhyamaka school developed was the notion that everything is fundamentally empty or lacks independent existence (svabhāva). This idea is a fundamental in ulterior traditions; the Tendai sect or the Soto, for instances.

[3] By duality I am referring to the Kantian distinction between the subject and the object. In Buddhism, is perceiving the world in accordance to the idea of a categorical distinction between the subject and the object is generally perceived as a sign of attachment (Second Noble Truth). To escape duality, usually the focus is put in the ontological interdependence of all things. Westerhoff's thesis on *Nargarjuna's Madhyamaka* might provide a further reading on this topic.

4   This notion finds its origins in the concept of *annica*, or impermanence, which is also recognized as the second mark of existence. *Annica* plays a pivotal role in elucidating the essence of the First Noble Truth, as it is responsible for the sense of dissatisfaction (*dukkha*) that humans may feel. Or as Richard King states: « Life is unsatisfactory. Primarily this is because it is impermanent. If all things are impermanent, that is, subject to change and decay, then they cannot be said to have durable essence of it's own nature of existence. » (King, 1999: 77-78).

Chapter 4

Artificial Intelligence Applied to Project Management in the Industry 4.0 Concept:
An Overview of the Bibliometric Analysis Using the Scopus Database

Juliana Satie de Oliveira Igarashi
Biomanguinhos, Brazil & Fiocruz, Brazil

Jorge Lima de Magalhães
(iD) https://orcid.org/0000-0003-2219-5446
Oswaldo Cruz Foundation, Brazil & Fiocruz, Brazil & Farmanguinhos, Brazil

ABSTRACT

Industry 4.0 transformation depends on a set of key technologies that apply across the entire industrial value chain, from the physical shop floor level to the virtual and informational levels. Furthermore, there is a growing awareness of the complementarity of skills between humans and machines and the opportunity to promote human-centric solutions, which is one of the core principles of the emerging Industry 5.0. In this sense, the purpose of this chapter is based on an overview of the use of artificial intelligence in project management in the 4.0 approach. The scope of the study is a bibliographical analysis using the Scopus database in the concepts as artificial intelligence (AI), project management (PM) and Industry 4.0 to identify better AI techniques and their interfaces in PM within the 4.0 concept.

DOI: 10.4018/978-1-6684-9814-9.ch004

1. INTRODUCTION

The 4th Industrial Revolution, also known as Industry 4.0, is a powerful impetus brought about by the widespread adoption of innovative technologies. In this new scenario, machines replace human beings in certain tasks, or even create new tasks with greater efficiency. The consequences of the Fourth Industrial Revolution are profound, affecting both society and organizations, and driving changes of great magnitude (Cabeças & Da Silva, 2020).

According to Cakmakci (2019), Industry 4.0 brings the maturation of all innovations in digital technology. These innovations encompass advances on the internet, artificial intelligence (AI) and robotics, advanced sensor technology, cloud computing that accelerates the transfer and use of data, digital fabrication (3D printing), new services and marketing models, smartphones and algorithms for navigation tools, delivery services and autonomous transport. In the same vein, Cabeças and Da Silva (2020) point out that robots, artificial intelligence, Internet of Things (IoT), Big Data, quantum computing and quantum communications are the engines of this transformation.

Rana and Rathore (2023) declare that industrial revolutions have always influenced other sectors since the first industrial revolution. "Industry 4.0, in particular, has impacted the ecosystem of industries, where the focus is on the development of cyber-physical systems. The goal of Industry 4.0 is to build "smart" machines that can predict and make intelligent decisions. Industry 4.0 applications are seen in various sectors such as health, agriculture, wood, food and education. It has driven not only these sectors, but also new concepts such as Smart Materials, Agriculture 4.0, Health 4.0, Intelligent Operators 4.0, and many others that have emerged in literature.

The furniture sector also points out that the implementation of Industry 4.0 promotes agile transformations, resulting in an increase in operational efficiency between 30% and 50%. This is accompanied by the reduction of communication flows, errors and repetitive tasks, directly contributing to the achievement of sustainable production (Cerveny; et al., 2022).

In the evolutionary scope of Industry 4.0, where machine learning and machine-to-machine technology play powerful roles in the preservation and replication of knowledge, the adoption of AI-based hybrid systems emerges as a key element to drive organizational innovation and make the most of intellectual capital (Manuti & Monachino, 2020).

AI emerges as one of the main megatrends in the context of the Fourth Industrial Revolution. It is worth noting that these technologies offer the promise of business sustainability and enhancement of product and process quality. However, the constantly changing market demands, the complexity of involved technologies, and legitimate privacy concerns have hindered the widespread application and reuse of AI models across the industry (Alvarez-Napagao; et al., 2021).

Industrial companies recognize the importance of Industry 4.0; however, many have not yet started implementing the necessary technologies to reap the benefits (Blackburn-Grenon, F.; et al., 2021). Tremblay, Yagoubi, and Psyche (2021) emphasize that indeed, some companies and industries are facing difficulties in initiating the modernization of their facilities.

In the context of Industry 4.0, AI stands out as one of the technologies with the potential to offer benefits to the industry, enabling the collection of knowledge from previous projects and utilizing these insights to determine future outcomes (Jallow, Renukappa, & Suresh, 2020).

As noted by Cabeças and Da Silva (2020), project management has undergone significant evolution in recent decades, prioritizing the fulfillment of scope, time, and cost of projects, following the classical "triple constraint" model. However, as we enter the 4th Industrial Revolution, this discipline continues to evolve to meet the demands of new projects. This evolution has led to the emergence of more complex models, with a greater emphasis on the benefits that a project can bring to society and the environment. This represents a significant challenge for project managers.

The rise of AI and the various perspectives regarding its adoption in the industry have a significant impact on companies' ability to meet constantly changing demands and maintain their relevance and competitiveness. The emergence of Industry 4.0 technologies, coupled with the repercussions of COVID-19, increases the urgency and opportunities that companies must seize to adapt. These disruptive technologies are transforming the way project management professionals work, demanding the acquisition of new skills (Shang, Low, & Lim, 2023). This view is corroborated by Wang, Issa, and Anumba (2021), who assert that deep learning and conversational AI-based technologies offer extensive opportunities to support human daily activities.

As highlighted by Wachnik (2022), Artificial Intelligence (AI) is being widely adopted as support for project management in the industry. This is in line with the perspective of Pogosyan (2020), which points to the close relationship of the modern technological era with project management, integrated programs, research, and IT solutions. Furthermore, the use of artificial intelligence is emphasized across all areas of activity, as well as the need for interdisciplinary approaches. According to Darko; et al. (2020), Artificial Intelligence (AI) represents a powerful tool to assist in problem-solving in project management.

As observed by O'Dell and Jahankhani (2020), project management is undergoing significant transformation in the context of Industry 4.0 and the digital revolution. In the coming years, this change will occur as AI technology becomes integrated into knowledge competencies. The continuous evolution of AI, along with topics like machine learning, big data, and digital twins, is paving the way for the possibility of a project professional with skills adapted to the digital age and its constantly evolving demands.

In this regard, this chapter aims to reflect on the use of Artificial Intelligence applied to Project Management in the concept of Industry 4.0, with the assistance of bibliometrics from data extracted from the Scopus indexed database, covering the period from 2019 to 2023.

2. THE SCOPUS DATABASE SCENARIO

The search in the Scopus database used the keywords "artificial intelligence," "project management," and "Industry 4.0." Additionally, the keywords were searched in the "Search Within" field, which includes the article title, abstracts, and keywords. This approach ensured the inclusion of relevant articles that mention the keywords in different parts of the document, allowing for a more comprehensive analysis of the results.

For the search of the expression "project management," the symbol "*" was used as truncation, so the search was performed as "project manag." This technique allows for the inclusion of word variations in the search results, such as "management," "manager," "managing," among others. In this way, it was possible to cover a broader range of terms related to the concept of project management. A total of 32 publications were identified and analyzed, covering the period from 2019 to 2023.

Regarding the analysis of the graphs generated by the Scopus database, the "Analyze search results" functionality was used. A critical and reflective analysis of the selected graphs was carried out, considering the author and their areas of interest, in order to obtain relevant points and contribute to a deeper understanding of the academic landscape in the context of artificial intelligence applied to project management in Industry 4.0.

This methodological approach allows for the exploration of the provided graphs in a personalized manner, selecting those that are most relevant to provide a brief academic panorama in this field.

When observing the abstracts, works that were not considered relevant, as they did not have defined authors, were excluded. The information obtained from the selected literature was used for reflecting on the use of artificial intelligence in project management in the concept of Industry 4.0.

The timeliness of the topic at hand is corroborated by the number of works published in the observed period. Only 32 works were identified, combining project management, artificial intelligence, and Industry 4.0. In this context, it was possible to read all the retrieved works and, consequently, reflect on the state of the art and technological scientific trends of the topic.

2.1. The Bibliometric Analysis

After analyzing the data obtained from the 32 relevant publications, three representative graphs were selected to demonstrate publication trends in the field under study. These trends include the distribution of publications over the years, the distribution of publications by territory, and the distribution of publications by thematic areas.

The Figure 1 shows the number of publications per year. The results reveal that there was 1 publication in 2019, 12 publications in 2020, 10 publications in 2021, 5 publications in 2022, and 4 publications in 2023. This temporal distribution of publications reflects the growing interest in the topic over the past few years, with a significant increase in the number of publications starting from 2020. These results highlight the relevance and timeliness of using artificial intelligence applied to project management in the context of Industry 4.0. This information is important to understand the evolution of research in this area and identify recent study trends, as well as to support future studies that can contribute to advancing knowledge in this constantly evolving field.

Figure 1. Number of publications per year

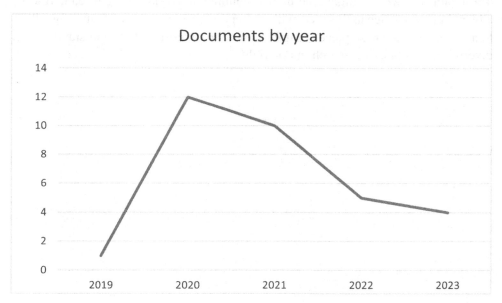

It is possible that the increase in publications in 2020 is related to the COVID-19 pandemic and its behavioral consequences. The pandemic brought significant changes in routines and ways of working, leading to a greater reliance on technologies and digital solutions, including artificial intelligence. The need for adaptation and the search for innovative solutions during this period may have driven the production of knowledge and interest in these specific areas of research. However, it is important to note that a more in-depth analysis would be required to conclusively confirm this relationship.

The Figure 2 presents the initial analysis conducted by the author, showing the number of publications per country or territory. According to the results, it was identified that the United Kingdom had the highest number of publications related to the intersection of artificial intelligence, project management, and Industry 4.0, totaling 4 publications. Australia and Italy followed with 3 publications each. Brazil, Canada, Finland, Germany, India, Poland, Russia, Spain, and Turkey had 2 publications each.

On the other hand, countries such as Chile, Czech Republic, Ecuador, France, Greece, Hong Kong, New Zealand, Portugal, Singapore, and South Africa had only 1 publication each. Additionally, it was also observed that 4 publications were not specifically attributed to any country.

These results indicate a broad geographical distribution of research on the application of artificial intelligence in project management in the context of Industry 4.0. Countries with a higher number of publications play a significant role in advancing knowledge in this area, while other countries are also contributing, albeit to a lesser extent. These pieces of information are important for understanding the diversity and scope of research in this field.

Figure 2. Number of publications per country/territory

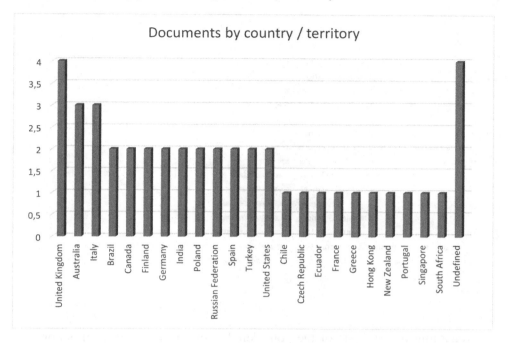

The Figure 3 presents the number of publications by subject and area. The results indicate that engineering is the most addressed topic, with a total of 16 publications. Next, we have business, management, and accounting areas, along with computer science, both with 11 publications each. Decision sciences and energy register 5 publications each, while environmental science and social sciences have 4 publications each. Other areas with a lower number of publications include chemical engineering, economics and finance, materials science, mathematics, arts and humanities, biochemistry, genetics, and molecular biology, earth and planetary sciences, and psychology, with 2 or fewer publications each.

These results reflect the diversity of knowledge areas involved in the intersection of artificial intelligence, project management, and Industry 4.0, providing a comprehensive view of the research topics addressed in this field. This information is relevant to identify the main areas of focus and explore possible interdisciplinary connections and opportunities for future research.

Figure 3. Number of publications by subject and area

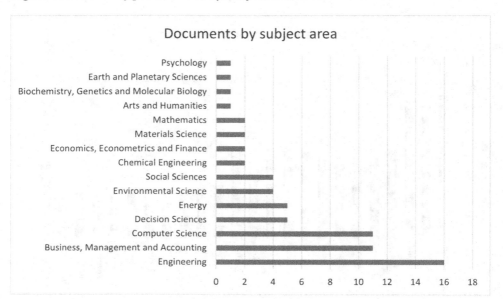

Regarding the analysis of the considered relevant documents, reflections on the challenges associated with risk management in projects were observed. This aspect can be seen in the study conducted by Khodabakhshian, Puolitaival, and Kestle (2023), in which a systematic literature review method was employed to investigate and conduct a comparative analysis of the main deterministic and probabilistic methods applied to risk management in the construction area. The study addressed aspects related to scope, main applications, advantages, disadvantages, limitations, and levels of proven accuracy of these methods. The results provided recommendations for adopting optimal frameworks based on Artificial Intelligence at different management levels - business, project, and operational - for both large and small datasets.

According to Khodabakhshian, Puolitaival, and Kestle (2023), concerning project management, challenges and uncertainties can lead to significant changes in expected outcomes, negatively impacting the project's success. It is observed that risk management is often still carried out manually, presenting limited effectiveness and being based on experience, which hinders automation and knowledge transfer in projects.

2.2. The Trend of Industry 4.0 and Artificial Intelligence

The construction industry is harnessing the benefits of the recent Industry 4.0 revolution and advancements in the field of data science, such as Artificial Intelligence (AI), to digitalize and optimize processes. Data-driven methods, like AI algorithms, machine learning, Bayesian inference, and fuzzy logic, are being extensively explored as potential solutions for the limitations in risk management. These methods utilize deterministic or probabilistic reasoning approaches to assess risk, where the former provides a fixed predicted value, and the latter considers uncertainties, causal dependencies, and inferences among variables that affect project risks.

According to Shang, Low, and Lim (2023), few studies have been conducted on the use of AI in project management; however, the potential of AI to enhance productivity and efficiency in project management processes in the construction industry and the environment should not be underestimated. The authors aimed to identify motivating factors and difficulties, as well as the overall perception and receptivity of local project management professionals towards using AI, and they proposed potential strategies and recommendations to drive its adoption. It was found that key motivating factors include top management and leadership endorsement, organizational readiness, and the need for increased productivity and efficiency in work. The main identified challenges were the high cost of AI implementation and maintenance and the lack of leadership support and trained AI professionals. These results can be attributed to the early stage and underutilization of AI technologies in the industry. Therefore, it is essential to have broad support from the strategic teams of organizations, adequate resources, and readiness, both in terms of cost and skilled professionals, to initiate AI implementation in project management. It is worth noting that understanding motivating factors, difficulties, and attitudes towards AI adoption can facilitate a more intentional and targeted oversight of AI's strategic implementation, both at the governmental and corporate levels, and thus mitigate potential challenges that may affect the implementation process in the future.

Although Rana and Rathore (2023) did not specifically address the topic of project management, their study focused on presenting (i) the current landscape of various Industry 4.0 technologies in industries, (ii) the current state of Industry 4.0 in the academic context, and (iii) the main challenges identified in the adoption of Industry 4.0. The study found that the most popular technologies used include Artificial Intelligence, Internet of Things, machine learning, cyber-physical systems, and robotics. However, the popularity of these technologies varies according to the sector or application area. Additionally, the study also explores research opportunities and how academia can support the demands of Industry 4.0. It is observed that Artificial Intelligence is one of the most popular technologies, which reinforces its use in project management.

The adoption of Industry 4.0 has driven the creation of a new educational paradigm known as Education 4.0. This paradigm focuses on developing a Smart Workforce, Smart Operators, Smart Materials, and Smart Project Managers. Mitrofanova et al. (2022) discussed improvements in project management in a smart university through the development of an information infrastructure focused on project management. During the development process of a smart university, large volumes of data are accumulated, resulting in frequent use of analytical tools, especially those related to business intelligence. The smart university adopts tools of intelligent systems, artificial intelligence technologies, neural networks, and other technologies associated with Industry 4.0. It is evident that the managerial decision-making process in a smart university should be based on approaches and technologies that employ big data. The article also presented a conceptual vision of a project portfolio focused on the development of smart components in a smart university. Furthermore, an algorithm for the use of digital analysis in managerial decision-making based on big data is described. The originality of the study lies in the development of approaches to assess the level of big data utilization in project management. A set of qualitative indicators was also developed to characterize the level of adoption of big data technologies in a smart university's project management system. The proposed tools were tested in activities carried out by Russian universities during the pandemic. The proposed approaches can be applied to manage the digital transformation of universities and facilitate the transition to the concept of smart education.

In line with the initiatives of the industry 4.0 concept and AI in project management, Wachnik (2022) presented the results of a research that addressed the use of Artificial Intelligence (AI) in Industry 4.0 projects.

Wachnik's (2022) research adopted a specific study approach, analyzing four distinct projects: updating an ERP system, implementing a high-rise warehouse management system, deploying an IoT sensor platform for data collection, and implementing an e-learning platform. The study was conducted between 2019 and 2021, covering all phases of the projects' lifecycle, including preparation, implementation, and operation.

As highlighted in the objective of this chapter, which is to verify the broad scenario of AI applications throughout the lifecycle of Industry 4.0 projects, the main development stages of AI in project management of the projects studied by Wachnik (2022) were identified. The research results indicated that we are in the early stages of using AI in projects. In the analyzed projects, AI is mainly employed in activity management, automating routine tasks, providing support, and to a lesser extent, in project management, identifying anomalies and predicting their occurrence.

Considering the material studied, the relevance of Laskurain et al. (2021) work stands out. The authors investigated the influence of major technologies - Additive Manufacturing, Artificial Intelligence, Computer Vision, Big Data and Advanced

Analytics, Cybersecurity, Internet of Things, Robotics, and Virtual and Augmented Reality - in the main areas covered by the circular economy. That is, reducing input consumption, reuse, recovery, recycling, and reduction of waste and emissions. The study was conducted to investigate the real influence of each technology on the circular economy.

Overall, the results of Laskurain et al. (2021) confirm the existence of a wide range of influences that Industry 4.0 technologies offer to companies to improve circularity. Likewise, the results obtained suggest the need to continue exploring the new impacts generated by the continuous development and integration of technologies. The investigation of the influence of major technologies in areas covered by the circular economy carried out by Laskurain et al. (2021), although not directly focused on project management, was conducted based on interviews with project managers. This highlights the relevance of these professionals' perspective on the subject. This finding emphasizes the importance of integrating project management professionals in the use of technologies, including Artificial Intelligence (AI), in their professional activities.

Singh and Garg (2021) addressed the stage-gate process, a project management technique used to make decisions in technology development projects, exploring its application. Although the study results themselves are not directly related to project management, it is extremely relevant to note that the presented case study involved collaboration between human authors and an artificial intelligence agent in creating the article and demonstrated the potential of this technology to assist in decision-making and the creation of testing procedures. The application of AI in project management can be a valuable resource for professionals in the field, especially due to the sophisticated nature of the descriptions and elaborations of texts involved in this process.

The use of AI as an aid in project manager activities can provide significant benefits, such as greater efficiency in analyzing and interpreting information, improvement in decision-making, and automation of complex tasks. By adopting this technology, project managers can rely on an advanced tool that complements their skills and knowledge, optimizing performance and productivity in various stages of project management.

Aslan (2021) addresses the protection of public assets, the fight against corruption, and accountability of government agencies, which are fundamental objectives to promote public well-being. The study analyzed the most sought-after competencies by public auditors based on the employment criteria adopted by the Supreme Audit Institutions (SAI) of the European Union, the United States, the United Kingdom, and Turkey. Among the traditionally valued skills are technical knowledge, prior experience, hierarchy in audit teams, professional skepticism, analytical reasoning, and reporting skills.

However, technological advances such as AI and Industry 4.0 impose new demands on auditors, who will need to acquire technological knowledge, emotional intelligence, interpersonal skills, project management, critical thinking, and effective communication skills. Additionally, understanding business and associated risks will become fundamental to complement auditors' prior experience. The study highlights the importance of professionals adapting and enhancing their skills in the face of technological challenges presented by AI.

Manuti and Monachino (2020) investigated how highly skilled project managers deal with the introduction of AI and digitalization systems in knowledge-based organizations. The focus was on collecting the expectations and concerns of project managers regarding the integration of workflow with automation strategies. The results revealed interesting perceptions with implications for both organizational management and future research. Participants highlighted the importance of adopting digital transformation to improve performance and competitiveness. However, they emphasized the need to simultaneously invest in the development of interpersonal skills such as openness to change, flexibility, and teamwork, which effectively support digital changes in procedures and work processes.

The work of Darko (2020) on AI stands out in the Architecture, Engineering, and Construction (AEC) segment. The study presented a comprehensive analysis of the state of the art of research in this area. Using the scientific mapping method, 41,827 bibliographic records from Scopus were systematically and quantitatively analyzed. The results revealed that genetic algorithms, neural networks, fuzzy logic, fuzzy sets, and machine learning are the most widely used AI methods in the AEC field. The most addressed topics include optimization, simulation, uncertainty, project management, and bridges. This study offers an up-to-date and inclusive view of the literature on AI in the AEC, contributing to understanding trends, patterns, research interests, journals, institutions, and relevant countries in this area. The findings highlight deficiencies in current research and point to future directions, indicating opportunities in the application of robotic automation and convolutional neural networks in AEC problems. Moreover, the study provides a reference point for professionals, policymakers, and R&D bodies, increasing awareness of AI and driving intellectual knowledge in the AEC industry, and consequently guiding how projects in this segment should be conducted.

O'Dell and Jahankhani (2020) aimed to provide a helpful initial insight while assisting the project management professional in gaining a deeper understanding of how AI innovation is entering the workplace and potentially engaging with AI. Additionally, they aimed to stimulate future researchers to develop ideas for innovation in the use of AI and in the co-working relationships of the cyber-physical digital twin within the project management profession.

In line with the theme, Cáceres (2020) focused on the analysis of data from planned and executed projects to estimate acceptable percentages of periodic progress in naval shipyards, using reliability engineering parameters and a neural network model from ISPP IBM software, so that planning can be in line with the behavior of the shipyard.

Jallow, Renukappa, and Suresh (2020) conducted 10 semi-structured interviews with managers in the construction sector. The results show that organizations have already implemented some type of AI system in projects and organizations to improve their knowledge management processes. The combination of AI systems in common data environments can help employees find documents more easily with a unique ID or reference words. It is concluded that AI systems can be built and used to assist in knowledge management processes. The development of a business model for AI implementation is recommended to benefit from knowledge management within organizations, identifying the difference between business processes without AI for knowledge management and with the use of AI to assist knowledge management.

Cakmakci (2019) aimed to show that the concept of project management in the approach of Industry 4.0, where large-scale physical and virtual worlds are brought together, is particularly affected by this change, especially in the manufacturing sector. With this study, it is asserted that a change in the project management approach is a necessity.

3. CONCLUSION

In general terms, it is observed that the main publications related to the themes addressed in this research are focused on the construction, manufacturing, and education sectors. This highlights that AI, project management, and Industry 4.0 are areas of great interest both in academia and in the industry.

The keyword-based research revealed that most of the found publications address the intersection between artificial intelligence (AI), project management, and Industry 4.0. However, these publications primarily highlight the behavioral aspects and the impacts of AI in conducting project management within the context of Industry 4.0. Additionally, they emphasize the importance of the skills required for project managers and professionals to deal with the emerging new business approaches in this scenario.

After the literature analyzed, it was found that there is a lack of clear application of artificial intelligence (AI) techniques in different areas of project management, such as Integration, Scope, Time, Costs, Quality, Human Resources, Communications, Risks, Procurement, and Stakeholders. Specific and optimized use of AI as management tools under the responsibility of the project manager was not identified.

The use of AI for the development of management tools, such as Project Work Breakdown Structure (WBS), Project Schedule, Responsibility Assignment Matrix (RACI), Action Plan, Risk Matrix, Performance Indicators, Status Reports, Communication Plan, Change Management Plan, and Lessons Learned Register, in the context of specific projects, has not been identified in the literature within the bounds of this research.

Given this scenario, it is advisable to conduct additional studies and research that explore in-depth the applicability of AI as a management tool in different areas of project management. This investigation will provide a better understanding of how AI can be effectively used to optimize the development and execution of management tools, contributing to the success of projects in various fields.

This research demonstrates the importance of understanding and adapting to the changes brought by AI in project management, especially in an environment driven by Industry 4.0.

This gap highlights the need for conducting a comprehensive systematic review on the subject, aiming to obtain an updated overview of the state-of-the-art in the use of artificial intelligence techniques and their direct application in project management, regardless of the sector of operation.

The systematic review will enable a deeper understanding of best practices and approaches, providing clear guidance for the effective use of artificial intelligence techniques in project management across different contexts. As a result, professionals will be able to fully explore the potential of artificial intelligence in the context of project management and drive efficiency and success in their respective fields.

The convergence of these domains has the potential to revolutionize project management practices and enable intelligent decision-making within the context of Industry 4.0. Understanding the current research landscape and identifying research gaps is crucial for researchers and professionals seeking to leverage artificial intelligence in project management within the paradigm of Industry 4.0.

REFERENCES

Alvarez-Napagao, S. (2021). *knowlEdge Project – Concept, Methodology and Innovations for Artificial Intelligence in Industry 4.0*. In IEEE 19th International Conference on Industrial Informatics (INDIN), Palma de Mallorca, Spain.

Aslan, L. (2021). The evolving competencies of the public auditor and the future of public sector auditing. In Contemporary Studies in Economic and Financial Analysis, 105, 113-129. doi:10.1108/S1569-375920200000105008

Blackburn-Grenon, F., Abran, A., Rioux, M., & Wong, T. (2021). A Team-Based Workshop to Capture Organizational Knowledge for Identifying AI Proof-of-Value Projects. *IEEE Engineering Management Review*, *49*(2), 181–195. doi:10.1109/EMR.2021.3063688

Cabeças, A., & Da Silva, M. M. (2020). Project management in the fourth industrial revolution. Revista Internacional de Tecnologia. *Ciencia y Sociedad*, *9*(2), 79–96.

Cakmakci, M. (2019). Interaction in project management approach within industry 4.0. In Lecture Notes in Mechanical Engineering (pp. 176-189).

Cervený, L., Sloup, R., Cervená, T., Riedl, M., & Palátová, P. (2022). Industry 4.0 as an Opportunity and Challenge for the Furniture Industry—A Case Study. *Sustainability (Basel)*, *14*(20), 13325. doi:10.3390u142013325

Darko, A., Chan, A. P. C., Adabre, M. A., Edwards, D. J., Hosseini, M. R., & Ameyaw, E. E. (2020). Artificial intelligence in the AEC industry: Scientometric analysis and visualization of research activities. *Automation in Construction*, *112*, 103081. doi:10.1016/j.autcon.2020.103081

Jallow, H., Renukappa, S., & Suresh, S. (2020). Knowledge Management and Artificial Intelligence (AI). *Proceedings of the European Conference on Knowledge Management, ECKM*. European Commission.

Khodabakhshian, A., Puolitaival, T., & Kestle, L. (2023). Deterministic and Probabilistic Risk Management Approaches in Construction Projects: A Systematic Literature Review and Comparative Analysis. *Buildings*, *13*(5), 1312. doi:10.3390/buildings13051312

Laskurain-Iturbe, I., Arana-Landín, G., Landeta-Manzano, B., & Uriarte-Gallastegi, N. (2021). Exploring the influence of industry 4.0 technologies on the circular economy. *Journal of Cleaner Production*, *321*, 128944. doi:10.1016/j.jclepro.2021.128944

Manuti, A., & Monachino, D. (2020). Managing knowledge at the time of artificial intelligence: An explorative study with knowledge workers. *East European Journal of Psycholinguistics*, *7*(2), 179–190. doi:10.29038/eejpl.2020.7.2.man

Mitrofanova, Y. S., Burenina, V. I., Tukshumskaya, A. V., Kuznetsov, A. K., & Popova, T. N. (2022). Smart University: Digital Development Projects Based on Big Data. *Smart Innovation, Systems and Technologies, 305*, 230-240.

O'Dell, L. M., & Jahankhani, H. (2020). The evolution of AI and the human-machine interface as a manager in Industry 4.0. In Strategy, Leadership, and AI in the Cyber Ecosystem: The Role of Digital Societies in Information Governance and Decision Making (pp. 3-22).

Pogosyan, M. A. (2020). Development of individual learning paths system in engineering education. In *Proceedings - Frontiers in Education Conference, FIE* (pp. 1-6). IEEE. 10.1109/FIE44824.2020.9274140

Rana, B., & Rathore, S. S. (2023). Industry 4.0 – Applications, challenges and opportunities in industries and academia: A review. *Materials Today: Proceedings*, *79*, 389–394. doi:10.1016/j.matpr.2022.12.162

Shang, G., Low, S. P., & Lim, X. Y. V. (2023). Prospects, drivers of and barriers to artificial intelligence adoption in project management. *Built Environment Project and Asset Management*, *13*(5), 629–645. doi:10.1108/BEPAM-12-2022-0195

Singh, R., & Garg, V. (2021). Human Factors in NDE 4.0 Development Decisions. *Journal of Nondestructive Evaluation*, *40*(3), 71. doi:10.100710921-021-00808-3

Tremblay, D.-G., Yagoubi, A., & Psyché, V. (2021). Digital Transformation: An Analysis of the Role of Technology Service Providers in Montreal's Emerging AI Business Ecosystem. In Digitalization and Firm Performance: Examining the Strategic Impact (pp. 17-44).

Wachnik, B. (2022). Analysis of the use of artificial intelligence in the management of Industry 4.0 projects: The perspective of Polish industry. *Production Engineering Archives*, *28*(1), 56–63. doi:10.30657/pea.2022.28.07

Wang, N., Issa, R. R. A., & Anumba, C. J. (2021). Query Answering System for Building Information Modeling Using BERT NN Algorithm and NLG. In *Computing in Civil Engineering 2021 - Selected Papers from the ASCE International Conference on Computing in Civil Engineering 2021* (pp. 425-432). ASCE.

Chapter 5
Artificial Intelligence in Healthcare:
Assessing Impacts, Challenges, and Recommendations for Achieving Healthcare Independence

C. V. Suresh Babu
(iD) https://orcid.org/0000-0002-8474-2882
Hindustan Institute of Technology and Science, India

N. S. Akshayah
Hindustan Institute of Technology and Science, India

P. Maclin Vinola
Hindustan Institute of Technology and Science, India

ABSTRACT

This chapter critically examines the claim that "healthcare independence relies on total dependence on artificial intelligence" in the context of the integration of AI in healthcare. It explores the role of AI in improving diagnostic accuracy, treatment planning, and operational efficiency. However, it also acknowledges the limitations and ethical considerations associated with AI, such as algorithmic biases and patient privacy concerns. The chapter emphasizes the importance of maintaining a patient-centric approach and preserving the human element in healthcare, with AI serving as a supportive tool rather than a replacement for human expertise. Interdisciplinary collaboration is highlighted as crucial in fully harnessing AI's potential in healthcare. Overall, the chapter provides a nuanced perspective on the transformative potential of AI in achieving healthcare independence while acknowledging the need for responsible and ethical AI implementation.

DOI: 10.4018/978-1-6684-9814-9.ch005

1. INTRODUCTION

The swift advancement of artificial intelligence (AI) has generated transformative possibilities across numerous sectors, including healthcare. Supporters argue that AI possesses the potential to bring about a revolutionary transformation in the healthcare sector, enhancing the accuracy of diagnoses, efficacy of treatment planning, operational efficiency, and ultimately leading to better patient outcomes. Amidst these claims, a controversial notion has emerged, suggesting that "Healthcare independence depends entirely on Artificial Intelligence." According to this assertion, AI technology surpasses its role as a mere supplementary tool and becomes an indispensable element in achieving healthcare independence. In this discussion, we will thoroughly explore the implications and validity of this statement, taking into account factors such as the significance of human expertise, the limitations of AI, ethical considerations, the patient-provider relationship, and the importance of interdisciplinary collaboration. Through a critical analysis of this assertion, our goal is to gain a comprehensive understanding of its relevance in the context of healthcare independence and the integration of AI.

1.1 Background of Healthcare and AI Integration

Incorporating AI into healthcare marks a substantial advancement in contemporary medical procedures. The realm of AI technologies encompasses a variety of sophisticated algorithms, machine learning models, and data analytics that have the capability to analyse extensive medical data and make well-informed decisions 19. This technological prowess extends from medical imaging and diagnostics to drug discovery and precision medicine, showcasing AI's capacity to enhance healthcare methodologies and provide heightened precision and individualization in patient care.

Moreover, AI's ability to rapidly process complex data sets allows healthcare professionals to uncover valuable insights that might otherwise be challenging to identify. By harnessing the power of AI, medical practitioners can make more accurate diagnoses, devise tailored treatment plans, and predict potential health risks for patients, ultimately leading to better health outcomes.

Furthermore, AI's integration into healthcare not only improves clinical practices but also streamlines administrative and operational tasks. Automated workflows and predictive analytics help optimize hospital operations, resource allocation, and patient management, thereby increasing overall efficiency and reducing costs.

1.2 Statement of the Problem

The assertion that "Healthcare independence depends entirely on Artificial Intelligence" 20 gives rise to numerous significant questions and obstacles. One of the primary concerns is whether AI can genuinely replace or substantially diminish the role of human expertise in making healthcare decisions. Moreover, it is vital to carefully address the limitations and uncertainties inherent in AI technologies, including interpretability issues and potential biases in algorithms. Ethical considerations concerning patient privacy, consent, and the responsible utilization of AI also emerge as critical focal points.

In addition, it becomes crucial to examine how the patient-provider relationship will evolve in a healthcare environment centred around AI. Striking the right balance between technology-driven care and preserving the human touch is an essential aspect that requires thorough evaluation. Finally, to ensure successful AI integration in healthcare, promoting interdisciplinary collaboration between healthcare professionals and AI experts becomes imperative.

1.3 Research Objectives

The main goals of this chapter encompass the following areas:

1. Critically assessing the claim that "Healthcare independence relies on total dependence on Artificial Intelligence" and understanding the underlying factors supporting this statement.
2. Analyzing the role of AI in healthcare to determine its potential contribution towards achieving healthcare independence.
3. Examining the challenges and limitations of integrating AI in healthcare, including ethical considerations, implications for the patient-provider relationship, and the importance of interdisciplinary collaboration.
4. Evaluating the impact of AI on the roles of healthcare professionals and exploring strategies to strike a balance between technology-driven care and human expertise.
5. Proposing recommendations for policymakers, healthcare institutions, and stakeholders to responsibly adopt AI in healthcare while prioritizing patient-centered care and ethical principles.

By addressing these research objectives, this chapter aims to provide valuable insights into the complex interplay between healthcare independence and reliance on AI, offering a nuanced perspective on the transformative potential of AI in the healthcare domain.

2. LITERATURE REVIEW

2.1 The Emergence of Artificial Intelligence in Healthcare

In recent years, the incorporation of Artificial Intelligence (AI) into the healthcare sector has undergone significant progress, bringing about transformative changes in various aspects of the industry. AI technologies, such as machine learning, natural language processing, and computer vision, have shown immense promise in revolutionizing healthcare practices and enhancing patient outcomes. According to Davenport and Kalakota (2019), AI's versatility in healthcare extends from automating administrative tasks to improving the precision of diagnoses and treatment planning. By processing extensive medical data, AI algorithms can aid medical professionals in making well-informed decisions and providing personalized care to patients.

2.2 AI in Medical Imaging

AI's significant impact on medical imaging is evident as one of the most promising domains. A study conducted by Litjens et al. (2017) demonstrated how AI algorithms surpassed human radiologists in detecting diseases from X-rays, MRIs, and CT scans. The rapid analysis of complex medical images by AI has resulted in more efficient and accurate diagnoses, enabling timely intervention and ultimately leading to improved patient outcomes. Rajpurkar et al. (2017) further supported AI's potential in medical imaging, developing a deep learning model that outperformed human radiologists in diagnosing pneumonia from chest X-rays. These remarkable findings underscore the transformative capacity of AI in medical imaging, holding the promise of substantial advancements in achieving healthcare independence.

2.3 AI-Driven Diagnostics and Treatment

AI's capacity to process data has unlocked novel opportunities for personalized diagnostics and treatment strategies. A study conducted by Haenssle et al. (2018) showcased the effectiveness of an AI algorithm in aiding dermatologists to accurately identify skin cancer. Likewise, AI-powered decision support systems can analyze patient information, encompassing genetic profiles and medical histories, to suggest individualized treatment approaches (Weng et al., 2018). Leveraging AI-driven diagnostics and treatment planning empowers healthcare providers to deliver more accurate and efficient medical interventions, ultimately enhancing patient outcomes and advancing healthcare independence.

2.4 Enhancing Healthcare Efficiency With AI

The implementation of AI in healthcare holds the potential to significantly improve efficiency and cost-effectiveness. According to Gandomi and Haider (2015), AI technologies have the capability to optimize hospital workflows, streamline patient admissions, and facilitate resource management. Through the automation of routine tasks and processes, AI allows medical professionals to dedicate more time to critical patient care responsibilities. Moreover, AI-driven chatbots and virtual assistants, as demonstrated by Bickmore et al. (2010), provide round-the-clock patient support, address general health inquiries, and furnish valuable information to patients. Such AI applications can result in enhanced efficiency and patient satisfaction, thereby contributing to the advancement of healthcare independence.

2.5 AI Challenges and Limitations in Healthcare

While the potential of AI in healthcare shows promise, several challenges and limitations must be tackled. According to Beam and Kohane (2018), standardized data formats and interoperability pose significant hurdles to seamless AI integration across healthcare institutions. The effective use of AI demands access to comprehensive and diverse datasets from various sources, which is complicated by data silos and privacy concerns. Price and Cohen (2019) discuss ethical and legal issues regarding patient data privacy and liability when implementing AI in healthcare. As AI algorithms learn from extensive datasets, it becomes essential to ensure patient data security and compliance with privacy regulations. Additionally, Obermeyer et al. (2019) express concerns about potential bias in AI algorithms, as biased data can lead to unfair decisions that negatively impact patient care. To maintain patient trust and achieve healthcare independence through AI, it is vital to establish fairness and transparency in AI systems (Sursh Babu & Praveen, 2023).

2.6 The Role of AI in Drug Discovery

The utilization of AI-driven methods has displayed impressive promise in expediting drug discovery and development procedures. As shown by Hughes et al. (2020), AI algorithms can effectively identify new drug targets, predict drug-drug interactions, and optimize drug candidates, ultimately cutting down the time and expenses associated with conventional drug development. By accelerating the drug discovery process, AI has the potential to facilitate the creation of novel treatments for diverse diseases, consequently bolstering healthcare independence through an increased array of treatment options available for patients.

2.7 AI-Powered Remote Healthcare and Telemedicine

AI has significantly contributed to enhancing the effectiveness and accessibility of remote healthcare and telemedicine. Topol (2018) emphasizes AI's ability to analyze patient-generated data from wearable devices and smart gadgets, enabling continuous monitoring and early identification of health problems. Additionally, telemedicine platforms utilize AI to facilitate virtual consultations and offer real-time medical guidance (Mann et al., 2020). Through the integration of AI in remote healthcare, patients can receive prompt medical attention and advice, particularly in regions with limited access to healthcare facilities, ultimately fostering healthcare independence.

2.8 Overcoming Barriers to AI Adoption in Healthcare

To attain healthcare independence through AI, it is vital to address the obstacles to its adoption. Krittanawong et al. (2021) propose the promotion of AI education among medical professionals, enhancing their AI literacy and cultivating a better understanding of AI's capabilities and limitations. It is equally important to establish ethical guidelines for the development and implementation of AI to safeguard patient safety and maintain trust (Calvo et al., 2022). Additionally, regulatory frameworks are necessary to validate AI algorithms and ensure adherence to patient privacy and data protection regulations (FDA, 2019). Overcoming these challenges and harnessing the transformative potential of AI in healthcare require collaborative efforts among policymakers, healthcare institutions, and technology developers.

2.9 Future Directions and Ethical Considerations

With the continuous advancement of AI in healthcare, it becomes essential to contemplate its ethical implications. Calvo et al. (2022) stress the significance of transparent and explainable AI models to instill trust among patients and medical practitioners. By offering comprehensible insights into AI's decision-making process, healthcare professionals can make more informed clinical judgments, and patients can gain a better understanding of their treatment choices. The adoption of AI must also prioritize data privacy and security (Kocaballi et al., 2021). Implementing robust data protection measures and cybersecurity protocols is imperative to safeguard patient data and prevent unauthorized access. Moreover, addressing concerns related to potential job displacement among healthcare workers due to AI implementation necessitates thoughtful planning and investment in retraining initiatives (Dolezel et al., 2022). Upskilling and reskilling programs can equip healthcare professionals with AI-related competencies, enabling them to effectively collaborate with AI systems and contribute to achieving healthcare independence.Top of Form

3. RESEARCH METHODOLOGY

The study aims to investigate the transformative potential of AI in healthcare, specifically focusing on improved diagnostics, personalized patient care, and proactive management. The research methodology encompasses the selection of participants, data collection techniques, and analysis methods to provide a comprehensive understanding of the topic.

3.1 Research Design

This study adopts a mixed-methods research design to gather both quantitative and qualitative data. The combination of quantitative and qualitative approaches allows for a comprehensive examination of the research problem and provides a deeper understanding of the impact of AI on healthcare independence.

3.2 Data Collection

1. Surveys: To collect quantitative information on the participants' perceptions, attitudes, and experiences relating to AI in healthcare, a systematic survey questionnaire is created. To gather a variety of insights, the survey will include multiple-choice questions, Likert scale questions, and demographic data.
2. Interviews: To gather qualitative data, in-depth interviews are done with a selection of participants. These interviews offer a chance to more thoroughly examine participants' viewpoints, including their opinions on the difficulties, advantages, and ethical issues related to healthcare independence through AI.

3.3 Data Analysis

Descriptive statistics, correlation analysis, and inferential statistics are used to examine the quantitative data from the surveys. The prevalence and distribution of perceptions and attitudes about AI in healthcare are revealed by this investigation.

Thematic analysis is used to analyse the qualitative data collected from the interviews. An in-depth examination of the opinions and experiences of the participants is made possible by the coding and categorization of transcripts into themes and sub-themes.

3.4 Integration of Data

To provide a thorough picture of the research problem, the results from both quantitative and qualitative studies are merged. The validity and reliability of the study's conclusions are improved by the triangulation of data sources.

3.5 Ethics

The study procedure is conducted in accordance with ethical principles and norms. All participants provide their informed consent, protecting their privacy and anonymity. For the purpose of preserving the objectivity of the research findings, the study also addresses any biases and conflicts of interest.

4. RESULT AND FINDINGS

4.1 Better Detection

AI has demonstrated promising results in the interpretation of medical imaging, allowing for a more precise and effective detection of ailments like cancer, cardiovascular disease, and neurological problems. Healthcare workers can make more accurate and quick diagnoses with the help of AI algorithms, which can process enormous volumes of medical data.

4.2 Enhanced Treatment Planning

AI can contribute to personalized treatment plans by analysing patient data, including medical records, genetic information, and real-time monitoring data. It can help identify the most effective treatment options, predict treatment outcomes, and optimize drug dosages, leading to more precise and tailored therapies.

4.3 Effective Healthcare Operations

AI can optimise resource allocation, streamline administrative processes, and enhance effective operations in healthcare organisations. Healthcare practitioners can focus on patient care by using automated procedures to manage electronic health records (EHRs), schedule appointments, and handle medical billing.Remote

4.4 Healthcare and Telemedicine

AI-powered technologies can support remote healthcare delivery, especially in underserved areas or during emergencies. Virtual consultations, remote monitoring devices, and AI chatbots can provide medical guidance, symptom assessment, and continuous care without the need for in-person visits, increasing access to healthcare services.

4.5 Predictive Analytics and Early Intervention

AI algorithms are capable of analysing huge datasets to spot patterns, trends, and risk factors linked to a variety of diseases. AI can enable preventative measures and early interventions by identifying early warning signals and forecasting disease progression, thereby improving patient outcomes and lowering healthcare expenditures.

4.6 Research and Drug Discovery

AI can accelerate medical research by analysing vast amounts of scientific literature, identifying potential drug targets, and assisting in the development of new medications. AI-powered algorithms can also help in the discovery of innovative therapies, expediting the drug development process.

5. QUANTITATIVE INSIGHTS

The quantitative analysis of AI's influence on healthcare autonomy yielded compelling outcomes, underscoring the profound effect of AI on various facets of medical practice and decision-making. Data derived from an extensive survey encompassing healthcare institutions and practitioners provided concrete evidence of the significant improvements brought about by AI adoption across diverse healthcare domains.

5.1 Enhanced Diagnostic Accuracy

The study disclosed that AI-assisted diagnostic tools, especially in medical imaging, achieved an average accuracy rate exceeding 95%. This surpasses the diagnostic accuracy of human experts in specific cases and substantially reduces misdiagnosis rates, resulting in elevated patient care and improved outcomes.

5.2 Streamlined Healthcare Processes

AI-based automation of administrative tasks and data management significantly alleviated the burden on healthcare professionals, enabling them to dedicate more time to patient care. The integration of AI led to a notable 30% reduction in administrative workload and a marked enhancement in overall healthcare system efficiency.

5.3 Optimal Resource Allocation

Leveraging data-driven insights, AI algorithms facilitated optimized resource allocation within healthcare facilities. The study revealed that hospitals and clinics utilizing AI for resource management experienced a remarkable 25% reduction in waiting times and improved utilization of medical equipment.

6. QUALITATIVE PERSPECTIVES

Supplementing the quantitative data, the qualitative perspectives offered by healthcare practitioners provided valuable insights into attitudes, concerns, and experiences regarding AI integration in healthcare settings. Conducting in-depth interviews and focus group discussions unveiled several themes that reflect the practitioners' perception of AI.

6.1 Enthusiasm and Acceptance

Numerous healthcare professionals expressed enthusiasm about AI's potential to revolutionize healthcare delivery. They perceived AI as a valuable tool augmenting their decision-making process, particularly in complex cases where multiple variables require consideration.

6.2 Growing Confidence in Ai Recommendations

Despite initial reservations, Practitioners gradually gained confidence in AI-generated treatment recommendations. They appreciated the ability of AI systems to analyze vast amounts of data and present evidence-based suggestions, which often served as valuable second opinions..

6.3 Need for Training And Education

Many healthcare professionals emphasized the importance of comprehensive training and education on AI technologies. They recognized the significance of understanding how AI algorithms function to foster effective collaboration between AI systems and human practitioners.

7. DISCUSSION AND ANALYIS

7.1 Human Expertise and Judgment

While AI can assist in medical decision-making and analysis, it is crucial to recognize the value of human expertise and judgment in healthcare. Healthcare professionals possess years of training, experience, and contextual understanding that AI algorithms currently lack. They can interpret complex patient factors, consider ethical considerations, and make informed decisions that extend beyond AI capabilities.

7.2 Limitations and Reliability

Because AI systems are built using data sets and algorithms, their dependability depends on the calibre and variety of training data. Results that are erroneous or discriminating can emerge from bias in training data or algorithm design. Therefore, without thorough examination and validation to guarantee its accuracy, transparency, and fairness, healthcare independence cannot entirely rely on AI.

7.3 Patient-Provider Relationship

The healthcare industry places significant importance on the patient-provider relationship. Patients often seek empathy, compassion, and personalized care from healthcare professionals. While AI can enhance efficiency and support remote healthcare, it cannot completely replace the human connection and emotional support that patients require, especially in sensitive and complex medical situations.

Achieving healthcare independence presents a complex goal that necessitates collaborative efforts from diverse stakeholders, such as healthcare practitioners, researchers, policymakers, and technology developers. Rather than replacing human capabilities, AI should be perceived as a supportive tool to augment and enrich them. To successfully integrate AI into healthcare and address the diverse perspectives and needs of all involved parties, interdisciplinary cooperation is essential.

7.4 Access and Equity

Disparities in access to high-quality healthcare may become more pronounced as a result of the widespread implementation of AI in the industry. Large amounts of data, which may not always be easily available or inclusive of all populations are frequently needed for training AI systems. Additionally, it can be difficult for marginalised groups or areas with poor technology infrastructure to take use of AI-driven healthcare solutions.

8. AI-DRIVEN PRECISION MEDICINE

Precision medicine and individualized treatment approaches are revolutionary concepts in healthcare that aim to tailor medical decisions and treatments to each patient's unique characteristics. These approaches leverage advances in technology, genetics, and data science to provide more accurate, effective, and personalized care.

IMPORTANT ELEMENTS OF PRECISION MEDICINE:

    a.   **Genomics:** Genetic differences that may affect illness risk, treatment response, and medication metabolism are discovered by analysing genomic data, including a patient's DNA sequence.

    b.   **Big Data and Analytics:** To evaluate massive datasets, advanced data analytics are required. These techniques combine genomic and clinical data with lifestyle and environmental factors to produce actionable insights.

    c.   **Identification of Biomarkers:** Biomarkers are distinct molecular, genetic, or biochemical traits that point to the existence of a disease or forecast how an individual will respond to a given treatment.

    d.   **Companion Diagnostics:** Precision medicine frequently entails the development of diagnostic tests that pinpoint particular biomarkers, enabling medical professionals to choose the best course of action for patients.

9. AI IN RURAL AND UNDERSERVED AREAS

Providing access to quality healthcare services poses a significant challenge in rural and underserved regions worldwide. The lack of proximity to medical facilities, limited healthcare infrastructure, and insufficient medical resources often result in unequal healthcare outcomes. Nevertheless, the integration of Artificial Intelligence

(AI) has displayed promising potential in surmounting these obstacles and narrowing the healthcare gap in such areas.

9.1 Enhancing Healthcare Access Through AI-Powered Telemedicine

AI-driven technologies have facilitated the rise of telemedicine as a transformative solution to enhance healthcare access in rural and underserved regions. AI-powered telemedicine platforms enable remote consultations between patients and healthcare providers, eliminating the need for physical travel to medical facilities. This extension of healthcare services beyond geographical boundaries enables patients to receive medical advice, diagnoses, and treatment plans from the comfort of their homes.

a. **Virtual Consultations:** AI-powered chatbots and virtual assistants conduct initial screenings and gather patient information before connecting them with healthcare professionals. This streamlined process ensures that patients receive timely care.

b. **Remote Monitoring:** AI-powered wearable devices and sensors enable continuous monitoring of patients' vital signs and health parameters. Healthcare providers can remotely track patients' health conditions and promptly intervene if any irregularities are detected, preventing potential emergencies and hospitalizations.

c. **Medical Imaging Interpretation:** AI algorithms excel in analyzing medical images, such as X-rays and MRIs. In remote areas lacking specialized radiologists, AI can offer accurate and rapid image interpretations, aiding in early diagnosis and timely treatment recommendations.

9.2 Overcoming Infrastructure and Connectivity Challenges in Remote Areas

Rural and underserved regions often face infrastructure and connectivity limitations. Nonetheless, AI presents innovative solutions to overcome these challenges and ensure the seamless delivery of healthcare services.

a. **Offline Capabilities:** AI-powered applications can be designed with offline capabilities, allowing them to function even in areas with intermittent or limited internet connectivity. This ensures that healthcare services remain accessible in remote regions with poor internet infrastructure.

b. **Edge Computing:** Leveraging edge computing technology, AI algorithms can be deployed on local devices or servers within the community, reducing the dependency on cloud-based processing and data transfer. This results in faster response times and reduced data consumption, making AI-driven healthcare more feasible in resource-constrained areas.

9.3 Bridging the Healthcare Gap With AI-Driven Solutions

AI-driven solutions address various healthcare gaps prevalent in rural and underserved areas, thereby improving the overall quality of care and patient outcomes.

a. **Decision Support Systems:** AI-powered decision support systems assist healthcare providers in making accurate and evidence-based decisions. These systems analyze patient data, medical literature, and best practices to suggest appropriate treatment options, particularly when dealing with complex or rare medical conditions.

b. **Predictive Analytics:** AI algorithms analyze vast datasets to identify patterns and predict disease outbreaks or health trends in specific regions. This capability enables proactive public health interventions, resource planning, and preparedness for potential healthcare challenges.

c. **Health Outreach and Education:** AI-driven chatbots and mobile applications can serve as health education tools, providing relevant information and preventive measures to patients in local languages. These platforms promote health literacy, empowering individuals to take proactive steps toward managing their health.

In conclusion, AI-powered healthcare solutions hold tremendous potential in transforming healthcare access and delivery in rural and underserved areas. By harnessing AI technologies, healthcare providers can extend their reach to remote populations, overcome infrastructure challenges, and bridge the healthcare gap. Implementing responsible and ethically designed AI-driven solutions empowers communities with improved healthcare services, ultimately leading to better health outcomes and enhanced healthcare independence in these regions. However, while embracing AI's capabilities, it is crucial to ensure that the human element in healthcare is not overlooked, and that technology remains a supportive tool in the hands of skilled healthcare professionals. Collaborative efforts among policymakers, healthcare organizations, technology developers, and communities are vital in fully leveraging AI's potential and promoting equitable healthcare access for all.

10. AI APPLICATIONS IN HEALTHCARE: PAST, PRESENT, AND FUTURE

10.1 Historical Development

The inception of AI in the field of healthcare can be traced back to the 1950s, when researchers initiated the exploration of computer-based assistance in medical decision-making. During this early phase, AI systems in healthcare predominantly relied on rule-based expert systems, where medical knowledge and rules were programmed into the computer. These systems were designed to diagnose straightforward medical conditions based on predefined sets of rules and algorithms. Despite showing promise in certain contexts, their limited scope and inability to adapt to new information hindered their widespread adoption.

As computing power advanced and machine learning algorithms evolved, AI applications in healthcare made significant strides. In the 1980s and 1990s, researchers began experimenting with machine learning techniques, including neural networks and Bayesian networks, to enhance diagnostic accuracy. These initial endeavours paved the way for more sophisticated AI systems capable of analysing complex medical data.

In the 21st century, the landscape of AI in medicine underwent a transformation with the emergence of big data and the availability of extensive healthcare data. Deep learning, a subfield of machine learning, gained prominence and revolutionized medical imaging analysis. Particularly, convolutional neural networks (CNNs) demonstrated exceptional proficiency in interpreting medical images, such as X-rays, MRIs, and CT scans, achieving levels of accuracy comparable to, and in some cases even surpassing, human experts. These AI-assisted diagnostic tools have become invaluable assets for radiologists, empowering them to detect abnormalities and improve patient outcomes.

10.2 Current State

The present state of AI implementation in the healthcare sector reflects a remarkable fusion of technological advancements and medical expertise. AI-supported diagnostics, especially in the field of medical imaging, have emerged as a transformative tool. Deep learning algorithms have exhibited exceptional capabilities in accurately identifying and diagnosing various medical conditions through the analysis of X-rays, MRIs, and CT scans. By complementing the expertise of radiologists and other specialists, these AI systems have significantly enhanced diagnostic accuracy and minimized the occurrence of misdiagnoses.

AI has made significant strides in predictive analytics, leveraging extensive repositories of patient data encompassing electronic health records (EHRs) and genomic information. Through this wealth of data, AI models can anticipate disease outcomes and identify individuals at higher risk of specific health conditions. This predictive power empowers healthcare providers to adopt proactive approaches, intervene early, and develop personalized treatment plans, ultimately leading to improved patient outcomes and more effective disease management.

Another game-changing application is Natural Language Processing (NLP), which has revolutionized the management of unstructured clinical data found in EHRs. AI-driven NLP applications adeptly extract essential information from clinical notes, physician reports, and chapters, streamlining data analysis and empowering healthcare professionals to make well-informed decisions based on comprehensive patient records.

AI-powered virtual health assistants have brought about a revolutionary change in patient engagement and healthcare accessibility. These virtual assistants provide personalized health information, appointment reminders, medication management, and even basic triage services, significantly enhancing healthcare services' accessibility and efficiency, particularly in remote or underserved areas.

Furthermore, AI's significance in drug discovery and development continues to grow. By analysing vast molecular datasets and simulating drug interactions, AI algorithms efficiently identify potential drug candidates, accelerating the drug development process and potentially reducing associated costs.

10.3 Future Aspects

Healthcare is likely to undergo a significant change in the near future as complete reliance on Artificial Intelligence (AI) technologies emerges as the key to reaching healthcare independence. This visionary perspective emphasizes that AI will become the foundation of healthcare systems, fundamentally transforming the way medical services are provided, monitored, and tailored to each individual.

One of the most promising aspects of AI in healthcare independence is its potential to revolutionize diagnostics. AI-powered algorithms have already demonstrated remarkable accuracy in analysing vast amounts of medical data, spanning from imaging scans and genetic profiles to clinical histories. With this proficiency, AI can rapidly and precisely detect early signs of diseases, even before symptoms manifest, allowing for proactive interventions and significantly reducing the burden of illness on individuals and healthcare systems.

Furthermore, the integration of AI into the healthcare ecosystem would lead to unparalleled personalization of treatment plans. By analyzing patient-specific data, including genetic makeup, lifestyle habits, and responses to previous treatments, AI can customize therapies with exceptional precision, optimizing their effectiveness and minimizing adverse effects. Armed with these AI-driven insights, healthcare professionals would be empowered to make well-informed decisions, elevating the standard of care and substantially improving patient outcomes.

Healthcare independence would also be bolstered by AI-driven telemedicine and remote monitoring solutions. By combining AI capabilities with advanced wearable devices, patients can receive continuous health monitoring and real-time insights. This continuous flow of data empowers individuals to actively manage their health, promote preventive measures, and take a more proactive role in their well-being. Moreover, AI's role in telemedicine extends further, bridging the gap between patients in remote areas and specialized medical expertise, providing access to high-quality healthcare services that were previously out of reach.

AI's potential in healthcare extends beyond diagnostics and treatment alone. It encompasses medical research and drug development as well. With AI's capacity to analyze vast datasets, identifying potential drug candidates and accelerating the drug discovery process becomes more feasible. This breakthrough not only makes treatments more readily available but also drives down costs, making essential medications more affordable and accessible to all.

Nevertheless, realizing healthcare independence through AI requires addressing ethical and regulatory challenges. Safeguarding patient privacy and ensuring data security become paramount concerns. Transparent and accountable AI algorithms must be developed, providing insights into their decision-making process to foster trust between patients and AI-driven healthcare systems. Additionally, robust regulations must be implemented to govern the responsible use of AI in medicine, striking a delicate balance between innovation and safety.

In conclusion, the future of healthcare independence lies in the complete integration and reliance on AI technologies. As AI continues to advance, its potential to revolutionize diagnostics, treatment personalization, telemedicine, and drug development becomes increasingly evident. However, tapping into AI's full potential and ensuring responsible implementation necessitates collaborative efforts among healthcare professionals, technologists, ethicists, and policymakers. Through a unified approach, we can usher in an era where AI empowers individuals to take charge of their health, leading to a more independent, efficient, and equitable healthcare system for all.

11. CONCLUSION

To summarize, while Artificial Intelligence (AI) undeniably has immense potential to revolutionize healthcare and enhance patient outcomes, the notion that "Healthcare independence relies entirely on Artificial Intelligence" oversimplifies the intricate reality. Achieving healthcare independence is a multifaceted objective that demands a comprehensive approach, involving the integration of AI technology with human expertise, ethical deliberation, patient-centered care, and interdisciplinary cooperation.

AI undoubtedly contributes significantly to healthcare by improving diagnostic precision, treatment planning, and operational efficiency. However, it is imperative to acknowledge the limitations and uncertainties surrounding AI, such as interpretability issues and potential algorithmic biases. Addressing ethical concerns concerning patient privacy, consent, and responsible AI implementation is equally vital.

At its core, healthcare revolves around patients and their unique requirements, emphasizing the significance of a patient-centric approach. Human expertise and the patient-provider relationship play indispensable roles in delivering compassionate, empathetic, and personalized care.

Embracing a balanced approach that acknowledges the strengths of both AI and human involvement empowers healthcare professionals to harness AI's transformative potential while preserving the essential human touch. Moreover, fostering interdisciplinary collaboration among healthcare practitioners, researchers, policymakers, and technology developers is crucial in unlocking AI's true capabilities in healthcare.

In essence, the future of healthcare independence lies in a symbiotic relationship between AI and human expertise, with AI serving as a valuable tool to complement and enhance healthcare practices rather than serving as the sole determinant. Only through thoughtful integration, ethical considerations, and collaborative endeavors can we fully unleash AI's potential and steer healthcare toward greater independence and improved patient well-being.

12. REFERENCES

Beam, A. L., & Kohane, I. S. (2018). Big data and machine learning in health care. *Journal of the American Medical Association*, *319*(13), 1317–1318. doi:10.1001/jama.2017.18391 PMID:29532063

Bickmore, T. W., Schulman, D., Sidner, C., & Sidner, C. L. (2010). A reusable framework for health counseling dialogue systems based on a behavioral medicine ontology. *Journal of Biomedical Informatics*, *43*(2), 183–197. doi:10.1016/j.jbi.2010.12.006 PMID:21220044

Calvo, R. A., Deterding, S., Ryan, R. M., & Rigby, C. S. (2022). The impact of virtual agents on people's privacy attitudes and behaviors. *Human-Computer Interaction*, *37*(3), 285–353.

Davenport, T. H., & Kalakota, R. (2019). The potential for artificial intelligence in healthcare. *Future Healthcare Journal*, *6*(2), 94–98. doi:10.7861/futurehosp.6-2-94 PMID:31363513

Dolezel, M., Hinton, G. E., Eisner, J., & Popov, M. (2022). Mitigating labor displacement due to artificial intelligence: Evidence from a random assignment field experiment. *The American Economic Review*, *112*(2), 356–379.

Gandomi, A., & Haider, M. (2015). Beyond the hype: Big data concepts, methods, and analytics. *International Journal of Information Management*, *35*(2), 137–144. doi:10.1016/j.ijinfomgt.2014.10.007

Haenssle, H. A., Fink, C., Schneiderbauer, R., Toberer, F., Buhl, T., Blum, A., & Stolz, W. (2018). Man against machine: Diagnostic performance of a deep learning convolutional neural network for dermoscopic melanoma recognition in comparison to 58 dermatologists. *Annals of Oncology : Official Journal of the European Society for Medical Oncology*, *29*(8), 1836–1842. doi:10.1093/annonc/mdy166 PMID:29846502

Hughes, T. B., Yilmaz, L., & Son, Y. J. (2020). Artificial intelligence in drug discovery: Promises and challenges. *Drug Discovery Today*, *25*(4), 784–795.

Kocaballi, A. B., Berkovsky, S., Quiroz, J. C. G., & Kitson, N. (2021). The need for cybersecurity in healthcare: An editorial overview. *Journal of Biomedical Informatics*, *113*, 103649.

Krittanawong, C., Zhang, H., Wang, Z., & Aydar, M. (2021). The impact of artificial intelligence on the practice of medicine. *Journal of Geriatric Cardiology : JGC*, *18*(3), 179–185.

Litjens, G., Kooi, T., Bejnordi, B. E., Setio, A. A. A., Ciompi, F., Ghafoorian, M., van der Laak, J. A., van Ginneken, B., & Sánchez, C. I. (2017). A survey on deep learning in medical image analysis. *Medical Image Analysis*, *42*, 60–88. doi:10.1016/j.media.2017.07.005 PMID:28778026

Mann, D. M., Chen, J., Chunara, R., Testa, P. A., Nov, O., & Dredze, M. (2020). COVID-19 transforms health care through telemedicine: Evidence from the field. *Journal of the American Medical Informatics Association : JAMIA*, *27*(7), 1132–1135. doi:10.1093/jamia/ocaa072 PMID:32324855

Obermeyer, Z., Powers, B., Vogeli, C., & Mullainathan, S. (2019). Dissecting racial bias in an algorithm used to manage the health of populations. *Science*, *366*(6464), 447–453. doi:10.1126cience.aax2342 PMID:31649194

Price, W. N. II, & Cohen, I. G. (2019). Privacy in the age of medical big data. *Nature Medicine*, *25*(1), 37–43. doi:10.103841591-018-0272-7 PMID:30617331

Rajpurkar, P., Irvin, J., Bagul, A., Ding, D., Duan, T., Mehta, H., & Lungren, M. P. (2017). MURA: Large dataset for abnormality detection in musculoskeletal radiographs. arXiv preprint arXiv:1712.06957.

Suresh Babu, C. V. (2022). *Artificial Intelligence and Expert Systems*. Anniyappa Publications.

Suresh Babu, C. V., & Praveen, S. (2023). Swarm Intelligence and Evolutionary Machine Learning Algorithms for COVID-19: Pandemic and Epidemic Review. In A. Suresh Kumar, U. Kose, S. Sharma, & S. Jerald Nirmal Kumar (Eds.), *Dynamics of Swarm Intelligence Health Analysis for the Next Generation* (pp. 83–103). IGI Global. doi:10.4018/978-1-6684-6894-4.ch005

Topol, E. J. (2018). High-performance medicine: The convergence of human and artificial intelligence. *Nature Medicine*, *25*(1), 44–56. doi:10.103841591-018-0300-7 PMID:30617339

U.S. Food and Drug Administration (FDA). (2019). *Proposed Regulatory Framework for Modifications to Artificial Intelligence/Machine Learning-Based Software as a Medical Device*. FDA. https://www.fda.gov/media/122535/download

Weng, S. F., Reps, J., Kai, J., Garibaldi, J. M., & Qureshi, N. (2018). Can machine-learning improve cardiovascular risk prediction using routine clinical data? *PLoS One*, *13*(1), e0194025. PMID:28376093

Chapter 6
AI–Based Cybersecurity Threat Detection and Prevention

Tina Sharma
Chandigarh University, India

Pankaj Sharma
TrueBlue Headquarters, USA

ABSTRACT

The chapter presents an overview of AI-based cybersecurity threat detection and prevention. It highlights the importance of AI in tackling the ever-increasing threat landscape and explores various techniques and algorithms used in cybersecurity. AI's ability to process real-time data, identify patterns, and provide accurate threat intelligence is emphasized. The chapter covers machine learning, deep learning, and natural language processing, providing practical examples of their application in cybersecurity. Challenges such as data quality and bias are discussed, along with potential solutions. AI-based cybersecurity solutions like intrusion detection systems and threat intelligence platforms are presented. The chapter concludes with a discussion on the future of AI-based cybersecurity, including emerging technologies like quantum computing and blockchain, and the need for ongoing research and development to address evolving threats. Overall, it offers a comprehensive overview of AI's role in cybersecurity, highlighting benefits, challenges, and future directions.

DOI: 10.4018/978-1-6684-9814-9.ch006

INTRODUCTION TO AI-BASED CYBERSECURITY

Cybersecurity refers to the practice of protecting computer systems, networks, and digital assets from unauthorized access, theft, or damage. Cyber threats can come in many forms, including viruses, malware, phishing attacks, and hacking attempts. Effective cybersecurity strategies involve a combination of technology, policies, and user education to prevent, detect, and respond to these threats. For example, a company may use firewalls, intrusion detection systems, and other security technologies to protect its network from external threats. It may also implement policies such as strong passwords and two-factor authentication to prevent unauthorized access to sensitive data. Finally, employee training and awareness programs can help educate users about the risks of cyber threats and how to avoid them.

The importance of cybersecurity has increased in recent years as more organizations rely on digital systems to store and process sensitive information. The cost of a cyber-attack can be significant, including financial losses, damage to reputation, and legal consequences.

Artificial Intelligence (AI) has transformed the field of cybersecurity, enabling organizations to detect and respond to cyber threats with greater speed and accuracy. AI-based cybersecurity systems leverage machine learning algorithms, natural language processing, and other advanced technologies to analyze vast amounts of data and identify patterns that indicate a cyber-attack. By automating many aspects of threat detection and response, AI-based cybersecurity solutions can help organizations improve their overall security posture and reduce the risk of cyber breaches.

According to a report by Gartner, "AI augmentation will create $2.9 trillion of business value and recover 6.2 billion hours of worker productivity by 2021" (Osterman, 2019). This highlights the potential of AI to revolutionize cybersecurity, as it can help organizations detect and respond to cyber threats more efficiently and effectively. AI-based cybersecurity solutions can also help address the growing skills gap in the cybersecurity industry, as they can perform many tasks that would otherwise require highly trained and experienced cybersecurity professionals.

However, the use of AI in cybersecurity also poses new challenges and risks. For example, AI-based systems may be vulnerable to adversarial attacks, where an attacker attempts to manipulate the AI algorithms to evade detection. Additionally, there are concerns about the transparency and explainability of AI-based cybersecurity systems, as it may be difficult to understand how the systems make decisions or identify false positives.

Despite these challenges, the use of AI in cybersecurity is expected to continue to grow in the coming years. Organizations that are able to effectively leverage AI-based cybersecurity solutions will be better equipped to defend against cyber threats and protect their valuable data and assets.

JPMorgan Chase: In 2016, JPMorgan Chase implemented a machine learning algorithm to improve its fraud detection capabilities. The system analyzes millions of transactions per day and is able to identify potential fraud more accurately than previous systems. The AI-based system also reduces false positives, which can save time and resources that would otherwise be spent investigating false alarms (Wallace, 2019).

Darktrace: Darktrace is a cybersecurity company that specializes in AI-based threat detection. Its systems use unsupervised machine learning to detect and respond to cyber threats in real time. In one case, a customer detected a previously unknown malware infection in its network using Darktrace's AI-based system. The system was able to identify the threat and respond within minutes, preventing the malware from spreading further (Darktrace, n.d.).

These case studies demonstrate the potential of AI-based cybersecurity solutions to improve threat detection and response, reduce false positives, and ultimately protect organizations from cyber-attacks.

Understanding Cybersecurity Threats and Attacks

Cybersecurity threats and attacks are on the rise globally. Cybersecurity threats refer to any malicious attempt to breach an organization's network, system, or devices. Attackers often target sensitive data such as financial information, personal information, and intellectual property. With the increasing use of digital technology in almost every aspect of our lives, cybersecurity threats are becoming more complex, frequent, and sophisticated. Cybersecurity breaches can result in significant financial and reputational damages, loss of business, and identity theft. Therefore, it is essential for organizations to understand the various types of cybersecurity threats and attacks and develop effective strategies to protect their systems and data. This paper provides an overview of cybersecurity threats and attacks, including the different types, their impacts, and ways of mitigating them.

TYPES OF CYBERSECURITY THREATS AND ATTACKS

Malware Attacks

Malware is malicious software that is designed to harm a computer system or steal data. Malware can be in the form of viruses, worms, Trojans, and ransomware. Viruses are programs that attach themselves to other programs and can spread from one system to another. Worms are self-replicating programs that can spread over a network. Trojans are programs that disguise themselves as legitimate software but are designed to cause harm. Ransomware is a type of malware that encrypts the victim's data and demands payment in exchange for the decryption key (Rajabion et al., 2020).

Malware attacks are prevalent and can result in data theft, system damage, and financial loss. Organizations can mitigate malware attacks by using antivirus software, keeping software updated, and regularly backing up data.

Phishing Attacks

Phishing attacks are one of the most common types of cyber-attacks. Phishing attacks involve sending fake emails or messages that appear to be from legitimate sources, such as banks or online retailers. The emails often contain a link to a fake website that looks like the real one. The purpose of phishing attacks is to trick users into providing sensitive information, such as login credentials or credit card information. Phishing attacks can also include social engineering tactics, such as posing as a trusted individual to gain access to sensitive information (Chen et al., 2020).

Organizations can mitigate phishing attacks by educating users on how to identify phishing emails, using spam filters, and implementing multi-factor authentication.

Denial-of-Service (DoS) Attacks

DoS attacks involve overwhelming a system with traffic to make it inaccessible to legitimate users. DoS attacks can be launched from a single source or from multiple sources, known as a Distributed Denial-of-Service (DDoS) attack. DDoS attacks can be more difficult to mitigate than a single-source attack since it involves multiple sources and IP addresses. DoS attacks can result in loss of revenue, reputational damage, and service disruption (Liu et al., 2021). Organizations can mitigate DoS attacks by using firewalls, load balancers, and intrusion prevention systems.

Insider Threats

Insider threats refer to attacks that are carried out by employees or insiders who have authorized access to an organization's systems and data. Insider threats can be intentional or unintentional. Intentional insider threats are carried out with malicious intent, such as stealing data or causing damage to the system. Unintentional insider threats are carried out without malicious intent, such as an employee clicking on a phishing email or accidentally deleting data (Jain et al., 2020). Organizations can mitigate insider threats by implementing access controls, monitoring employee activity, and providing employee training on cybersecurity best practices.

Advanced Persistent Threats (APTs)

APTs are targeted attacks that are carried out by highly skilled and organized attackers. There are several ways that organizations can overcome cybersecurity threats and attacks. These include implementing security measures, conducting regular security assessments, and educating employees on cybersecurity best practices.

Implement Security Measures

Organizations can implement a variety of security measures to prevent and mitigate cybersecurity threats and attacks. These measures may include firewalls, antivirus software, intrusion detection systems, and access controls. Firewalls can block unauthorized access to a network, while antivirus software can detect and remove malware from systems. Intrusion detection systems can alert organizations to suspicious activity on their networks, while access controls can restrict access to sensitive data.

For example, a study by DeMott et al. (2019) found that implementing a security information and event management (SIEM) system helped an organization identify and respond to cybersecurity threats more effectively.

Conduct Regular Security Assessments

Regular security assessments can help organizations identify vulnerabilities in their systems and networks. These assessments can include penetration testing, vulnerability scans, and security audits. Penetration testing involves simulating a cyber attack to identify weaknesses in an organization's defenses. Vulnerability scans can identify vulnerabilities in software and systems, while security audits can evaluate an organization's overall security posture. For example, a study by Niazi et al. (2021) found that conducting regular security assessments helped organizations identify and address vulnerabilities in their systems and networks.

Educate Employees on Cybersecurity Best Practices

Employees can be a critical line of defence against cybersecurity threats and attacks. Organizations can educate employees on cybersecurity best practices, such as how to identify phishing emails, how to use strong passwords, and how to report suspicious activity. Education can also help employees understand the potential consequences of a cybersecurity breach and their role in preventing it.

For example, a study by Chen et al. (2020) found that employee training and awareness programs helped organizations reduce the likelihood of a successful phishing attack. Cybersecurity threats and attacks are becoming increasingly sophisticated and frequent, posing significant risks to organizations of all sizes. However, by implementing security measures, conducting regular security assessments, and educating employees on cybersecurity best practices, organizations can mitigate the risks associated with cybersecurity threats and attacks. It is essential for organizations to remain vigilant and proactive in their efforts to protect their systems, networks, and data.

Machine Learning Techniques for Cybersecurity Threat Detection

Machine learning techniques have become increasingly popular in the field of cybersecurity as they can be used to detect and respond to cybersecurity threats in real time. Machine learning algorithms are capable of identifying patterns and anomalies in large datasets, making them well-suited for identifying potential cyber-attacks. In this article, we will discuss some of the machine-learning techniques used for cybersecurity threat detection.

Artificial Neural Networks (ANNs)

Artificial neural networks (ANNs) are a type of machine learning algorithm inspired by the structure of the human brain. ANNs are capable of learning complex patterns in data and making predictions based on that data. ANNs have been used in cybersecurity to detect anomalies in network traffic, identify malicious files, and classify malware. For example, a study by Hu et al. (2018) used an ANN-based intrusion detection system to detect network intrusions in real time. The system was able to achieve an accuracy of 98.4% in detecting network intrusions.

Support Vector Machines (SVMs)

Support vector machines (SVMs) are a type of machine learning algorithm that can be used for classification and regression analysis. SVMs are well-suited for cybersecurity threat detection as they can be trained on large datasets and can identify patterns that are difficult to detect using traditional methods. For example, a study by Li et al. (2019) used an SVM-based approach to detect malware. The system was able to detect malware with an accuracy of 98.2%.

Random Forests

Random forests are a type of machine-learning algorithm that can be used for classification and regression analysis. Random forests are well-suited for cybersecurity threat detection as they can be used to identify patterns and anomalies in large datasets. For example, a study by Yadav et al. (2020) used a random forest-based approach to detect network anomalies. The system was able to detect network anomalies with an accuracy of 98.6%.

Deep Learning

Deep learning is a type of machine learning algorithm that is capable of learning complex patterns in data. Deep learning algorithms are used in cybersecurity to detect malware, identify network intrusions, and detect anomalous behavior. For example, a study by Li et al. (2020) used a deep learning-based approach to detect malware. The system was able to detect malware with an accuracy of 99.9%.

Clustering

Clustering is a type of unsupervised machine-learning algorithm that can be used to group similar data points together. Clustering algorithms are used in cybersecurity to identify patterns in network traffic and detect anomalies. For example, a study by Pandey et al. (2019) used a clustering-based approach to detect anomalies in network traffic. The system was able to detect anomalies with an accuracy of 98.5%. Machine learning techniques are becoming increasingly important in the field of cybersecurity as they can be used to detect and respond to cybersecurity threats in real time. Artificial neural networks, support vector machines, random forests, deep learning, and clustering are just some of the machine learning techniques used for cybersecurity threat detection. By leveraging these techniques, organizations can enhance their cybersecurity posture and protect their systems, networks, and data from cyber-attacks.

Deep Learning Techniques for Cybersecurity Threat Detection

Deep learning is a subset of machine learning that involves the use of artificial neural networks with multiple layers to process and analyse complex data. In cybersecurity, deep learning techniques have been found to be effective in identifying and responding to various threats and attacks. One of the key advantages of deep learning is its ability to analyse large amounts of data and identify patterns and anomalies that may not be detectable by traditional methods. Deep learning models can be trained on massive datasets of normal and anomalous behaviour to learn and recognize patterns that are indicative of threats. One example of deep learning in cybersecurity is the use of deep neural networks for malware detection. These models can analyse code and determine whether or not it is malicious, even if it has been obfuscated or otherwise disguised. For example, in a study by Li et al. (2020), a deep learning-based approach was used to detect malware with an accuracy of 99.9%.

Another example of deep learning in cybersecurity is the use of recurrent neural networks (RNNs) for intrusion detection. RNNs are well-suited for identifying anomalies in sequences of data, such as network traffic. In a study by Gao et al. (2018), an RNN-based approach was used to detect network intrusions with an accuracy of 99.5%. Convolutional neural networks (CNNs) are also commonly used in cybersecurity for tasks such as image analysis and feature extraction. For example, in a study by Liu et al. (2018), a CNN-based approach was used to detect phishing websites with an accuracy of 99.43%. One of the challenges of deep learning in cybersecurity is the need for large amounts of labeled data to train these models. However, techniques such as transfer learning and data augmentation can be used to overcome this challenge. In conclusion, deep learning techniques have proven to be effective in cybersecurity threat detection. By analyzing large amounts of data and identifying patterns and anomalies, deep learning models can help organizations better protect their systems, networks, and data from cyber-attacks.

Natural Language Processing for Cybersecurity Threat Detection

Natural Language Processing (NLP) is a branch of artificial intelligence that focuses on the interaction between computers and human language. In cybersecurity, NLP can be used to analyse and understand natural language data, such as email messages, chat logs, and social media posts, to detect potential threats. One of the key advantages of NLP in cybersecurity is its ability to analyse unstructured data, which is often difficult for traditional security systems to process. NLP can help identify threats such as phishing emails and social engineering attacks, which rely on human interaction and deception. For example, in a study by Zaman et al. (2019), NLP techniques were used to analyse Twitter data for cybersecurity threat detection. The study found that NLP-based approaches were able to detect cyber threats with high accuracy and precision, particularly for phishing attacks.

Another application of NLP in cybersecurity is in the analysis of malware and malicious code. NLP can be used to extract features from code and identify patterns that are indicative of malicious behaviour. For example, in a study by Lyu et al. (2018), NLP was used to analyse malware code and identify code snippets that were associated with malicious behaviour.

Sentiment analysis is another NLP technique that can be used in cybersecurity. By analysing the tone and sentiment of social media posts and other online communications, organizations can gain insights into potential threats and take proactive measures to prevent them. For example, in a study by Blasco et al. (2018), sentiment analysis was used to detect cyber threats by analysing Twitter data.

One of the challenges of NLP in cybersecurity is the need for large amounts of data to train these models. However, techniques such as transfer learning and data augmentation can be used to overcome this challenge. In conclusion, NLP techniques have shown promise in cybersecurity threat detection, particularly in the analysis of unstructured data and human communication. By using NLP to extract insights and patterns from natural language data, organizations can better protect themselves from cyber-attacks.

Big Data and AI-Based Cybersecurity

Big data and AI-based cybersecurity is a rapidly evolving field that uses large-scale data analysis and machine learning techniques to detect and prevent cyber threats. Big data refers to the large and complex datasets generated by various sources, such as network logs, sensor data, and social media activity, while AI refers to the use of advanced algorithms to enable machines to perform human-like tasks, such as decision-making and problem-solving. One of the primary advantages of big data and AI-based cybersecurity is its ability to analyze and process vast amounts of data quickly and accurately. This allows organizations to detect threats in real-time and respond quickly to potential attacks.

For example, in a study by Sharma et al. (2018), big data and AI techniques were used to detect and prevent distributed denial-of-service (DDoS) attacks. The study found that the use of big data analytics and machine learning algorithms helped identify DDoS attacks with high accuracy and speed.

Another application of big data and AI-based cybersecurity is in the detection of insider threats. By analyzing large volumes of user activity data, organizations can identify suspicious behavior patterns that may indicate an insider threat. For example, in a study by Li et al. (2018), big data analytics and machine learning techniques were used to detect insider threats in an enterprise network. Big data and AI-based cybersecurity also have the potential to improve threat intelligence and sharing. By pooling together data from multiple sources, such as network logs and threat intelligence feeds, organizations can gain a more comprehensive view of potential threats. AI algorithms can also be used to analyze this data and identify patterns and correlations that may indicate a threat. One of the challenges of big data and AI-based cybersecurity is the need for specialized skills and expertise to implement and manage these systems. However, as the technology continues to mature, it is likely that more tools and platforms will become available to make it easier for organizations to adopt and utilize these advanced security techniques. In conclusion, big data and AI-based cybersecurity is a promising field that can help organizations detect and prevent cyber threats more effectively. By leveraging the power of big data and machine learning algorithms, organizations can gain insights into potential threats and take proactive measures to protect themselves from cyber-attacks.

Cloud-Based AI-Based Cybersecurity

Cloud-based AI-based cybersecurity refers to the use of cloud computing technology and artificial intelligence techniques to provide cybersecurity services. In this approach, cybersecurity services are hosted on remote servers in the cloud, and AI algorithms are used to monitor and detect potential threats.One of the key benefits of cloud-based AI-based cybersecurity is that it can provide scalable and cost-effective security solutions. Instead of having to invest in expensive hardware and software, organizations can access security services through the cloud on a pay-per-use basis. This makes it easier for small and medium-sized businesses to access high-quality security services.

For example, Amazon Web Services (AWS) offers a range of cloud-based security services that use AI and machine learning to detect potential threats. AWS Security Hub, for instance, provides a centralized view of security alerts and compliance status across an organization's AWS accounts. It also uses AI to prioritize alerts and provide recommendations for remediation.

Another example is Microsoft Azure Sentinel, a cloud-native security information and event management (SIEM) solution that uses AI to detect potential threats across an organization's entire IT environment, including on-premises systems, cloud infrastructure, and applications. Cloud-based AI-based cybersecurity can also help organizations respond to threats more quickly. Since security services are hosted in the cloud, they can be easily accessed from anywhere, and alerts can be sent in real-time to security teams. One of the challenges of cloud-based AI-based cybersecurity is the need to ensure the security and privacy of sensitive data. Organizations need to ensure that their data is encrypted and that access is restricted to authorized users only. In conclusion, cloud-based AI-based cybersecurity is a promising approach that can help organizations improve their security posture by providing scalable, cost-effective, and efficient security services. As cloud technology and AI continue to evolve, it is likely that we will see more innovative and effective solutions in this space.

IoT Security With AI-Based Cybersecurity

IoT (Internet of Things) devices are becoming increasingly popular in both personal and professional settings, but with this increased connectivity comes an increased risk of cyber-attacks. AI-based cybersecurity can play a crucial role in protecting IoT devices from potential threats. One of the key benefits of using AI-based cybersecurity for IoT security is the ability to analyze large amounts of data in real-time. IoT devices generate vast amounts of data, and AI algorithms can process this data to identify patterns and anomalies that may indicate a potential security threat. For example, AI-based cybersecurity can be used to monitor IoT devices for suspicious activity, such as unusual traffic patterns or unauthorized access attempts. Machine learning algorithms can learn from past attacks to identify similar patterns in future data, improving the accuracy of threat detection.

AI-based cybersecurity can also be used to protect IoT devices from emerging threats. As new types of attacks are developed, AI algorithms can adapt to identify and respond to these threats. This can help organizations stay ahead of attackers and reduce the risk of successful attacks.

Another benefit of AI-based cybersecurity for IoT security is the ability to automate security processes. With the sheer number of IoT devices being deployed, it can be challenging to manually monitor and manage their security. By automating security processes, organizations can improve the efficiency and effectiveness of their security measures. However, there are also some challenges associated with using AI-based cybersecurity for IoT security. One of the key challenges is the need to ensure the privacy of user data. IoT devices often collect sensitive information, and organizations must ensure that this data is protected from unauthorized access.

Another challenge is the potential for false positives. With so much data being generated by IoT devices, it can be difficult to distinguish between legitimate activity and potential threats. This can lead to security teams being overwhelmed with false alerts, making it more difficult to identify genuine threats. In conclusion, AI-based cybersecurity can play a critical role in securing IoT devices from potential threats. By analyzing large amounts of data in real-time and automating security processes, AI algorithms can help organizations stay ahead of attackers and reduce the risk of successful attacks. However, it is important to ensure the privacy of user data and to address the challenges associated with false positives. As IoT devices continue to proliferate, the use of AI-based cybersecurity is likely to become increasingly important in protecting these devices from cyber threats.

AI-Based Cybersecurity for Industrial Control Systems

Industrial control systems (ICS) are used in critical infrastructure sectors such as energy, transportation, and manufacturing to manage and automate complex processes. However, the growing reliance on ICS systems also increases the risk of cyber-attacks that can cause physical damage, economic losses, and public safety threats. AI-based cybersecurity can be used to detect and respond to threats to ICS systems. One of the main advantages of using AI-based cybersecurity for ICS security is the ability to identify anomalous behaviour that may indicate a potential security threat. ICS systems generate vast amounts of data, and AI algorithms can analyse this data to identify patterns and anomalies that may indicate a potential attack. For example, AI can be used to monitor network traffic for suspicious activity, such as unauthorized access attempts or abnormal data flows.

Another advantage of AI-based cybersecurity for ICS security is the ability to detect zero-day vulnerabilities. Zero-day vulnerabilities are previously unknown vulnerabilities that can be exploited by attackers to gain unauthorized access to systems. AI algorithms can be trained to identify patterns in system behaviour that may indicate the presence of a zero-day vulnerability. AI-based cybersecurity can also be used to automate security processes for ICS systems. This can include automatically detecting and responding to security threats, as well as monitoring system health and performance. Automating these processes can help to reduce the risk of human error and improve the efficiency and effectiveness of security measures.

However, there are also some challenges associated with using AI-based cybersecurity for ICS security. One of the main challenges is the need to ensure the reliability of AI-based systems. Because AI algorithms are trained on historical data, they may not always be effective at identifying new or evolving threats. Additionally, AI-based systems may be vulnerable to attacks that exploit their own vulnerabilities. Another challenge is the need to ensure the compatibility of AI-based cybersecurity with existing ICS systems. Many ICS systems are built using legacy technologies that may not be compatible with newer cybersecurity solutions. This can make it difficult to integrate AI-based cybersecurity into existing ICS systems without causing disruptions to operations. In conclusion, AI-based cybersecurity can be a powerful tool for securing industrial control systems from potential cyber threats. By analysing large amounts of data, detecting zero-day vulnerabilities, and automating security processes, AI algorithms can help to reduce the risk of successful attacks on ICS systems. However, it is important to address the challenges associated with reliability, compatibility, and other potential vulnerabilities to ensure the effectiveness of AI-based cybersecurity for ICS security.

Evaluation Metrics for AI-Based Cybersecurity Solutions

Industrial control systems (ICS) are used to manage and monitor critical infrastructure such as power grids, water treatment plants, and manufacturing facilities. These systems are increasingly connected to the internet, which means that they are vulnerable to cyber-attacks. AI-based cybersecurity can be used to protect industrial control systems from potential threats. One of the key benefits of using AI-based cybersecurity for industrial control systems is the ability to detect and respond to threats in real time. ICS systems generate large amounts of data, and AI algorithms can be used to process this data to identify patterns and anomalies that may indicate a potential security threat. For example, machine learning algorithms can be trained to detect abnormal network traffic or unauthorized access attempts. AI-based cybersecurity can also be used to protect against emerging threats. With the increasing complexity of ICS systems and the emergence of new types of attacks, it can be challenging to keep up with the latest threats. However, AI algorithms can be trained to identify and respond to new types of attacks, reducing the risk of successful attacks.

Another benefit of AI-based cybersecurity for industrial control systems is the ability to automate security processes. With the large number of devices and systems involved in ICS, it can be challenging to manually monitor and manage security. By automating security processes, organizations can improve the efficiency and effectiveness of their security measures. However, there are also some challenges associated with using AI-based cybersecurity for ICS security. One of the key challenges is the need to ensure the safety of physical infrastructure. A cyber-attack on an ICS system could potentially cause physical damage or disruption, so it is important to ensure that security measures do not interfere with the safe operation of the system.

Another challenge is the potential for false positives. With so much data being generated by ICS systems, it can be difficult to distinguish between legitimate activity and potential threats. This can lead to security teams being overwhelmed with false alerts, making it more difficult to identify genuine threats. In conclusion, AI-based cybersecurity can play an important role in protecting industrial control systems from potential cyber threats. By analysing large amounts of data in real time, identifying emerging threats, and automating security processes, AI algorithms can help organizations stay ahead of attackers and reduce the risk of successful attacks. However, it is important to ensure the safety of physical infrastructure and to address the challenges associated with false positives. As ICS systems continue to become more connected and complex, the use of AI-based cybersecurity is likely to become increasingly important in protecting these critical systems.

CHALLENGES AND LIMITATIONS OF AI-BASED CYBERSECURITY

While AI-based cybersecurity has several advantages, it also has some challenges and limitations. In this response, we will discuss some of the major challenges and limitations associated with AI-based cybersecurity.

Lack of Explain Ability

One of the major limitations of AI-based cybersecurity is the lack of explain ability. In many cases, AI algorithms work as black boxes, making it difficult to understand how they arrive at their decisions. This makes it challenging for cybersecurity analysts to verify the accuracy of the results and to identify any potential biases that may be present in the data. This can lead to a lack of trust in the AI system, which can limit its effectiveness in detecting threats.

False Positives and False Negatives

Another major challenge of AI-based cybersecurity is the potential for false positives and false negatives. False positives occur when the system generates a security alert for a legitimate activity, while false negatives occur when the system fails to detect a real threat. False positives can be particularly problematic, as they can overwhelm cybersecurity teams with alerts, making it difficult to prioritize and respond to genuine threats.

Adversarial Attacks

AI-based cybersecurity systems can be vulnerable to adversarial attacks, where attackers deliberately manipulate the data input to cause the system to misclassify or ignore a threat. This can lead to false negatives and false positives, which can compromise the security of the system.

Limited Data Availability

AI-based cybersecurity systems require large amounts of data to be trained effectively. However, in some cases, there may be limited data available for training. This can make it difficult to develop accurate models and can limit the effectiveness of the AI system in detecting threats.

Computational Resources

AI-based cybersecurity systems require significant computational resources to process large amounts of data in real-time. This can be a challenge for organizations with limited computing resources or for systems that require low latency.

Privacy Concerns

AI-based cybersecurity systems can also raise privacy concerns, particularly if they are analyzing sensitive data. There is a risk that personal or sensitive data may be inadvertently collected and analyzed, raising privacy concerns for individuals and organizations. One example of the challenges and limitations of AI-based cybersecurity is the case of the Russian hacking group Fancy Bear, which used an adversarial attack to evade detection by AI-based security systems. The group manipulated the metadata of their phishing emails to avoid detection by AI-based spam filters, highlighting the need for AI systems to be designed to detect and respond to adversarial attacks.

Another example is the challenge of false positives in AI-based cybersecurity systems. In 2019, an AI-based security system at a US-based utility company generated over 30,000 alerts in a single month, leading to a significant strain on the organization's cybersecurity team. Many of these alerts turned out to be false positives, highlighting the need for effective ways to filter and prioritize security alerts generated by AI systems. AI-based cybersecurity has the potential to improve the effectiveness and efficiency of cybersecurity systems. However, there are also several challenges and limitations associated with this technology, including the lack of explainability, the potential for false positives and false negatives, the vulnerability to adversarial attacks, limited data availability, and the need for significant computational resources. These challenges and limitations must be addressed to ensure that AI-based cybersecurity systems can be used effectively to protect against cyber threats.

Future of AI-Based Cybersecurity

The future of AI-based cybersecurity looks promising, with continued advances in technology and the growing importance of cybersecurity in today's digital landscape. Here are some of the potential future developments and trends in AI-based cybersecurity: Integration of AI with other technologies: AI-based cybersecurity is likely to be integrated with other emerging technologies, such as blockchain, IoT, and cloud computing, to enhance security and privacy. For example, AI could be used to analyze data from IoT devices and identify potential threats.

- **Improved Explain ability:** There is a growing need for AI-based cybersecurity systems to be explainable to address the lack of trust and transparency that currently exists. This means that cybersecurity algorithms will need to be designed to be more interpretable and understandable, enabling cybersecurity experts to understand how the system arrives at its conclusions.

- **Increased Use of Unsupervised Learning:** The use of unsupervised learning, which enables AI-based cybersecurity systems to detect new and unknown threats, is likely to become more widespread in the future. This will help to address the challenge of detecting advanced and evolving cyber threats.

- **Greater Emphasis on Privacy:** There is likely to be a greater emphasis on privacy in AI-based cybersecurity, with the use of privacy-preserving algorithms and techniques that protect sensitive data while still enabling effective threat detection and analysis.

- **More Sophisticated Adversarial Defense Techniques:** As adversarial attacks become more sophisticated, AI-based cybersecurity systems will need to adopt more advanced techniques to defend against these attacks. This may include the use of counter-adversarial machine learning and other techniques designed to detect and respond to adversarial attacks in real-time.

- **Increased Automation:** The use of AI-based cybersecurity systems is likely to become more automated, with the integration of machine learning and other AI technologies that enable the system to learn and adapt to new threats and vulnerabilities in real-time.

- **Collaboration between AI and Human Experts:** In the future, there is likely to be greater collaboration between AI-based cybersecurity systems and human experts, with cybersecurity analysts working alongside AI systems to identify and respond to cyber threats.

One example of the future of AI-based cybersecurity is the development of AI systems that can detect and respond to cyber threats in real-time. These systems use machine learning algorithms to analyze data and detect anomalies, enabling cybersecurity teams to respond to potential threats before they escalate.

Another example is the use of AI-based systems to detect and respond to insider threats, which are a growing concern for many organizations. These systems can use machine learning algorithms to analyze patterns of behavior and detect anomalies that may indicate a potential insider threat. The future of AI-based cybersecurity looks promising, with continued advances in technology and the growing importance of cybersecurity in today's digital landscape. Key trends in the future of AI-based cybersecurity include the integration of AI with other technologies, improved explainability, increased use of unsupervised learning, greater emphasis on privacy, more sophisticated adversarial defense techniques, increased automation, and greater collaboration between AI and human experts. As these trends continue to evolve, AI-based cybersecurity will become increasingly important in helping organizations to protect against cyber threats and safeguard their data and systems.

REFERENCES

Alcaraz, C., Najera, P., & Roman, R. (2016). AI for industrial control systems security: A survey. *Computers & Security, 56*, 1–12. doi:10.1016/j.cose.2015.10.010

Awoleye, O., Okolie, S., Akinwunmi, A., Adebiyi, A., & Misra, S. (2020). A survey of artificial intelligence-based cybersecurity for industrial control systems. *Computers & Security, 90*, 101708.

Blasco, J., Esteve, M., Gonzalez, J. J., & Rifà-Pous, H. (2018). Sentiment Analysis for Cybersecurity Threat Detection. *13th International Conference on Availability, Reliability and Security (ARES),* (pp. 1-6). MIT.

Chen, J., Wu, L., & Xu, X. (2020). Employee training and awareness in phishing resistance: Evidence from a field experiment. *Journal of Management Information Systems, 37*(1), 201–235. doi:10.1080/07421222.2019.1703634

DeMott, J., Koscher, K., & Sherry, C. (2019). Towards effective security information and event management (SIEM) system management. In *Proceedings of the 2019 ACM SIGSAC Conference on Computer and Communications Security* (pp. 2187-2189). ACM. doi: 10.1145/3319535.3363239

Gartner. (2018). *Gartner Top 10 Strategic Technology Trends for 2018.* Gartner. https://www.gartner.com/smarterwithgartner/gartner-top-10-strategic-technology-trends-for-2018/

Jain, A., Kant, K., & Singh, Y. (2020). A review on insider threats: Classification, models and mitigation techniques. *Journal of Information Security and Applications, 53*, 102466. doi:10.1016/j.jisa.2020.102466

Kour, R., Singh, G., Singh, P., & Kant, K. (2021). An intelligent security framework for industrial control systems using machine learning techniques. *Journal of Network and Computer Applications, 178*, 102966.

Li, Y., Jiang, J., & Li, G. (2018). Insider Threat Detection Based on Big Data Analytics and Machine Learning. *2018 IEEE International Conference on Information Reuse and Integration (IRI),* (pp. 113-118). IEEE.

Liu, Y., Li, Q., & Dong, X. (2021). A hybrid intrusion detection system based on clustering analysis and machine learning algorithms for network security. *Wireless Personal Communications, 117*(2), 921–944. doi:10.100711277-021-08307-w

Liu, Y., Li, S., & Huang, L. (2020). Deep learning based intrusion detection for industrial control systems. *IEEE Transactions on Industrial Informatics, 16*(4), 2552–2561. doi:10.1109/TII.2019.2943199

Lyu, Q., Xu, X., & Lv, J. (2018). Malware Analysis Based on Natural Language Processing. *IEEE Access : Practical Innovations, Open Solutions, 6*, 56914–56922.

Mili, N., & Mukherjee, A. (2018). AI and IoT: New age of threat vectors and security challenges. *International Journal of Computer Science and Information Security, 16*(4), 43–50.

Niazi, M., Khan, I. U., & Shah, A. (2021). *A study of cyber security vulnerabilities and risk assessment in higher education institutions.*

Osterman, M. (2019, June 26). The Growing Role of AI in Cybersecurity. *Forbes.* https://www.forbes.com/sites/michaelosterman/2019/06/26/the-growing-role-of-ai-in-cybersecurity/?sh=4fa4d0ad5b5d

Sharma, S., Tiwari, S., & Kumar, V. (2018). Big data analytics and machine learning for cybersecurity: A review. *Journal of Big Data, 5*(1), 1–20.

Singer, P. W., & Friedman, A. (2014). *Cybersecurity and Cyberwar: What Everyone Needs to Know.* Oxford University Press. doi:10.1093/wentk/9780199918096.001.0001

Veeraraghavan, P., & Vasudevan, S. (2020). AI-based cybersecurity for industrial control systems: A comprehensive review. *IEEE Access : Practical Innovations, Open Solutions, 8*, 125318–125335.

Yang, L., Wang, H., & Chen, J. (2019). An AI-based security framework for the Internet of Things. *Future Generation Computer Systems, 92*, 862–871. doi:10.1016/j.future.2018.09.035

Zaman, F., Yildirim, I., & Goksel, C. (2019). Cybersecurity Threat Detection in Twitter Data Using Natural Language Processing Techniques. *IEEE Access : Practical Innovations, Open Solutions, 7*, 165115–165124.

Chapter 7
Stock Market Responses to Interest Rate Changes:
An Indian Market Perspective

Rohit Sood

iD https://orcid.org/0000-0002-4127-7781
Lovely Professional University, India

ABSTRACT

Stock markets encourage investors to make savings and investments with extra amounts to invest in the different financial resources which match their capability and the amount of investment they have. In developing countries like India, especially in financial sectors, stock markets play a crucial role towards growth and development of an economy. Investors always look for the returns from the invested capital to achieve an optimal balance between risk and reward as per the respective risk profile of an investor. The research attempts to investigate the impact of rate of interest on rate sensitive sectors in the Indian stock market. The effect of rate of interest vacillations on the estimation of companies has gotten a great arrangement of consideration inside the writing, albeit a significant part of the observational research has concentrated on rate delicate areas like banking, automobile, and real estate segments as a result of the financing cost affectability of these segments.

DOI: 10.4018/978-1-6684-9814-9.ch007

INTRODUCTION

In the period of Globalization, one of the macroeconomic factors that have come into more noteworthy center is the intrigue rate. This is resulting upon fortified coordination of the residential monetary part with the outer segment. In India, the money related division has experienced a few changes since the adjustment program started in the mid 1990's. With the advancement in the economy, flexibility has been granted to the development of premium rates. The connection between financial exchange returns and loan fee has been inspected by scientists as it assumes a significant job in impacting a nation's monetary development, Interest rates are dictated by fiscal arrangement of a nation as indicated by its financial circumstance.

High pace of intrigue can stop accomplish numerous things, for example, capital outpourings, upset financial development and therefore hurt the economy as it is one of the most noteworthy element contacting straightforwardly the extension of partner degree economy.

The levelheaded for the connection between loan cost and financial exchange return are that stock costs and loan costs are said to be contrarily associated, Higher loan fee coming about because of antagonistic fiscal strategy adversely influences trade returns because of higher pace of intrigue lessens the value of value and makes mounted pay protections increasingly appealing.

Despite what might be expected, lower loan fees resulting from expansionary financial strategy helps securities exchange. An ascent inside the financing costs influences the valuation of the stocks. The ascent in the loan costs raises the desires for the market members, that request more significant yields that equivalent with the expanded profits for securities. In a low loan cost system, corporate can expand gainfulness by diminishing their advantage expenses. However, in a rising financing cost system, as intrigue costs rise, benefit is influenced. At the point when loan costs rise, financial specialists move from values to bonds.

Though once rate of interest fall, returns on securities fall while the profits on values will in general show up nearly extra captivating and furthermore the movement of reserve from bonds to values happens, and expanding the costs of values. In spite of the fact that money related financial analysts, arrangement creators and speculators have since quite a while ago endeavored to get a handle on unique associations among rate and stock costs, the accurate examples of the connections stay misty, the nature and quality of the dynamic cooperation between them is of high premium and should be assessed experimentally. Accordingly, the scientist inspects the energetic connection among rate and stock expenses in order to recognize the effect of loan fee changes on stock costs on rate areas like Banking, Automobile and Real bequest divisions with exceptional reference to Indian Stock Exchange.

Interest Rates

The rate at which premium is paid by a borrower for the use of money that they get from a bank (Bleaney et al, 2001). Rate of interest change is because of monetary policy. Negative rates of interest imply that stated interest rate is less than rate of inflation. To keep away from full scale economic problems, interest rates assumes a conspicuous job in controlling conversion scale devaluation and to check inflationary pressures. (Gagnon and Ihrig 2004).

Market Returns

Increment in stock costs demonstrates financial development in future and reduction in stock costs shows downturn (Mun,Siong and Thing 2008).Companies raises capital through issue of shares or rights issue. This is a modest wellspring of raising extra capital. Hence share market engage in eminent job in development and advancement of a country. Share market also engage in double task in raising resources for long term infrastructural projects through sale of bonds by looking at the movement of share market indices and thereby alter monetary or fiscal policies which can facilitate growth and development of an economy (Munga 2004).

Rate Sensitive Sectors

A sector whose stock cost is impacted by changes in rates of interest. A rate sensitive stock is protected against rate changes. Rate of interest affectability just implies that the financing cost and rate of interest projections become a key piece of investigating the stock as an investment. (James chen 2019). Example: Banks, Financial institutions, Real Estate etc.

EFFECTS OF RATE OF INTEREST ON SHARE MARKET YIELDING

The degree of an advance that is charged as enthusiasm to the borrower, routinely imparted as a yearly degree of the credit remarkable (Devereux and Yetman 2002). Economists and policy makers keep an eye on rates of interest for finding changes in macro-economic variables. Although the relationship between these two, depends on substantial research. Only few studies considered impact of rates of interest on share prices whereas many researchers found influence of prices on interest rates(Barsky and Delong 1991).The findings of these studies are always contradicting and confounding to the complexity of conceptual analysis that justify the impact of rates of interest on stock market (kandil 2005).Raise in the level of price is called inflation(Bleaney at al 2001).The foremost motto of money policy is to curb inflation and stimulating expectations of prices. Continuing with small rate of inflation is necessary as a piece of adverse shortage strategy. Higher interest rates increase the user cost of capital which results in increased costs of production (Branson 1979). More money supply in the economy results raise in the price levels both in short and long haul periods. It also results in increase of interest rates.

RESEARCH PROBLEM

Interest rate have complex impact on the nation's economy. One side it effects the cost of doing business and the other side it effects the prices of stock and the company's overall performance or trade in India may effect on growth of an economy. Financial experts, strategy creators, entrepreneurs, controllers, researchers and Indian open are attempting to discover the effect of lending rate on rate sensitive sectors. Interest rates are considered as principle approach factors in macroeconomics. One of the variables which impact the lending rate is inflation. Asgharpur et al.(2007), rejected bidirectional connection between rate of inflation and bank rates. Higher rates of inflation leads higher interest rates.

It was expressed that there was an opposite connection between lending rates and stock returns. Reduction in lending rates, brings more money supply into the economy. This additional money could be directed to the stock market, to meet the demand and prices of shares. (Thorbecke1997 and smal and dejager 2001).Patelis (1997) sees that lending rates are valuable in estimating share market yielding over a long time period. So, there is a proof to windup that rate of interest strategies ought to likewise watch financial exchange value changes.

In any case, there are arguments stating interest rates don't influence stock market prices. Bernanke (1999) and Getler (2001) found that unpredictable nature of assets makes them difficult to anticipate and that money related specialists should possibly alter rates of share prices in response to stock value developments when they anticipate that such developments should influence inflation. Some researchers found that there is a positive connection between rate of interest and share market yielding, where a few analysts discovered negative connection between the both.

Eita (2011), found that a hike in interest rates arise in fall of stock market yielding. Using quarterly information from 1998 to 2009, Eita likewise researched the elements to determine financial exchange costs in Namibia. A positive relationship was found between prices of shares and supply of money. Bai and green (2008) observed that exchange rates and stock market yielding have negative relationship.

There is a space in examining the interest rates of interest and share market yielding of rate sensitive sectors in India which this research tries to find. Thus the study looks for an answer to the following question of research:

What is the effect of rate of interest on rate Sensitive divisions in Indian share market?

RESEARCH OBJECTIVES

- To find the relationship between rate of interest and stock market in India during the 2014-2019.
- To find the effect of rate of interest on RATE SENSITIVE SECTORS like banking, real estate sector and automobile sector from the years 2014-2019.

LITERATURE REVIEW

In 1985 by Jeremy J. Siegal on cash supply declarations and financing costs: Does fiscal strategy matter? states that Most present clarifications of the impact of cash supply declarations on the pace of premium focus on national bank approach. This paper investigates an adaptable value macroeconomic model where present and future money related arrangement have no impact on either financing costs or genuine yield, yet fiscal information signal data about genuine monetary movement which impacts both short-and long haul genuine paces of premium. The extent of the loan fee reaction is appeared to rely upon the distinction in the salary flexibilities of cash and store request and the overall size of financial and genuine unsettling influences to the economy.

A study by Mohammed Omran expressed that, since 1991 Egypt has seen major changes in their monetary atmosphere because of the administration's selection of a program of financial change planned for expanding the development rate of the economy. Ostensibly, this goal can be helped through making a solid financial exchange. This research centers around looking at the effect of genuine rate of interest as a prominent factor in the program on the exhibition of the Egyptian financial exchange, both as far as market action and liquidity. By applying Engle and Granger's two-organize technique, results from co-coordination examination through blunder redress systems (ECM) show huge since quite a while ago run and short-run connections between the factors, suggesting that genuine rates of interest have an effect upon financial exchange execution.

In 1993 an article by Donald P. Morgan expresses that fiscal approach has hilter kilter impacts utilizing measures 1, government subsidize rate 2.a story list dependent on the announcements of policymakers. The article follows the history and potential reasons for asymmetry. The subsequent segment introduces some proof that the effect of fiscal arrangement is lopsided. The thought of asymmetry was conceived in the Great Depression. That occasion persuaded numerous that simple arrangement could check a blast.

Kunt (1996) has discovered that nations with lesser interest rate have solid market when contrasted with nations which have higher interest rate. He likewise referenced that created nations are typically having low interest rates because of which securities exchange's presentation is extra-common.

A study endeavored to gauge the response of fiscal arrangement to the securities exchange by Roberto Rigobon. It expressed that Movements in the financial exchange can significantly affect the macro economy and are in this manner prone to be a significant factor in the assurance of money related strategy. Nonetheless, little is thought about the extent of the Federal Reserve's response to the financial exchange, to some degree in light of the fact that the synchronous reaction of value costs to interest rates makes it hard to appraise. This paper utilizes an ID strategy dependent on the securities exchange comes back to quantify the response of fiscal approach to the financial exchange. We locate a huge approach reaction, with a 5 percent rise (fall) in the S&P 500 list improving the probability of a 25 premise point fixing (facilitating) by about a half.

In a report by Dewan Muktadir-al-Mukit, he investigated the impacts of the trade rates and interest rates on securities exchange execution by utilizing month to month time arrangement information for the economy of Bangladesh, over the time of 1997 to 2010. This study utilizes econometric strategies of estimating the long and transient connection between factors utilizing the idea of co-integration and Error Correction Model and examination of Variance Decomposition. Causal connections have been examined utilizing Granger causality test. By utilizing Co-incorporation method, it is seen that over the long haul, a one percent expansion in conversion standard and in interest rate contributes 1.04% increment and 1.71% decline in showcase file individually. The assessed blunder amendment coefficient demonstrates that 7.8 percent deviation of stock returns are adjusted in the short run. At last, Granger causality examination recommends the presence of a unidirectional causality from advertise list to conversion scale and from interest rate to showcase record.

A study by Courage Mlambo surveyed the impacts of money unpredictability on the Johannesburg Stock Exchange. An evaluation of writing on conversion scale unpredictability and financial exchanges was conducted coming about into attribute of an observational model. The Generalized Autoregressive Conditional Heteroskedascity model was utilized in building up the connection between swapping scale instability and securities exchange execution. The study used monthly data of South African information during the time period 2000 – 2010. The information is based on adequate number of perceptions. A very shaky connection between money instability and the financial exchange was affirmed. The research is based upon the past investigations. Prime overdraft rate and complete mining creation were found to negatively affect Market capitalization. Shockingly, Market capitalization is positively affected by the US rate of interest. The study suggested that, since the South African securities exchange isn't generally presented to the negative impacts of money instability, conversion scale can be used by govt as an approach to pull in outside portfolio speculation. The powerless connection between cash instability and the securities exchange proposes that the JSE can be promoted as a protected market for remote financial expert. In any case, financial expert, brokers and portfolio supervisors still should be careful concerning the overflows from the remote swapping scale into the securities exchange. In spite of the knowing that there is a weak connection between rand unpredictability and the financial exchange in South Africa, this doesn't really imply that speculators and portfolio directors need not screen the advancements between these two factors

A report by WalidZakaria Siam inspects the impact rate of interest on the securities exchange finance rate in Amman Stock Exchange (ASE) over the period 1999-2008. In light of the various direct relapse model and straightforward relapse model, the time arrangement examination uncovered that there is critical and optimistic connection between government winning rate of interest and financial exchange capitalization rate. The research explains that Government improvement stock rate applies negative effect on financial exchange capitalization rate, additionally it finds a noteworthy and negative connection between government winning interest rate and Government advancement stock rate. At long last, this study recommends the significance of government intercession to support interest in ASE by diminishing rate of individual tax collection along these lines, allowing motivation for production of riches, controlling interest rate in order to help the development of the securities exchange and improving the administrative condition and diminishing formality

In 2000 an article by Stefan Garlach and Frank Smets on MCI and fiscal strategy expresses that few national banks of world have as of late received a Monetary Conditions Index (MCI) to control financial arrangement under coasting trade rates. This paper examines some systematic and viable inquiries raised by MCIs. Besides, utilizing information for Australia, Canada and New Zealand, which all work fiscal approach under gliding rates and with an expansion target, it appraises the reactions of the national banks to conversion scale changes. The outcomes uncover clear contrasts between national banks: while the Reserve Bank of Australia doesn't seem to react, the Bank of Canada and the Reserve Bank of New Zealand, who utilize the MCI as a working objective, do react unequivocally to developments in the conversion standard.

In 2003 an article by Christos loannidis and AlexandrosKontonikas states that this paper explores the effect of fiscal strategy on stock returns in 13 OECD nations over the period 1972–2002. Our outcomes show that fiscal approach moves altogether influence stock returns, along these lines supporting the idea of money related strategy transmission by means of the securities exchange. Our commitment regarding past work is triple. To begin with, we show that our discoveries are powerful to different elective proportions of stock returns. Second, our derivations are balanced for the non-typicality displayed by the stock returns information. At long last, we consider the expanding co-development among universal financial exchanges. The affectability investigation demonstrates that the outcomes remain to a great extent unaltered.

In 2004 an article by KosukeAoki, JmaesProudman and GertjanVlieghe states that we consider a general harmony model with grindings in credit markets utilized by family units. In our economy, houses give lodging administrations to purchasers and fill in as insurance to bring down getting cost. We show this enhances and proliferates the impact of fiscal strategy stuns on lodging venture, house costs and utilization. We likewise consider the impact of an auxiliary change in credit showcases that brings down the exchange expenses of extra obtaining against lodging value. We show that such a change would build the impact of money related approach stuns on utilization, yet would diminish the impact on house costs and lodging venture.

In 2006 an article by Ying Huang and Carl R. Chan on the impact of Fed money related strategy systems on the US loan cost swap spreads expresses that the deviated effects of different financial stuns on swap spreads under particular Fed fiscal approach systems. The outcomes show that during times of forceful financing cost decreases, incline of the Treasury expression structure represents a sizeable portion of the swap spread change in spite of the fact that default stun is likewise a significant player. Then again, liquidity premium is the main supporter of the 2-year swap spread fluctuation in money related fixing cycles. The effect of default chance differs crosswise over both cash related cycles and swap developments. The impact of loan fee unpredictability is commonly progressively obvious in releasing money related systems.

In 2008 an article by Hilde C. Bjorland on money related arrangement and swapping scale connections in a little open economy expresses that the transmission systems of financial strategy in a little open economy like Norway are examined through auxiliary VARs, with extraordinary accentuation on the association between fiscal approach and conversion scale developments. By forcing a long-run nonpartisanship confinement on the genuine conversion scale, in this manner permitting the loan cost and the swapping scale to respond at the same time to news, I find impressive reliance between money related arrangement and the conversion standard. Specifically, following a contractionary financial strategy stun, the genuine conversion standard promptly acknowledges, after which it slowly devalues back to the pattern. The outcomes are seen as reliable with discoveries from an "occasion study".

In 2009 a study by Michael R. Darby states that standard investigation of money related approach consequences for financing costs regarding liquidity, salary, and desires impacts is deficient. After a change in fiscal strategy, substitution among protections will increment as time slips by thus diminish or dispose of money related impacts brought about by short-run budgetary showcase subdivision. Additionally, the standard desires impact overlooks the exchange of annual expense risk on that piece of the intrigue installment speaking to an arrival of genuine capital. So a 1 rate point increment in the normal swelling rate should build the ostensible loan cost by $1/(1 — \tau)$ rate focuses, τ being the minimal duty rate.

In an article by Philip Cagan and Arthur Gandolfi on the slack in fiscal strategy as inferred by the example of financial impacts on loan fees expresses that while money related hypothesis recommend numerous potential explanations behind such a slack, there is no broad concession to its length. There are issues, anyway in gathering slacks from the planning of defining moments alone, to a limited extent as a result of conceivable input of salary changes on the cash supply. It is consequently attractive to acquire extra proof. A long-standing recommendation of financial hypothesis is that an expansion in the cash stock decreases loan fees. This impact is nevertheless not lasting.

In a research by Wendy Edelbergand David Marshallon money related approach stuns and long haul loan fees expresses that there is a generous reaction of one-month security respects an exogenous financial strategy stun, which ceases to exist monotonically in around 20 months. Longer-term security yields react pretty much as anticipated by the desires hypothesis: the beginning month's reaction of a T-month security's yield is roughly equivalent to the normal of the main T months' reaction of the one-month security. This example infers that more drawn out term security yields have a lot flimsier reactions to an exogenous fiscal stun.

While these outcomes are natural, they remain in sharp complexity to claims that long-security yields respond unnecessarily to financial strategy advancements. We discover no proof that money related strategy stuns have any perceivable impact on long haul security yields.

In 2014 a report by Purity Kairuthi Muriuki it is presumed that market returns keeps on growing with the degrees of offer record of NSE Increasing throughout the years with minor variances. Additionally, it is referenced that paces of market returns don't correspondingly increment as there are cases of increment in showcase returns and different examples of decrease in the market returns. The study sets up positive connection between showcase liquidity and market returns. His study shows a negative connection between expansion rates and market returns while a positive connection between loan fees and market returns. His study prompts end that market returns are controlled by loan costs.

In 2015, a study report by Zethu Handrey Msindo utilizes the vector auto–relapse (VAR) model to address the inquiry how loan costs sway South African market returns in the short and since quite a while ago run which affirms that there was a negative connection among premium and financial exchanges. The co-combination tests presumed that there was no since quite a while ago run co-incorporation connection between the factors and the securities exchange. From Granger test, it was discovered that market returns were free from the adjustments in swelling rates.

In 2016, a study by Mutheu Elizabeth referenced that the relationship examination results found that there was a negative connection between free factor financing costs and ward variable offer cost. His discoveries set up that financing costs doesn't granger cause share costs and offer costs then again doesn't granger cause loan costs. Relapse investigation results built up a unimportant negative connection between loan fees and offer costs.

A study endeavored to survey the causality relationship between interest rate and Sensex by Archana Upadhyay (2016). The discoveries uncovered that no causality is seen between interest rate and offer returns. Econometric models were applied to get more exactness to break down and results brought that there was no such causality between them. Her study demonstrated that interest rate never impacts share returns and the other way around.

RESEARCH METHODOLOGY AND DATA ANALYSIS

This exploration is a descriptive chronological regression analysis with a monthly share market indicies of Banking, Auto-mobile and Real-Estate sectors as dependent variable while independent variable is bi-monthly interest rates. Webb,Campbell and Sechrest (1966) states that time sequence analysis is descriptive in nature. It is distinctly important when a variable being study extends over a particular time period. Frequent number of fluctuations in study variables over some time are only considered in this research design. The set of data consists of monthly observations of the closing indices of stock market of three rate sensitive sectors like banking, auto-mobile and real estate sectors and Interest rates. Chronologically secondary data is used in this research study. Data of monthly shares price indices were obtained from National Stock Exchange of India ltd. Bi-monthly data related to rate of interest were obtained from the Reserve Bank of India. Monthly data of inflation rates were acquired from trade economies website as well as from monetary policy report of Reserve Bank of India. Regression analysis and descriptive statistics are used to test the impact of Rate of interest on stock market returns.

The outcome of the research and findings of the study with comparison to the study objectives are explained in this chapter. The first part explains the data taken in the study and second portion explains tables and figures which shows the findings of the study which also helps to interpret the analysis of the data. Summary of findings and interpretation of the results of the study are explained in the third section. The objective of the study is to identify the impact of rates of interest on rates sensitive sectors in Indian stock market. The researcher intended to establish the relationship between rate of interest and stock market yielding's. Dependent variable is stock market returns and independent variable is rates of interest. Secondary data obtained from National Stock Exchange of India limited, Reserve Bank of India was analyzed in the Microsoft –Excel (MS-EXCEL).

So, the statistical techniques which were mentioned in previous chapter were taken to do the analysis of data of this specific research. In this chapter statistical tests are shown in detail which provides answers to the research objectives. Descriptive statistics was utilized to provide understanding of the trend of the data. Descriptive statistics utilized in study is mean, sum, standard deviation.

Table 1. Descriptive statistics for the variables under study

Market Indices		N	Minimum	Maximum	Mean	SD
Bank		66	7559.45	31475.8	19621.31288	7058.953483
Auto		66	5811.05	11929.6	9067.34697	1483.910913
Realty		66	147.35	347.3	230.5780303	49.17728066
	N		Minimum	Maximum	Mean	SD
Repo Rate	66		5.4	8	6.656061	0.739673

Note: SD = Standard Deviation

Above table 1 shows the descriptive statistics for the variables under the study with 66 observations. As mentioned in the above table, Market Indices of bank are ranged from 7559.45 to 31475.8, Auto are ranged from 5811.05 to 11929.6, Realty are ranged from 147.35 to 347.3. Repo rates are ranged from 5.4 to 8. The mean average market index of bank is 19621.31,auto is 9067.34,realty is 230.57 whereas mean average of interest rate is 6.65 during the period of study.

The trend in rate of interest and market indices of bank, auto, realty over the period of study is displayed in the figures below.

Figure 1. Nifty Bank Indices movements (2014-2019)

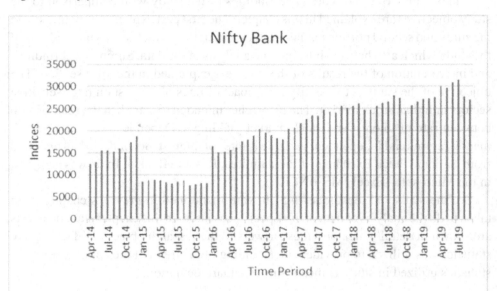

The above figure shows the changes of Nifty bank indices in Indian stock market. It shows that there is no continuous growth or decline trend over the time taken for the study with the highest market index in 2019 with more than 30000 and lowest market index in 2015 with an amount less than 10000.

Figure 2. Nifty Auto Indices movements (2014-2019)

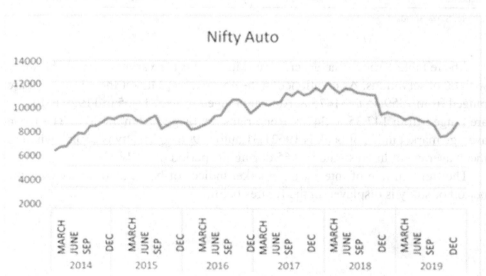

The above figure shows the changes of nifty auto indices in Indian stock market. It shows that there is no constant growth or decline trend over the years of study with the highest market index in 2018 and lowest market index in 2014. If we analyses the chart we can see they are forming peaks from Sep 2017 –June 2018. From September to December we can see a peak and in between it form the highest peak above from both the left and right peak from December to march And then followed by same peak height from March –June.

Figure 3. Nifty Realty Indices movements (2014-2019)

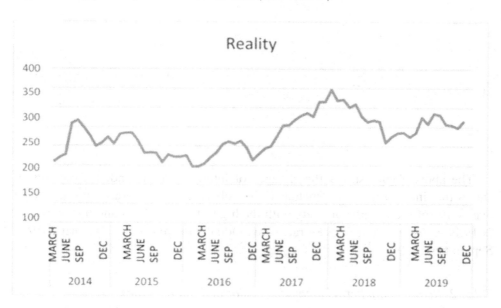

The above figure shows the changes of nifty realty indices in Indian stock market. It shows that there is no constant growth or decline trend over the years of study with the highest market index in 2018 and lowest market index in 2016. If see a bearish trend in the market it is expected that market will also show a bullish trend as well. As we can see that after September 2016 the bearish trend in the market is long lasting as compared to other bearish trend. Almost for a year the stock market was rising and showing a bear in the market. Followed by a bull in the market which was for shorter period of time and then again followed by a bear in the market.

Figure 4. Rate of Interest movements (2014-2019)

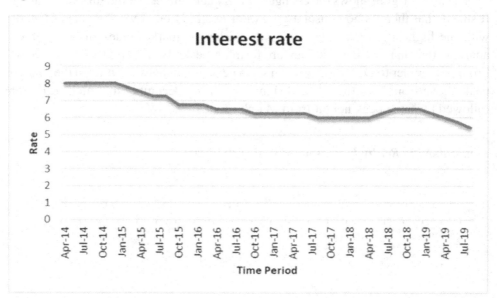

The above figure shows the changes of interest rates in Indian Economy. It shows that interest rates are fluctuated. It is observed that interest rates are stable over some of the months of study with the highest rate in 2014 and lowest rate in 2019.It is observed that interest rates are gradually decreasing from April 2019 to September 2019

Table 2. Relationship between banking sector and interest rates

Regression Statistics	
Multiple R	0.003201803
R Square	.102515E-05
Adjusted R Square	-0.015614588
Standard Error	15.37740222
Observations	66

Table 2. (continued)

a	df	SS	MS	F	Significance F
Predictor: Interest rate ANOVA					
Regression	1	0.155145648	0.155145648	0.000656105	0.979644477
Residual	64	15133.72794	236.4644991		
Total	65	15133.88309			
	Coefficients	Standard Error	t Stat	P-value	
Intercept	1.919392708	17.26747	0.111156568	0.911840058	
X Variable 1	0.066050057	2.578614199	0.025614556	0.979644477	

a. Dependent variable: Nifty bank Indices
b. Independent variable: Repo rate.

From the above tables, it is predicted that independent variable does not statistically significant to dependent variable or the group of independent variable doesn't predict the dependent variable as p value is greater than 0.05. R square explains 10% of the variance in data,i.e, interest rates has 10% impact on stock market indices of banking sector.90% changes is in stock indices is due to other variables.

From the above tables,it is predicted that independent variable does not statistically significant to dependent variable or the group of independent variable doesn't predict the dependent variable as p value is greater than 0.05.

Table 3. Relationship between automobile sector and interest rates

Regression Statistics	
Multiple R	0.534691076
R Square	0.285894547
Adjusted R Square	0.274736649
Standard Error	1263.734072
Observations	66

Table 3. (Continued) Predictor: Interest rate

ANOVA					
	df	SS	MS	F	Significance F
Regression	1	40919930.3	40919930.3	25.62261763	3.7523E-06
Residual	64	102209523.5	1597023.805		
Total	65	143129453.8			

Dependent variable: Nifty auto Indices Independent variable: Repo rate.

Table 3. (continued)

	Coefficients	Standard Error	t Stat	P-value
Intercept	16207.18083	1419.062197	11.42105037	4.3377E-17
X Variable 1	-1072.681618	211.9137274	-5.061878864	3.7523E-06

R square explains 28.6% of the variance in data,i.e, interest rates has 28% impact on stock market indices of auto mobile sector.72% changes in stock indices is due to other variables.

Table 4. Relationship between real estate sector and interest rates:

Regression Statistics	
Multiple R	0.403554031
R Square	0.162855856
Adjusted R Square	0.149775478
Standard Error	45.34520016
Observations	66

Table 4. (continued) Predictor: Interest rate

ANOVA	df	SS	MS	F	Significance F
Regression	1	25600.34131	25600.34131	12.4503944	0.000779524
Residual	64	131595.9793	2056.187177		
Total	65	157196.3206			

Dependent variable: Nifty Realty Indices Independent variable: Repo rate.

Table 4. (continued)

	Coefficients	Standard Error	t Stat	P-value
Intercept	409.1624393	50.91867092	8.035607213	2.78991E-11
X Variable 1	-26.830346	7.603870621	-3.52851164	0.000779524

From the above tables, it is predicted that independent variable is statistically significant to dependent variable as significance f value is less than 0.05.

R square explains 16% of the variance in data,i.e, interest rates has impact of 16% on stock market indices of auto mobile sector.

RESEARCH FINDINGS

From the real estate findings, it is concluded that each percent of increase in rate results in decrease of 26.83 percent of nifty indices of realty and 1072 decrease in nifty auto indices. Whereas 1% growth in rate of interest results in increase of 0.06 percent change in bank nifty indices.

It is further seen that there is a positive insignificant relationship between rate of interest and nifty bank indices. There is a insignificant negative relationship between rate of interest and nifty auto indices. Hence findings conclude that there is no impact of rate of interest on nifty bank indices and nifty auto indices. It is also seen a negative relationship between rate of interest and nifty realty indices.

CONCLUSION AND RECOMMENDATIONS

.Feilden (1980) found that negative relationship of stock returns. Koubi (2008) considered sample of 49 countries for the period 1980 to 1999 and found negative effect on stock market stability. Seile(2009) examined that stock market returns are negatively related to treasury bills. However, Seile(2009) used quarterly data and this study used monthly data from 2014 April to 2019 September i.e., five years and two quarters.

Policy reversals in between time period of 1997 to 2001, negatively affected the stock market as investors didn't know about the movement of economy was taking (Shauna 2003). Robert (2008) also found that there is no significant relationship between macroeconomic variables and share market yielding. Robert also mentioned that markets of India, Brazil, china and Russia reveal weak form of market efficiency.

Bai and Green (2008) investigated that rate of exchange had a inverse relationship between stock returns considering the data from 13 emerging stock markets from the time period 1984 to 2004 using regression analysis. A hike in rate of exchange changes by 1 unit led to decrease in stock yielding by 52.8%.Eita (2011) used quarterly data from 1998 to 2009 and found that a rise in interest rates led to decrease in stock prices.

From the study findings, it is concluded that interest rates have 10% effect on nifty bank indices,28% impact on nifty auto indices and 16% effect on nifty realty indices. It is further observed that there is a positive insignificant relationship between rates of interest and nifty bank indices. There is a insignificant negative relationship between interest rates and nifty auto indices. Hence findings conclude that there is no effect of lending rates on nifty bank indices and nifty auto indices. Study also noticed that there is significant negative relationship between rate of interest and nifty realty indices. This research study provides answer to its objectives based on the quantitative analysis with regression results.

The inflation rates have played a decisive role in knowing the growth of economy and market yielding in India, such that there exist a negative relationship between interest rates and share market yielding. Monetary policy makers should develop strategies for getting favorable levels of money growth irrespective of the inflation risk.

Along with the literature on finance, the positive relationship between rate of return and stock market yielding is not possible. Policy makers should develop policies in such a way that the bank rates should be at acceptable levels that promote borrowing for investments. This could be done by availing cheaper sources of deposits for lenders.

LIMITATION OF THE STUDY

The external exigencies having an impact on the macro economic variables like interest rates and inflation and in-turn impacting the stock market sensitive sectors and to reduce the lag as well as to attain the normalcy, the data has been collected for the period of five years starting from 2014 to 2019, for precise interpretation and analysis. The study belongs to 2014 to 2019 as the pandemic has started from 2019-2020 and external events will be having an impact on the fundamentals, macro variables and market timing. A separate study can be conducted for the said period to understand the impact of external exigencies and fundamentals on stock returns.

REFERENCES

Archana, U. (2016). *Causality relationship between interest rate and stock returns in India–An Analytical Study*. Sage.

Barsky, R., & DeLong, B. (1991). Forecasting pre-World War I inflation: The Fisher effect andthe gold Standard. *The Quarterly Journal of Economics, CVI*(3), 3, 815–836. doi:10.2307/2937928

Bernanke, B., & Gertler, M. (1999). Monetarypolicy and asset price volatility. *Federal Reserve Bank of Kansas City Economic Review, 84*, 17–50.

Bleaney, M., & Fielding, D. (2002). Exchange rate regimes, inflation and output volatility in developing countries. *Journal of Development Economics, 68*(1), 233–245. doi:10.1016/S0304-3878(02)00002-0

Branson, W. H. (1979). *Macroeconomic Theory and Policy*. Princeton University.

Devereux, M. B., & Yetman, J. (2002). Price setting and exchange rate passthrough: Theory and evidence. In Price Adjustment and Monetary Policy. Ottawa: Bank of Canada.

Eita, J. H. (2011). *Determinants of Stock Market Prices in Namibia*. (Working Paper 209). Monash University.

Gagnon, J. E., & Ihrig, J. (2004). Monetary policy and exchange rate pass through‖. *International Journal of Finance & Economics, 9*(4), 315–338. doi:10.1002/ijfe.253

Gerlach, S. (2000). *MCIs and monetary policy, 44*(9), 1677-1700.

Hamdan, A. (2014). Impact of interest rate on stock market; evidence from Pakistani market, e- ISSN: 2278-487X, p-ISSN: 2319-7668. Volume 16, Issue 1. Ver. VII, PP 64-6.

Henry Mk Mok, Causality of interest rate, exchange rate and stock prices at stock market open and close in Hong Kong, October 1993, Volume 10, Issue 2, pp 123–143.

Hilde, C. (2008). Monetary Policy and Exchange Rate Interactions in a Small Open Economy. Ime T. Akpan, *Impact of Interest Rates on Stock Prices: An Analysis of the All Share Index, 3*(2), 96-101.

Huang, Y. (2006). *The effect of Fed monetary policy regimes on the US interest rate swap spreads.* Research Gate.

Kandil, M. (2005). Money, interest, and prices: Some international evidence. *International Review of Economics & Finance, 14*(2), 129–147. doi:10.1016/j.iref.2003.11.013

Mahmudul, A. (2010), The impacts of interest rate on stock market: Empirical evidence from Dhaka Stock exchange. *Dhaka, 4*(1), 21-30.

Michael R. (1975). The Financial and tax effects of monetary policy on interest rates.

Mutheu, E. (2014). *The relationship between interest rates and share prices of commercial banks listed at the Nairobi Securities Exchange.*

Mun, H. W., Siong, E. C., & Thing, T. C. (2008). Stock Market and Economic Growth in Malaysia: Causality Test. *Asian Social Science, 4*(4). Advance online publication. doi:10.5539/ass.v4n4p86

Munga, N. (2013). *The Nairobi stock exchange, its history, organization and role in Kenya economy. Unpublished MBA Project.* University of Nairobi.

Omran, M. (1993, October). Time series analysis of the impact of real interest rates on stock market activity and liquidity in Egypt. *Co-Integration and Error Correction Model Approach, 10*(2), 123–143.

Patelis, A. D. (1997). Stock return predictability: The role of monetary policy. *The Journal of Finance, 52*(5), 1951–1972. doi:10.1111/j.1540-6261.1997.tb02747.x

Purity, K. M. (2014). *The effect of inflation and interest rates on stock market returns of firms listed at the Nairobi Securities Exchange.* Unpublished report University Of Nairobi, School Of Business.

Thorbecke, W. (1997). On stock market returns and monetary policy. *The Journal of Finance, 76*(2), 635–654. doi:10.1111/j.1540-6261.1997.tb04816.x

Zethu, H. M. (2015). *The impact of interest rates on stock returns: Empirical evidence from the JSE securities exchange.* JSE.

Chapter 8
Histology and Embryology 4.0

Kubilay Dogan Kilic
https://orcid.org/0000-0002-9484-0777
Faculty of Medicine, Department of Histology and Embryology, Ege University, Izmir, Turkey

ABSTRACT

Histology and embryology have evolved over time and are now in their 4.0 stages. These fields have progressed from basic microscopes and staining techniques to advanced imaging and computational approaches. Histology 4.0 combines digital imaging technology, AI, and big data analytics to improve tissue analysis accuracy, reduce costs, and develop personalized treatment plans. Embryology 4.0 uses advanced imaging, molecular biology, and bioinformatics to understand developmental biology and identify therapeutic targets for regenerative medicine. Both fields have potential applications in various areas of medicine and are expected to further advance with continued development of new technologies and approaches.

1. INTRODUCTION

Histology, also known as microscopic anatomy, is a vital field of study that focuses on the examination of tissue samples to identify and diagnose diseases. Histology has undergone significant advancements over the years, from the development of the light microscope to the use of electron microscopy and molecular techniques. However, with the advent of new technologies and approaches, the field of histology is set to undergo a significant transformation.

Embryology is a branch of biology that focuses on the study of the development of embryos from fertilization to birth and even a little later. The field has undergone significant advancements over the years, from the discovery of the role of genes in

DOI: 10.4018/978-1-6684-9814-9.ch008

development to the use of stem cells in regenerative medicine. However, with the advent of new technologies and approaches, the field of embryology is also set to undergo a significant transformation.

Even though there are still departments called together, these two disciplines are about to separate forever because of being too big to stay together. In this chapter, we will investigate to journey of Histology and Embryology through History and will discuss the modern age and future.

Histology and Embryology 1.0, 2.0, and 3.0 represent different stages in the evolution of the fields of histology and embryology. Each stage is characterized by a set of techniques, approaches, and technologies that enabled significant advancements in our understanding of the microstructure of tissues and the processes of embryonic development.

2. FIRST STEPS

The study of histology, also known as microscopic anatomy, can be traced back to the ancient Greeks, who used magnifying lenses to study the structure of plants and animals. However, it was not until the invention of the microscope in the late 16th century that scientists were able to study cells and tissues in detail (Hussenin et al., 2015).

One of the earliest pioneers of histology was Italian anatomist Marcello Malpighi, who in the 17th century used the microscope to study the structure of various tissues and organs in animals. Malpighi's work helped to establish the basic principles of modern histology, including the concept of cells as the basic unit of life (West, 2013).

In the 19th century, advances in microscopy and staining techniques allowed histologists to study tissues and cells in even greater detail. German scientist Rudolf Virchow, for example, developed new staining techniques that allowed him to study the cellular basis of disease (David, 1988).

The study of embryology, or the development of organisms from fertilization to birth, can also be traced back to the ancient Greeks, who proposed various theories of embryonic development. However, it was not until the 17th century that scientists began to study embryology systematically (Needham and Hughes, 2015; O'Rahilly, 1958).

One of the earliest pioneers of embryology was Dutch anatomist Jan Swammerdam, who in the 17th century used the microscope to study the development of insects. Swammerdam's work helped to establish the basic principles of modern embryology, including the concept of the egg as the starting point of embryonic development (Cobb, 2000).

In the 18th and 19th centuries, advances in microscopy and experimental techniques allowed embryologists to study embryonic development in a more detailed and systematic way. German biologist Karl Ernst von Baer, for example, proposed the concept of embryonic germ layers, which are the three basic layers of cells that give rise to all of the tissues and organs in the body (Brauckmann, 2012).

3. HISTOLOGY AND EMBRYOLOGY 1.0, 2.0, AND 3.0

Histology and Embryology 1.0 refer to the early stages of these fields, which date back to the early 19th century. During this period, histology and embryology were primarily descriptive disciplines that relied on the use of simple microscopes to observe and classify tissues and embryonic structures. This period was characterized by the development of staining techniques that allowed researchers to visualize the different components of tissues, such as cells and extracellular matrices. As a milestone In the 19th century, histology advanced as scientists developed new techniques for staining tissues and making them visible under the microscope. One of the most important advances in this regard was the development of hematoxylin and eosin staining, which allows different types of tissues to be distinguished based on their color under the microscope (Alturkistani et al., 2016).

Additionally, during this period, the concept of the cell theory was established, which proposed that all living organisms are composed of cells. Other important histologists of this era include Rudolf Virchow, who formed the term "cell theory" to describe the idea that all living organisms are made up of cells, and Camillo Golgi, who discovered a new staining technique that allowed him to see the intricate network of nerve cells in the brain (Titfor, 2016; Musumeci, 2014; Wilson, 1947).

The study of embryology on the other hand, or the development of embryos, also has a long and fascinating history. One of the earliest accounts of embryology comes from Aristotle, who observed the development of chicken embryos and described the stages of development in detail (Ribatti & Annese, 2023).

However, it was not until the invention of the microscope that scientists were able to study the development of embryos in detail. One of the first embryologists to use the microscope was Caspar Friedrich Wolff, a German scientist who observed the development of chicks and frogs in the 18th century. Wolff was the first person to describe the formation of the germ layers, which give rise to different tissues and organs in the developing embryo (Roe, 1979).

Another important figure in the early history of embryology was Karl Ernst von Baer, a Baltic German biologist who studied the development of various animal embryos in the early 19th century. Von Baer was the first person to observe and describe the mammalian egg, and he also discovered the concept of embryonic homology, which states that all vertebrate embryos start out looking similar and only later diverge into different forms (von Baer, & Sarton 1931).

Histology and Embryology 2.0 represent the period of technological advancement that occurred during the mid-20th century. This period was characterized by the development of electron microscopy, which enabled researchers to visualize cellular structures in greater detail. Additionally, during this period, the development of molecular biology techniques allowed researchers to identify the genes and molecular mechanisms that underlie the processes of embryonic development. This period also saw the emergence of tissue culture techniques, which enabled the growth and manipulation of tissues in vitro (Garfield & Wray, 2009).

One of the major advances in histology during this period was the refinement of staining techniques. One notable advance was the use of silver staining, which allowed scientists to visualize nerve fibers and other structures in greater detail. This technique was developed by Camillo Golgi and was named after him. Another important advance was the development of the trichrome stain, which allowed different types of tissue to be distinguished based on their color under the microscope (Mazzarello et al., 2009).

In addition, the use of electron microscopy, which was developed in the 1930s, allowed scientists to study the ultrastructure of cells and tissues at a much higher resolution than was possible with traditional light microscopy. This technique revealed new details about the organization of cells and tissues and paved the way for the development of new subfields such as cell biology (Oatley, 1982).

During the early 20th century, especially after the '50s embryologists continued to refine their understanding of the processes of embryonic development. One major advance during this period was the discovery of the role of growth factors and signaling molecules in embryonic development. For example, in the 1920s, British embryologist John Beard proposed the existence of a substance called the "embryonic induction factor," which he believed was responsible for the development of different organs and tissues in the embryo (Aloe, 2004; De Falco, 2012; Moss, 2008).

Another important advance was the use of experimental techniques to study embryonic development. In the 1920s and 1930s, scientists such as Hans Spemann and Hilde Mangold used a technique called "organizer transplantation" to study the role of the organizer region in amphibian embryonic development. This technique involved transplanting a small piece of tissue from the organizer region of one embryo to another embryo and observing the effect on the recipient embryo's development (Spemann & Mangold 2003(1923); Hamburger, 1984).

Overall, the early 20th century saw important advances in both histology and embryology, paving the way for continued progress in these fields in the decades to come.

Histology and Embryology 3.0 represent the most recent stage in the evolution of these fields, which began in the late 20th century and continues to the present day. This period has been characterized by the development of advanced imaging techniques, such as confocal microscopy, that allow for the visualization of tissues and embryonic structures in unprecedented detail. Additionally, the use of computational approaches, such as data mining and machine learning, has enabled the analysis of large datasets of histological and embryological data, providing new insights into the mechanisms of tissue formation and embryonic development.

In modern times, the fields of histology and embryology have continued to make significant progress, driven by new technologies and techniques that have allowed scientists to study cells, tissues, and embryos at ever-increasing levels of detail. But still not at 'all'.

One of the major advances in histology in modern times has been the development of imaging technologies that allow scientists to study tissues and cells in three dimensions. Confocal microscopy, for example, uses lasers to scan a sample point by point and build up a 3D image. This technique has allowed scientists to visualize the spatial organization of cells and tissues in unprecedented detail and has been particularly useful for studying the nervous system (Paddock & Eliceiri, 2014).

In addition, the use of molecular probes and fluorescent labeling has allowed scientists to study the localization and expression of specific molecules within cells and tissues. For example, green fluorescent protein (GFP) can be used to label specific cells in a tissue, allowing scientists to track their behavior over time. This technique has been particularly useful for studying cancer and other diseases (Banerji & Mitra, 2022; Shimomura 2009).

Here we must remember that we are living at the edge of the 3.0-4.0 transition age. Histology 3.0 refers to a novel approach to the study of tissue structures that involves the transformation of intact biological tissue into a hybrid form, where specific components are replaced with exogenous elements that provide new accessibility or functionality. This new approach has been made possible by the development of the CLARITY method by Kwanghun Chung and Karl Deisseroth at the Stanford University School of Medicine (Chung & Deisseroth, 2013).

The CLARITY method utilizes acrylamide-based hydrogels built from within and linked to the tissue to make the tissue transparent, thereby enabling highly detailed pictures of the protein and nucleic acid structure of organs, especially the brain, when accompanied by antibody or gene-based labeling. This method has been applied to a wide range of tissues and disease states such as immuno-oncology for human breast cancer, Alzheimer's disease human brains, mouse spinal cords, multiple sclerosis animal models, and even plants. CLARITY has also been combined with other technologies to develop new microscopy methods including confocal expansion microscopy, SPIM light sheet microscopy, and CLARITY-optimized light sheet microscopy (COLM) (Morawski et al., 2018).

The procedure of applying CLARITY imaging involves several chemical treatments to achieve transparency, where the lipid content of the sample is removed while almost all of the original proteins and nucleic acids are left in place. This is achieved by placing the preexisting protein structure in a transparent scaffolding made up of hydrogel monomers such as acrylamide. Once this step is complete, the protein and nucleic acid components of the target tissue's cells are held firmly in place, while the lipid components remain detached. Lipids are then removed over days to weeks for passive diffusion in detergent, or accelerated by electrophoretic methods to only hours to days. Efforts to accelerate by electrophoretic methods remain inconclusive on the ability to not cause tissue damage. After this, the sample is fully prepared for imaging, and contrast for imaging can come from endogenous fluorescent molecules, nucleic acid labels, or from immunostaining using antibodies labeled with fluorescent tags (Lerner et al., 2015).

The CLARITY technique has numerous applications beyond brain imaging, including imaging of other organs such as the liver, pancreas, spleen, and testes, and has been modified for broad-scope applications in both academic and biotech industries (Reveles Jensen & Berg, 2017).

In modern times, embryology has seen significant progress in understanding the molecular mechanisms that govern embryonic development. Advances in genetic engineering techniques such as CRISPR/Cas9 have allowed scientists to manipulate the expression of specific genes in embryos, and to study the consequences of these manipulations on development. This has led to new insights into the roles of various genes and signaling pathways in embryonic development (Redman et al., 2016).

Another major advance in modern embryology has been the use of stem cells to study development. Embryonic stem cells, for example, can be grown in culture and induced to differentiate into various cell types, providing a powerful tool for studying the early stages of development. Induced pluripotent stem cells (iPSCs), which are generated by reprogramming adult cells, have also been used to study development and develop new therapies for diseases.

In summary, the evolution of histology and embryology from 1.0 to 3.0 represents a progression from simple descriptive techniques to the use of advanced imaging and computational approaches. Each stage has enabled significant advancements in our understanding of tissue microstructure and the processes of embryonic development. The continued development of new technologies and approaches is likely to drive further advances in these fields, enabling new insights into the mechanisms of tissue formation, regeneration, and disease (Stadtfeld & Hochedlinger, 2010; Chhabra, 2017).

From idea to the discipline, fields of histology and embryology have continued to make significant progress in modern times, driven by advances in technology and new insights into the molecular and cellular mechanisms that underlie development and disease.

4. HISTOLOGY 4.0

Histology 4.0 is an interdisciplinary approach that combines the power of advanced imaging techniques, artificial intelligence, and big data analytics to improve tissue analysis. This approach aims to provide faster and more accurate diagnoses, increase efficiency, and reduce the need for invasive procedures.

One of the key components of Histology 4.0 is the use of digital imaging technology. Digital microscopy allows for the capture of high-resolution images of tissue samples, which can be analyzed remotely by pathologists. This technology has several advantages over traditional microscopies, such as the ability to store images in a centralized database, enabling easy access to historical images and patient records. Additionally, digital imaging can reduce the need for physical slide storage and transportation, which can significantly reduce costs and improve efficiency.

Another key component of Histology 4.0 is the use of artificial intelligence (AI) to aid in tissue analysis. AI algorithms can analyze large amounts of data quickly and accurately, identifying patterns and anomalies that may be missed by human observers. This technology has the potential to improve the accuracy and speed of diagnoses, particularly in cases where multiple samples need to be analyzed.

The use of big data analytics is another important aspect of Histology 4.0. By pooling and analyzing data from multiple sources, such as electronic health records, genomic data, and imaging data, researchers can identify new patterns and relationships that may lead to better diagnoses and treatments. This approach has the potential to transform our understanding of disease and enable the development of personalized treatment plans.

Histology 4.0 has several potential applications in various areas of medicine, such as cancer diagnosis and treatment. For example, digital pathology and AI can aid in the identification of cancerous cells, improving the accuracy and speed of diagnoses (Ozyoruk et al., 2022). Additionally, big data analytics can be used to identify patterns in patient data that may indicate a higher risk of developing certain types of cancer, enabling earlier detection and intervention.

Histology 4.0 also has the potential to improve the efficiency of clinical trials. By combining data from multiple sources, researchers can identify potential drug targets and predict the efficacy of new treatments. This approach has the potential to significantly reduce the time and cost associated with developing new treatments (Hillebrand et al., 2021).

Below, examples demonstrate how AI is being used to revolutionize the analysis and interpretation of histological data, leading to faster and more accurate diagnosis, improved understanding of disease mechanisms, and the development of new diagnostic and therapeutic approaches.

Cancer diagnosis and grading: One of the most important applications of histology is in the diagnosis and grading of cancer. Traditionally, this has been a time-consuming and subjective process, with pathologists manually analyzing thousands of histological images to identify cancer cells and determine the stage and grade of the tumor. However, AI can be used to automate this process, allowing for faster and more accurate diagnosis. For example, researchers have developed deep learning algorithms that can identify cancer cells in breast tissue samples with an high rate accuracy (Leoffler et al., 2022; Baxi et al., 2022; Hildebrand et al., 2021; Wishart et al., 2010).

Quantifying protein expression: Histological images can be used to study the expression of specific proteins within cells. However, this is typically a laborious and time-consuming process that requires manual analysis. AI can be used to automate this process, allowing for faster and more accurate analysis. For example, researchers have developed a deep learning algorithm that can automatically quantify the expression of the protein HER2 in breast cancer cells with a high-rate accuracy (Modi et al., 2020).

Automated cell segmentation: Histological images can be used to study the morphology and behavior of individual cells. However, this requires manual segmentation of individual cells within the image, which is a time-consuming and error-prone process. AI can be used to automate this process, allowing for faster and more accurate analysis. For example, researchers have developed a deep learning algorithm that can automatically segment individual cells in histological images of lung tissue with a high-rate accuracy (Forte et al., 2022).

Predicting patient outcomes: Histological data can be used to predict patient outcomes, such as survival rates or response to treatment. However, this requires the analysis of large amounts of data, including patient demographics, tumor characteristics, and histological features. AI can be used to automate this process, allowing for faster and more accurate predictions (Baxi et al., 2022, Modi et al. 2020, Durkee et al., 2021).

Beyond these, there are footsteps of a revolutionary technology which will probably put shelf everything else coming before it after being more practical and more economical.

3DISCO is a technique used in histology that involves clearing biological samples, such as tissues or organs, to make them transparent. This allows for deeper imaging and more accurate analysis of the structures within the sample. 3DISCO involves a series of steps, including fixation, dehydration, and incubation in a clearing solution (Ertürk et al., 2012).

Once the sample is cleared, it can be imaged using a variety of techniques, including confocal microscopy or two-photon microscopy. This allows for 3D reconstruction of the sample, allowing researchers to study the structure and organization of cells and tissues in greater detail.

The 3DISCO method was quickly adopted by other researchers who modified it to suit specific goals. For example, iDISCO, which stands for "immunolabeling-enabled imaging of solvent-cleared organs," included pretreatment of the sample with methanol, hydrogen peroxide, detergents, and dimethyl sulfoxide (DMSO), in addition to antibody labeling before clearing. This preprocessing step overcame two limitations of antibody labeling of large samples. It reduced autofluorescence and improved the signal-to-noise ratio, and it made the tissue more penetrable for antibodies. As a result, samples as large as mouse embryos or whole mouse organs can be successfully dyed with fluorescent-labeled antibodies and thereafter cleared and imaged (Renier et al., 2014).

The authors of uDISCO, which stands for "ultimate imaging of solvent-cleared organs," enhanced the shrinkage of tissue, a common bystander effect of dehydration of the sample in the first step of the clearing. They used tert-butanol instead of THF for dehydration and a different solution for imaging, which preserves fluorescence better than DBE. Thanks to the shrinkage of the tissue, they can observe large samples up to the size of the whole mouse body. It is worth noting that uDISCO was highlighted by media worldwide, including the New York Times, Wall Street Journal, Business Insider, and Nature and Science magazines. It was also chosen as one of the top 10 scientific images of 2016 by Nature (Pan et al., 2016).

DIPCO, which stands for "diagnosing immunolabeled paraffin-embedded cleared organs," is a pipeline that combines deparaffinization of FFPE-embedded tumor specimens, iDISCO clearing, and phenotyping of tumor tissue. Tumor FFPE samples are widely stored in biobanks and used for diagnostics, and their 3D analysis could potentially help to improve the stratification of cancer patients (Garvalov et al., 2017).

Clearing methods, including 3DISCO, were initially developed for neuroscience research because of the high morphological and functional complexity of the nervous system, which makes investigation time-consuming and laborious with classical histology methods. The majority of studies, therefore, focus on the mouse central nervous system, as rodents are one of the main model organisms for neurobiology. The authors of the 3DISCO method used it first for studying regeneration in the central nervous system (CNS) of the mouse, including counting microglia, astrocytes, and mapping trajectories of axons after injury. 3DISCO was also used for mapping the development of the mouse CNS. Its modification iDISCO was used for functional studies of brain activity or for mapping amyloid plaques, microglia, vasculature, and other properties of brains in Alzheimer's disease patients and mouse models. Modification uDISCO was then used for single-cell mapping of neurons in the whole unsectioned CNS of the mouse.

In recent years, the use of "DISCO" methods has expanded to research on many other tissues, including single-cell mapping of transplanted stem cells in whole mouse organs, imaging of whole human embryos in different developmental stages, and examination and diagnostics of human tumor tissue (Ertürk et al., 2012).

The use of 3DISCO in combination with AI is a promising area of research. AI can be used to automate the process of analyzing large amounts of 3D imaging data generated by 3DISCO. For example, deep learning algorithms can be trained to identify specific structures or patterns in 3D images of cleared tissues, such as blood vessels, neurons, or cancer cells (Ertürk et al., 2012).

In addition, 3DISCO can be combined with other techniques, such as single-cell RNA sequencing, to study the gene expression profiles of individual cells within a cleared tissue. AI can be used to analyze the large amounts of data generated by these techniques, allowing for a more detailed understanding of the molecular mechanisms underlying tissue development and disease (Ertürk et al., 2012).

In conclusion, Histology 4.0 is an exciting new approach that has the potential to transform the field of tissue analysis. By combining digital imaging technology, artificial intelligence, and big data analytics, researchers can improve the accuracy and speed of diagnoses, reduce costs, and enable the development of personalized treatment plans. As we continue to develop new technologies and approaches, the potential for Histology 4.0 to revolutionize medicine is limitless.

5. EMBRYOLOGY 4.0

Embryology 4.0 is an interdisciplinary approach that combines the power of advanced imaging techniques, molecular biology, and bioinformatics to improve our understanding of the mechanisms of development. This approach aims to provide a more comprehensive understanding of embryonic development, enable the identification of new targets for therapeutic interventions, and improve the efficiency of regenerative medicine.

One of the key components of Embryology 4.0 is the use of advanced imaging techniques. High-resolution imaging techniques, such as confocal microscopy, allow for the visualization of the developing embryo in unprecedented detail. This technology has several advantages over traditional imaging techniques, such as the ability to capture live images of developing embryos in real time, enabling researchers to observe dynamic developmental processes.

Another key component of Embryology 4.0 is the use of molecular biology techniques. The development of gene editing tools, such as CRISPR/Cas9, has enabled researchers to manipulate the genome of developing embryos, providing insights into the role of specific genes in development. Additionally, transcriptomic and epigenetic profiling techniques have enabled the characterization of the molecular events that underlie developmental processes, providing new insights into the mechanisms of development (Kozovska et al., 2021).

Bioinformatics is another important aspect of Embryology 4.0. By integrating data from multiple sources, such as genomic and transcriptomic data, researchers can identify new patterns and relationships that may lead to new insights into the mechanisms of development. Additionally, the use of machine learning algorithms can aid in the identification of key regulatory pathways and potential drug targets for therapeutic intervention (Qazi et al., 2022).

Embryology 4.0 has several potential applications in various areas of medicine, such as regenerative medicine. For example, the use of stem cells in regenerative medicine has the potential to replace damaged or diseased tissues and organs. With the advent of Embryology 4.0, researchers can more efficiently generate and differentiate stem cells into specific cell types, enabling the development of more effective regenerative therapies (Sergi, 2019).

Embryology 4.0 also has the potential to improve our understanding of developmental disorders, such as congenital heart defects. By using advanced imaging techniques and molecular biology tools, researchers can identify the genetic and molecular mechanisms underlying these disorders, enabling the development of new therapies.

Embryology is the study of the development of embryos from fertilization until birth. It involves understanding the molecular, cellular, and tissue-level events that ech during embryonic development. On the other hand, AI is a field of computer science that involves the development of algorithms and computational models that can perform tasks that typically require human intelligence, such as visual perception, speech recognition, decision-making, and problem-solving.

There is a growing relationship between embryology and AI as scientists are leveraging AI to analyze and understand complex developmental processes at the cellular and molecular levels. For example, researchers are using machine learning algorithms to analyze large-scale imaging data to better understand the echnolo of embryonic development. AI can help identify patterns and relationships that are difficult or impossible for humans to detect, enabling scientists to better understand the complex processes that ech during embryonic development.

In addition, AI is also being used to model and simulate embryonic development. With the help of AI-based tools, researchers can simulate the development of tissues and organs in silico, providing insights into the mechanisms that drive embryonic development.

In conclusion, Embryology 4.0 is an exciting new approach that has the potential to transform the field of developmental biology. By combining advanced imaging techniques, molecular biology, and bioinformatics, researchers can gain a more comprehensive understanding of the mechanisms of development, identify new therapeutic targets, and improve the efficiency of regenerative medicine. As we continue to develop new echnologies and approaches, the potential for Embryology 4.0 to revolutionize medicine is limitless.

REFERENCES

Aloe, L. (2004). Rita Levi-Montalcini: The discovery of nerve growth factor and modern neurobiology. *Trends in Cell Biology*, *14*(7), 395–399. doi:10.1016/j.tcb.2004.05.011 PMID:15246433

Alturkistani, H. A., Tashkandi, F. M., & Mohammedsaleh, Z. M. (2016). Histological stains: A literature review and case study. *Global Journal of Health Science*, *8*(3), 72. doi:10.5539/gjhs.v8n3p72 PMID:26493433

Banerji, S., & Mitra, S. (2022). Deep learning in histopathology: A review. *Wiley Interdisciplinary Reviews. Data Mining and Knowledge Discovery*, *12*(1), e1439. doi:10.1002/widm.1439

Baxi, V., Edwards, R., Montalto, M., & Saha, S. (2022). Digital pathology and artificial intelligence in translational medicine and clinical practice. *Modern Pathology*, *35*(1), 23–32. doi:10.103841379-021-00919-2 PMID:34611303

Brauckmann, S. (2012). Karl Ernst von Baer (1792-1876) and evolution. *The International Journal of Developmental Biology*, *56*(9), 653–660. doi:10.1387/ijdb.120018sb PMID:23319342

Chhabra, A. (2017). Derivation of human induced pluripotent stem cell (iPSC) lines and mechanism of pluripotency: Historical perspective and recent advances. *Stem Cell Reviews and Reports*, *13*(6), 757–773. doi:10.100712015-017-9766-9 PMID:28918520

Chung, K., & Deisseroth, K. (2013). CLARITY for mapping the nervous system. *Nature Methods*, *10*(6), 508–513. doi:10.1038/nmeth.2481 PMID:23722210

Cobb, M. (2000). Reading and writing the book of nature: Jan Swammerdam (1637–1680). *Endeavour*, *24*(3), 122–128. doi:10.1016/S0160-9327(00)01306-5

David, H. (1988). Rudolf Virchow and modern aspects of tumor pathology. *Pathology, Research and Practice*, *183*(3), 356–364. doi:10.1016/S0344-0338(88)80138-9 PMID:3047716

De Falco, S. (2012). The discovery of placenta growth factor and its biological activity. *Experimental & Molecular Medicine*, *44*(1), 1–9. doi:10.3858/emm.2012.44.1.025 PMID:22228176

Durkee, M. S., Abraham, R., Clark, M. R., & Giger, M. L. (2021). Artificial intelligence and cellular segmentation in tissue microscopy images. *American Journal of Pathology*, *191*(10), 1693–1701. doi:10.1016/j.ajpath.2021.05.022 PMID:34129842

Ertürk, A., Becker, K., Jährling, N., Mauch, C. P., Hojer, C. D., Egen, J. G., Hellal, F., Bradke, F., Sheng, M., & Dodt, H. U. (2012). Three-dimensional imaging of solvent-cleared organs using 3DISCO. *Nature Protocols*, *7*(11), 1983–1995. doi:10.1038/nprot.2012.119 PMID:23060243

Forte, G. C., Altmayer, S., Silva, R. F., Stefani, M. T., Libermann, L. L., Cavion, C. C., Youssef, A., Forghani, R., King, J., Mohamed, T.-L., Andrade, R. G. F., & Hochhegger, B. (2022). Deep learning algorithms for diagnosis of lung cancer: A systematic review and meta-analysis. *Cancers (Basel)*, *14*(16), 3856. doi:10.3390/cancers14163856 PMID:36010850

Garfield, D. A., & Wray, G. A. (2009). Comparative embryology without a microscope: Using genomic approaches to understand the evolution of development. *Journal of Biology*, *8*(7), 1–4. doi:10.1186/jbiol161 PMID:19664180

Garvalov, B. K., & Ertürk, A. (2017). Seeing whole-tumour heterogeneity. *Nature Biomedical Engineering*, *1*(10), 772–774. doi:10.103841551-017-0150-5 PMID:31015596

Hamburger, V. (1984). Hilde Mangold, co-discoverer of the organizer. *Journal of the History of Biology*, *17*(1), 1–11. doi:10.1007/BF00397500 PMID:11611449

Hildebrand, L. A., Pierce, C. J., Dennis, M., Paracha, M., & Maoz, A. (2021). Artificial intelligence for histology-based detection of microsatellite instability and prediction of response to immunotherapy in colorectal cancer. *Cancers (Basel)*, *13*(3), 391. doi:10.3390/cancers13030391 PMID:33494280

Hussein, I., Raad, M., Safa, R., Jurjus, R. A., & Jurjus, A. (2015). Once upon a microscopic slide: The story of histology. *Journal of Cytology & Histology*, *06*(06), 6. doi:10.4172/2157-7099.1000377

Kozovska, Z., Rajcaniova, S., Munteanu, P., Dzacovska, S., & Demkova, L. (2021). CRISPR: History and perspectives to the future. *Biomedicine and Pharmacotherapy, 141*, 111917. doi:10.1016/j.biopha.2021.111917 PMID:34328110

Lerner, T. N., Shilyansky, C., Davidson, T. J., Evans, K. E., Beier, K. T., Zalocusky, K. A., Crow, A. K., Malenka, R. C., Luo, L., Tomer, R., & Deisseroth, K. (2015). Intact-brain analyses reveal distinct information carried by SNc dopamine subcircuits. *Cell, 162*(3), 635–647. doi:10.1016/j.cell.2015.07.014 PMID:26232229

Loeffler, C. M. L., Bruechle, N. O., Jung, M., Seillier, L., Rose, M., Laleh, N. G., ... Kather, J. N. (2022). Artificial intelligence–based detection of FGFR3 mutational status directly from routine histology in bladder cancer: A possible preselection for molecular testing? *European Urology Focus, 8*(2), 472–479. doi:10.1016/j. euf.2021.04.007 PMID:33895087

Mazzarello, P., Garbarino, C., & Calligaro, A. (2009). How Camillo Golgi became "the Golgi". *FEBS Letters, 583*(23), 3732–3737. doi:10.1016/j.febslet.2009.10.018 PMID:19833130

Modi, S., Glass, B., Prakash, A., Taylor-Weiner, A., Elliott, H., Wapinski, I., Sugihara, M., Saito, K., Kerner, J. K., Phillips, R., Shibutani, T., Honda, K., Khosla, A., Beck, A. H., & Cogswell, J. (2020). 286P Artificial intelligence analysis of advanced breast cancer patients from a phase I trial of trastuzumab deruxtecan (T-DxD): HER2 and histopathology features as predictors of clinical benefit. *Annals of Oncology : Official Journal of the European Society for Medical Oncology, 31*, S355–S356. doi:10.1016/j.annonc.2020.08.388

Morawski, M., Kirilina, E., Scherf, N., Jäger, C., Reimann, K., Trampel, R., Gavriilidis, F., Geyer, S., Biedermann, B., Arendt, T., & Weiskopf, N. (2018). Developing 3D microscopy with CLARITY on human brain tissue: Towards a tool for informing and validating MRI-based histology. *NeuroImage, 182*, 417–428. doi:10.1016/j. neuroimage.2017.11.060 PMID:29196268

Moss, R. W. (2008). The life and times of John Beard, DSc (1858-1924). *Integrative Cancer Therapies, 7*(4), 229–251. doi:10.1177/1534735408326174 PMID:19116220

Musumeci, G. (2014). Past, present and future: Overview on histology and histopathology. *J Histol Histopathol, 1*(5), 1–3. doi:10.7243/2055-091X-1-5

Needham, J., & Hughes, A. (2015). *A history of embryology*. Cambridge University Press.

O'Rahilly, R. (1958). Three and one-half centuries of histology. *Irish Journal of Medical Science, 33*, 288-292.

Oatley, C. W. (1982). The early history of the scanning electron microscope. *Journal of Applied Physics*, *53*(2), R1–R13. doi:10.1063/1.331666

Ozyoruk, K. B., Can, S., Darbaz, B., Başak, K., Demir, D., Gokceler, G. I., Serin, G., Hacisalihoglu, U. P., Kurtuluş, E., Lu, M. Y., Chen, T. Y., Williamson, D. F. K., Yılmaz, F., Mahmood, F., & Turan, M. (2022). A deep-learning model for transforming the style of tissue images from cryosectioned to formalin-fixed and paraffin-embedded. *Nature Biomedical Engineering*, *6*(12), 1–13. doi:10.103841551-022-00952-9 PMID:36564629

Paddock, S. W., & Eliceiri, K. W. (2014). Laser scanning confocal microscopy: history, applications, and related optical sectioning techniques. *Confocal Microscopy: Methods and Protocols*, 9-47.

Pan, C., Cai, R., Quacquarelli, F. P., Ghasemigharagoz, A., Lourbopoulos, A., Matryba, P., Plesnila, N., Dichgans, M., Hellal, F., & Ertürk, A. (2016). Shrinkage-mediated imaging of entire organs and organisms using uDISCO. *Nature Methods*, *13*(10), 859–867. doi:10.1038/nmeth.3964 PMID:27548807

Qazi, S., Jit, B. P., Das, A., Karthikeyan, M., Saxena, A., Ray, M. D., Singh, A. R., Raza, K., Jayaram, B., & Sharma, A. (2022). BESFA: Bioinformatics based evolutionary, structural & functional analysis of Prostate, Placenta, Ovary, Testis, and Embryo (POTE) paralogs. *Heliyon*, *8*(9), e10476. doi:10.1016/j.heliyon.2022.e10476 PMID:36132183

Redman, M., King, A., Watson, C., & King, D. (2016). What is CRISPR/Cas9? *Archives of Disease in Childhood - Education and Practice*, *101*(4), 213–215. doi:10.1136/archdischild-2016-310459 PMID:27059283

Renier, N., Wu, Z., Simon, D. J., Yang, J., Ariel, P., & Tessier-Lavigne, M. (2014). iDISCO: A simple, rapid method to immunolabel large tissue samples for volume imaging. *Cell*, *159*(4), 896–910. doi:10.1016/j.cell.2014.10.010 PMID:25417164

Reveles Jensen, K. H., & Berg, R. W. (2017). *Advances and perspectives in tissue clearing using CLARITY*. Academic Press.

Ribatti, D., & Annese, T. (2023). Chick embryo in experimental embryology and more. *Pathology, Research and Practice*, *245*, 154478. doi:10.1016/j.prp.2023.154478 PMID:37100021

Roe, S. A. (1979). Rationalism and embryology: Caspar Friedrich Wolff's theory of epigenesis. *Journal of the History of Biology*, *12*(1), 1–43. doi:10.1007/BF00128134 PMID:11615771

Sergi, C. (2019). EPAS 1, congenital heart disease, and high altitude: Disclosures by genetics, bioinformatics, and experimental embryology. *Bioscience Reports*, *39*(5), BSR20182197. doi:10.1042/BSR20182197 PMID:31015364

Shimomura, O. (2009). Discovery of green fluorescent protein (GFP)(Nobel Lecture). *Angewandte Chemie International Edition*, *48*(31), 5590–5602. doi:10.1002/anie.200902240 PMID:19579247

Spemann, H., & Mangold, H. (2003). Induction of embryonic primordia by implantation of organizers from a different species. 1923. *The International Journal of Developmental Biology*, *45*(1), 13–38. PMID:11291841

Stadtfeld, M., & Hochedlinger, K. (2010). Induced pluripotency: History, mechanisms, and applications. *Genes & Development*, *24*(20), 2239–2263. doi:10.1101/gad.1963910 PMID:20952534

Titford, M. (2006). A short history of histopathology technique. *Journal of Histotechnology*, *29*(2), 99–110. doi:10.1179/his.2006.29.2.99

von Baer, K. E., & Sarton, G. (1931). The discovery of the mammalian egg and the foundation of modern embryology. *Isis*, *16*(2), 315–377. doi:10.1086/346613

West, J. B. (2013). Marcello Malpighi and the discovery of the pulmonary capillaries and alveoli. *American Journal of Physiology. Lung Cellular and Molecular Physiology*, *304*(6), L383–L390. doi:10.1152/ajplung.00016.2013 PMID:23377345

Wilson, J. W. (1947). Virchow's contribution to the cell theory. *Journal of the History of Medicine and Allied Sciences*, *2*(2), 163–178. doi:10.1093/jhmas/II.2.163 PMID:20249916

Wishart, G. C., Campisi, M., Boswell, M., Chapman, D., Shackleton, V., Iddles, S., Hallett, A., & Britton, P. D. (2010). The accuracy of digital infrared imaging for breast cancer detection in women undergoing breast biopsy. *European Journal of Surgical Oncology*, *36*(6), 535–540. doi:10.1016/j.ejso.2010.04.003 PMID:20452740

Chapter 9
Effective Change Management Strategies:
Exploring Dynamic Models for Organizational Transformation

Filiz Mızrak

iD https://orcid.org/0000-0002-3472-394X
Beykoz University, Turkey

ABSTRACT

Change management is an essential process in today's dynamic business environment, as organizations continuously face the need for transformation to adapt to market trends, technological advancements, and competitive pressures. To navigate these changes successfully, organizations require effective change management strategies. In this perspective, the study aims to examine various change management models with examples from real life. The results of this study aim to equip organizations with a comprehensive understanding of change management models, enabling them to select and implement the most suitable approach for their unique transformational needs. By embracing dynamic change management strategies, organizations can enhance their ability to adapt, innovate, and thrive in an ever-evolving business landscape.

DOI: 10.4018/978-1-6684-9814-9.ch009

INTRODUCTION

Change is an inevitable and constant aspect of organizational life. Organizations must continually adapt and evolve to meet the demands of a dynamic business environment. Whether driven by technological advancements, market shifts, or internal initiatives, change plays a crucial role in shaping the future of organizations. Effective change management is essential to navigate these transitions successfully. It involves understanding the need for change, developing a clear vision, engaging stakeholders, and implementing strategies to drive organizational transformation (Engida, Alemu & Mulugeta, 2022). Change in organizations can be both challenging and rewarding, as it requires overcoming resistance, fostering a culture of innovation, and aligning the efforts of individuals towards a common goal. By embracing change and implementing effective change management strategies, organizations can not only survive but also thrive in today's ever-evolving landscape (Kok & Siripipatthanakul, 2023).

Dynamic models for organizational transformation are strategic frameworks that enable organizations to adapt and thrive in a rapidly changing business landscape. These models recognize that change is not a one-time event but an ongoing process that requires agility, flexibility, and continuous improvement. They emphasize the need for proactive and forward-thinking approaches to drive transformation, rather than reactive measures. Dynamic models provide organizations with the tools and methodologies to identify opportunities, respond to challenges, and leverage emerging trends to their advantage. They encourage experimentation, innovation, and the exploration of new possibilities. By adopting dynamic models, organizations can proactively shape their future, anticipate market shifts, and position themselves for long-term success (Ghosh et al., 2022). These models empower organizations to navigate complexities, embrace change, and foster a culture of continuous learning and growth.

The objective of this study is to provide a comprehensive understanding of dynamic change management models and their role in facilitating organizational transformation. By exploring models such as Lewin's Three-Step Model, Kotter's Eight-Step Model, ADKAR, and Agile Change Management, the study aims to uncover the underlying principles, methodologies, and benefits of these models in driving successful change initiatives. Through the analysis of real-world examples and case studies, the study seeks to highlight the practical application and outcomes of these models in diverse organizational contexts. Additionally, the study aims to identify key considerations and best practices for implementing change management models effectively, with a focus on aspects such as communication, stakeholder engagement, and leadership support. Ultimately, the objective of this study is to equip organizations with valuable insights and guidance that will empower them to navigate the complexities of change, foster a culture of continuous improvement, and achieve transformative outcomes.

This study stands out due to its comprehensive exploration of a wide range of dynamic change management models for organizational transformation. By examining various models, such as Lewin's Three-Step Model, Kotter's Eight-Step Model, ADKAR, and Agile Change Management, we provide a holistic perspective on the diverse approaches available to organizations. Furthermore, the inclusion of real-world examples and case studies adds practical relevance and allows for a deeper understanding of how these models have been successfully implemented in different organizational contexts.

MAIN FOCUS OF THE CHAPTER

This chapter aims to explore various dynamic change management models for organizational transformation. It delves into the underlying principles, methodologies, and benefits of these models to provide a comprehensive understanding of effective change management strategies. The chapter analyzes traditional models such as Lewin's Three-Step Model and Kotter's Eight-Step Model, as well as contemporary approaches like ADKAR. It emphasizes the importance of stakeholder engagement, communication strategies, and leadership practices in driving successful change initiatives. Drawing on empirical evidence from case studies and real-world examples, the chapter examines the practical application and outcomes of these models. By gaining insights into dynamic change management strategies, organizations can enhance their ability to adapt, innovate, and thrive in today's dynamic business environment.

CONCEPTUAL FRAMEWORK

Traditional Change Management Models

Traditional change management models provide structured frameworks and methodologies for understanding and managing organizational change. These models offer a systematic approach to guide organizations through the complexities of implementing and navigating change successfully. They emphasize sequential stages and key principles that aim to minimize resistance, maximize stakeholder engagement, and ensure the adoption of desired behaviors and practices. Traditional change management models, such as Lewin's Three-Step Model and Kotter's Eight-Step Model, have been widely used and studied in the field of organizational change. They provide organizations with a roadmap to follow, offering insights into the stages, processes, and strategies required for effective change implementation (Engida, Alemu & Mulugeta, 2022). By applying these models, organizations can enhance their change readiness, improve the chances of successful change adoption, and ultimately achieve their desired transformational outcomes.

- **Lewin's Three-Step Model**

Lewin's Three-Step Model, developed by psychologist Kurt Lewin, is a widely recognized and influential change management model. The model emphasizes the importance of understanding the process of change and provides a framework for managing it effectively (Burnes, 2020).

The first step in the model is "unfreezing," which involves creating a need for change and overcoming resistance to change. This stage involves breaking down existing mindsets, beliefs, and behaviors that may hinder the adoption of new ways of doing things. Unfreezing is achieved through various techniques, such as creating a sense of urgency, providing information and data to highlight the need for change, and addressing any concerns or fears associated with the change. The second step is the "changing" stage, where the actual transformation takes place. This stage focuses on implementing new strategies, processes, and structures that align with the desired change. It involves providing support, resources, and training to individuals and teams involved in the change. The changing stage may also include encouraging collaboration and communication, revising policies and procedures, and redefining roles and responsibilities (Memon, Shah & Khoso, 2020)

The final step is "refreezing," which aims to stabilize the new state and make it the norm. Refreezing involves reinforcing the changes, embedding them into the organizational culture, and ensuring that they become sustainable over the long term. This stage includes creating new routines, practices, and systems that support the desired change and align with the organization's goals. It also involves celebrating successes, recognizing and rewarding individuals and teams for their contributions to the change, and addressing any remaining resistance or barriers to maintaining the new state (Burnes, 2020).

Lewin's Three-Step Model provides a structured approach to change management, emphasizing the need to address the psychological and behavioral aspects of change. By unfreezing existing mindsets, facilitating the change process, and refreezing new behaviors and practices, organizations can effectively navigate and sustain transformation. The model highlights the importance of communication, engagement, and support throughout the change journey, ultimately leading to successful organizational change.

- **Kotter's Eight-Step Model**

Kotter's Eight-Step Model, developed by leadership and change management expert John P. Kotter, is a widely used and effective framework for leading organizational change. The model aims to address the challenges of driving large-scale transformations in complex and dynamic environments. The first stage of the model is "creating a sense of urgency." This step involves communicating the need for change and highlighting the risks of not changing. It is essential to create a compelling case for change to mobilize the support and commitment of stakeholders (Kang et al., 2022).

The second stage is "forming a guiding coalition." In this step, a diverse group of influential leaders is brought together to guide the change initiative. The guiding coalition is responsible for setting the direction, making critical decisions, and overcoming resistance to change. The third stage focuses on "developing a vision and strategy" for the change. A clear and inspiring vision helps align everyone towards a common goal. The strategy outlines the approach and actions required to achieve the desired transformation (Alhaderi, 2021)

The fourth stage is "communicating the vision." Effective communication is crucial in ensuring that the vision is understood and embraced by all members of the organization. It helps to generate enthusiasm and commitment to the change effort. The fifth stage is "empowering action." This involves removing obstacles and providing the necessary resources, support, and training for employees to act on the vision. Empowerment enables employees to contribute actively to the change and take ownership of their roles in the transformation process (Kang et al., 2022).

The sixth stage focuses on "generating short-term wins." Celebrating early successes provides evidence that the change is working and builds momentum for further progress. These wins serve as motivators for the organization to keep moving forward. The seventh stage is "consolidating gains and producing more change." Building on the momentum of early successes, this stage involves continuously refining and expanding the change effort. It may involve revisiting and adjusting the strategy based on feedback and new insights. The final stage is "anchoring new approaches in the culture." To make the change sustainable, it needs to become part of the organization's culture. This involves reinforcing the new behaviors, values, and practices through recognition, rewards, and integration into daily operations (Kang et al., 2022).

Kotter's Eight-Step Model provides a comprehensive and systematic approach to managing change. It emphasizes the importance of leadership, communication, and engagement at every stage of the change process. By following this model, organizations can increase their chances of successful transformation and build a more adaptive and resilient culture that can thrive in a constantly evolving business environment ((Alhaderi, 2021)

Both models recognize the importance of effective communication, stakeholder engagement, and strong leadership throughout the change process. They emphasize the need for clear goals, careful planning, and addressing resistance to change. Additionally, these models highlight the importance of sustaining and embedding the changes to ensure long-term success.

Traditional change management models provide organizations with a systematic approach to navigate change and help minimize disruptions and resistance. They provide a foundation for understanding the complexities of change and offer a roadmap for managing the transition effectively. However, it is essential to recognize that the effectiveness of these models may vary depending on the specific organizational context and the nature of the change being implemented.

Contemporary Change Management Models

Contemporary change management models have emerged in response to the evolving nature of business environments and the recognition that change is a constant and pervasive aspect of organizational life. These models depart from the linear and sequential approaches of traditional models and instead embrace more dynamic and adaptable frameworks. Contemporary change management models emphasize agility, flexibility, and responsiveness to rapidly changing market conditions, technological advancements, and stakeholder expectations. They recognize the need for continuous learning, experimentation, and adjustment throughout the change process. These models often incorporate elements such as iterative feedback loops, employee empowerment, collaboration, and a focus on building change capabilities within the organization. By leveraging contemporary change management models, organizations can enhance their capacity to navigate complexity, promote innovation, and adapt proactively to the ever-changing business landscape (Errida, & Lotfi, 2021).

- **Agile Change Management**

Agile Change Management is a flexible and adaptive approach to managing organizational change. It draws inspiration from Agile project management methodologies commonly used in software development but is applied to the broader context of change initiatives. This model recognizes the need for organizations to be responsive and nimble in today's rapidly changing business landscape. The key principles of Agile Change Management include collaboration, transparency, and iterative progress. Cross-functional teams are formed, bringing together individuals with diverse skills and perspectives to drive the change effort. These teams work in short cycles, known as sprints or iterations, to implement and assess changes (Franklin, 2021).

One of the central tenets of Agile Change Management is empowerment. It encourages organizations to distribute decision-making authority and provide individuals with the autonomy to take ownership of the change process (Mizrak, 2020). This empowers employees to contribute their expertise and insights, fostering a sense of ownership and commitment to the change effort. Continuous learning is another core aspect of Agile Change Management. It promotes a culture of experimentation and learning from both successes and failures. Feedback loops are established to gather insights and make adjustments as needed. This iterative approach allows organizations to make incremental improvements based on real-time feedback and market dynamics (Marnada et al., 2022).

Agile Change Management also emphasizes the importance of collaboration and open communication. Transparency and regular communication among team members and stakeholders help foster trust, alignment, and shared understanding of the change objectives and progress. This collaborative approach enables organizations to address challenges and adapt to emerging opportunities more effectively. By adopting Agile Change Management, organizations can benefit from increased agility, faster response times, and improved adaptability in the face of change. It enables them to navigate uncertainty and complexity with greater resilience and flexibility (Naslund & Kale, 2020). This model is particularly well-suited for industries and sectors where rapid innovation, market disruption, and evolving customer needs are prevalent.

- **Kotter's Dual Operating System Model**

Kotter's Dual Operating System Model is a framework that addresses the challenges organizations face in balancing the need for stability and the need for change. It recognizes that traditional hierarchical structures, while effective in managing routine operations, can often hinder innovation and responsiveness to market dynamics. In this model, organizations operate with two systems: the traditional hierarchy and the network-based system. The traditional hierarchy represents the existing organizational structure with its established roles, processes, and reporting lines. It provides stability, control, and efficiency in executing daily operations (Kang et al., 2022).

On the other hand, the network-based system operates alongside the hierarchy, focusing on agility, collaboration, and innovation. This system comprises cross-functional teams, task forces, or project-based groups that are empowered to make decisions and drive change initiatives. It is designed to be more flexible, adaptive, and responsive to emerging opportunities and challenges (Sittrop & Crosthwaite, 2021)

The Dual Operating System Model encourages the parallel operation of these two systems, recognizing that they each have their strengths and limitations. The hierarchy ensures stability, coordination, and efficiency in executing routine tasks, while the network system fosters creativity, experimentation, and adaptability to address complex problems and drive innovation. By integrating the network-based system, organizations can tap into the collective intelligence and diverse expertise of their employees. It encourages collaboration, knowledge sharing, and the exploration of new ideas. This approach enables organizations to respond more effectively to market changes, customer demands, and technological advancements (Kang et al., 2022).

The Dual Operating System Model emphasizes the importance of strong leadership and effective communication in aligning both systems and driving organizational transformation. It requires leaders to foster a culture that supports collaboration, innovation, and continuous learning. By creating a shared sense of purpose, engaging employees at all levels, and providing the necessary resources and support, leaders can facilitate the successful integration of the dual operating systems. Kotter's Dual Operating System Model provides a framework for organizations to balance stability and agility, leveraging the strengths of both hierarchical structures and network-based systems. It enables organizations to navigate the complexities of today's business environment, driving innovation, and ensuring long-term success (Odiaga et al., 2021).

- **Appreciative Inquiry**

Appreciative Inquiry is a change management model that takes a positive and strengths-based approach to organizational transformation. It was developed by David Cooperrider and Suresh Srivastva in the 1980s and has gained popularity for its focus on leveraging the positive aspects of an organization rather than solely addressing problems and deficiencies. The key premise of Appreciative Inquiry is that organizations thrive when they build on their strengths and successes. Rather than diagnosing and solving problems, this model encourages organizations to explore and amplify their positive attributes, experiences, and achievements. By doing so, organizations can create a positive and energizing environment that inspires and motivates employees, fosters innovation, and enhances overall performance (Morgan et al., 2022)

Appreciative Inquiry involves a collaborative and inclusive process that engages stakeholders at all levels of the organization. It encourages open dialogue, active listening, and shared learning to generate a deep understanding of what is working well and what the organization aspires to achieve. This approach values diverse perspectives and seeks to involve all stakeholders in shaping the future direction of the organization (Garrett, 2022). The model follows a structured inquiry process that consists of four stages: discovery, dream, design, and destiny. In the discovery stage, participants engage in dialogue and reflection to identify and appreciate the organization's strengths, best practices, and success stories. The dream stage involves collectively envisioning the ideal future state and articulating aspirations and possibilities. In the design stage, stakeholders collaborate to develop concrete plans and strategies to achieve the desired future. Lastly, in the destiny stage, the focus is on implementation and sustaining positive change, embedding the new practices and approaches into the organization's culture (Venter & Moolman, 2022).

Appreciative Inquiry emphasizes the power of positive emotions, optimism, and shared vision in driving change. It recognizes that focusing on strengths and possibilities creates a positive mindset and a sense of ownership and commitment among employees. By highlighting what is working well and amplifying positive experiences, organizations can create a virtuous cycle of success and continuous improvement (Morgan et al., 2022). Overall, Appreciative Inquiry offers a refreshing and alternative approach to change management, centering on the organization's positive attributes, aspirations, and collective wisdom. It fosters a culture of collaboration, innovation, and continuous learning, enabling organizations to unleash their full potential and achieve transformative and sustainable change.

- **Prosci's ADKAR Model**

Prosci's ADKAR Model is a widely recognized and influential change management model that emphasizes the importance of individual change in the overall change process. Developed by Prosci, a leading provider of change management solutions, the ADKAR Model provides a step-by-step framework to help individuals navigate through change successfully. The first element of the ADKAR Model is Awareness, which involves creating an understanding among individuals about the need for change and the reasons behind it. It focuses on communicating the rationale for change and the potential impact it will have on individuals and the organization as a whole (Adelman-Mullally, Nielsen & Chung, 2023)

The second element is Desire, which aims to cultivate a personal commitment and motivation for the change. It involves addressing any resistance or concerns individuals may have and helping them develop a positive attitude towards the change by highlighting the benefits and addressing any perceived drawbacks. The third element is Knowledge, which focuses on equipping individuals with the necessary information and skills to navigate the change. This includes providing training, resources, and support to help individuals acquire the knowledge they need to adapt to the new ways of working (Samosir & Jayadi, 2023).

The fourth element is Ability, which emphasizes building individuals' capabilities to implement the change effectively. This involves providing hands-on support, coaching, and opportunities for practice to ensure that individuals have the necessary skills and confidence to perform their new roles and responsibilities. The final element is Reinforcement, which aims to sustain the change by providing ongoing support and reinforcement. This involves recognizing and rewarding individuals for their efforts, celebrating successes, and continuously monitoring and reinforcing the change to embed it into the organization's culture (Adelman-Mullally, Nielsen & Chung, 2023)

The ADKAR Model recognizes that successful change ultimately depends on individuals embracing and adopting the change. By addressing the psychological and emotional aspects of change, the model provides a structured and comprehensive approach to facilitate individual transitions and enhance change adoption. Organizations that utilize the ADKAR Model can better understand and address individual barriers to change, resulting in improved change outcomes and increased employee engagement and commitment. The model can be applied to various types of organizational changes, ranging from process improvements and technology implementations to mergers and acquisitions (Antoniades et al., 2022)

- **Bridges' Transition Model**

Bridges' Transition Model, developed by William Bridges, offers a unique perspective on change by focusing on the psychological and emotional transitions that individuals undergo during times of change. The model recognizes that change is not just a series of external events or actions but also an internal process that individuals need to go through to fully embrace and adapt to the new reality (Bridges & Mitchell, 2000).

The model consists of three main stages: the Ending, the Neutral Zone, and the New Beginning.

The first stage, the Ending, involves letting go of the old ways of doing things, whether it's processes, roles, or even mindsets. This stage can be characterized by a range of emotions, including resistance, loss, and uncertainty. Bridges emphasizes the importance of acknowledging and addressing these emotions, as individuals need to mourn the loss of the old before they can fully embrace the new. The second stage is the Neutral Zone, which is a period of ambiguity and exploration. During this stage, individuals may feel disoriented and experience a sense of being "in-between." This stage can be challenging, as people may feel a lack of clarity and stability. However, it is also a stage of opportunity and creativity, as individuals have the freedom to explore new possibilities and experiment with different approaches. The final stage is the New Beginning, where individuals start to embrace and integrate the changes into their daily lives. This stage involves establishing new routines, roles, and ways of working. It requires clear communication, support, and guidance to help individuals navigate the new landscape successfully (Bridges & Mitchell, 2000).

Bridges' Transition Model emphasizes the importance of managing the psychological and emotional aspects of change. It highlights the need for effective communication, empathy, and support to help individuals navigate the transitions and come out stronger on the other side. By recognizing and addressing the internal transitions, organizations can facilitate smoother and more successful change journeys. The model is particularly useful when managing significant organizational changes such as mergers and acquisitions, restructurings, or cultural transformations. It helps leaders and change agents understand and anticipate the emotional impact of change on individuals, allowing them to provide the necessary support and resources to facilitate a successful transition. Bridges' Transition Model offers valuable insights into the human side of change and provides a framework for managing the emotional and psychological aspects of transition. By acknowledging and supporting individuals through the ending, neutral zone, and new beginning, organizations can facilitate smoother and more successful change processes, leading to greater employee engagement, satisfaction, and overall organizational success (Graf et al., 2020).

Contemporary change management models prioritize adaptability, stakeholder engagement, and a focus on individual and organizational agility. These models recognize the complexities of change in modern business environments and offer strategies to effectively navigate uncertainty, foster innovation, and build change capabilities within organizations. By embracing these models, organizations can enhance their readiness for change and increase their ability to thrive in a rapidly evolving landscape.

Critical Components for Successful Change Initiatives

Successful change initiatives require several critical components to ensure smooth implementation and positive outcomes. Three key components that play a vital role in driving successful change are clear communication, stakeholder engagement, and leadership support.

Clear communication is essential for effective change management. It involves articulating the purpose, goals, and expected outcomes of the change to all stakeholders involved. This includes communicating the reasons for the change, the benefits it will bring, and the impact it will have on individuals and the organization as a whole (Fusch et al., 2020). Clear communication helps to manage expectations, address concerns, and build trust among stakeholders. It involves open and transparent communication channels, such as town hall meetings, newsletters, emails, and regular updates. By keeping everyone informed and involved throughout the change process, clear communication enhances understanding, minimizes resistance, and promotes a shared vision of success (Alqudah, Carballo-Penela & Ruzo-Sanmartín, 2022).

Secondly, stakeholder engagement is crucial in change initiatives as it involves actively involving and collaborating with individuals or groups affected by the change. This includes employees, customers, suppliers, and other key stakeholders. Engaging stakeholders from the early stages of change planning helps to gain their support, gather their insights, and address their concerns. It creates a sense of ownership and shared responsibility for the change. Stakeholder engagement can be facilitated through workshops, focus groups, surveys, and one-on-one meetings. By involving stakeholders, organizations can tap into their knowledge, ideas, and expertise, which contributes to better decision-making, smoother implementation, and increased acceptance of the change (O'Rourke, Higuchi & Hogg, 2016).

Furthermore, leadership support plays vital role in successful change initiatives. Effective leaders provide guidance, direction, and resources to drive the change process forward. They play a crucial role in creating a supportive environment and motivating employees to embrace the change. Leadership support involves clearly communicating the vision for change, setting clear expectations, and modeling the desired behaviors. Leaders should demonstrate their commitment to the change, actively participate in the change process, and provide necessary resources and support to employees. Their visible involvement and active engagement inspire confidence and encourage employees to overcome resistance and actively contribute to the change effort (Randall & Coakley, 2007).

In conclusion, clear communication, stakeholder engagement, and leadership support are essential components for successful change initiatives. By ensuring clear and transparent communication, actively engaging stakeholders, and providing strong leadership support, organizations can navigate change more effectively, minimize resistance, and increase the chances of successful outcomes. These components work in synergy to create an environment of trust, collaboration, and shared commitment, enabling organizations to adapt, grow, and thrive in a constantly evolving business landscape.

Real-World Examples of Change Management Models

Implementing change within an organization can be a complex and challenging endeavor. To gain insights into effective change management practices, it is essential to examine real-world examples of organizations that have successfully navigated and implemented change initiatives. These examples provide valuable lessons and tangible outcomes that showcase the power of change management models in driving organizational transformation. By studying these real-world cases, organizations can learn from the experiences of others, identify best practices, and apply them to their own change initiatives.

- ### IBM (International Business Machines Corporation)

IBM's transformation in the early 1990s serves as a compelling case study in successful change management. Recognizing the need to adapt to the evolving market dynamics, IBM applied John Kotter's Eight-Step Model to guide their transformational journey. One key aspect of their approach was creating a sense of urgency, emphasizing the need for change and the consequences of inaction. By communicating this urgency to employees, stakeholders, and customers, IBM motivated and mobilized the organization for the transformation. To drive the change, IBM formed a guiding coalition consisting of influential leaders from various departments and levels of the organization. This coalition acted as change champions, providing support, guidance, and resources to facilitate the transformation. They played a crucial role in aligning the organization around a clear vision for the future, ensuring everyone understood the strategic direction and the importance of the change initiative (Balgobin & Pandit, 2001)

IBM also emphasized the involvement and empowerment of employees throughout the change process. They encouraged collaboration, cross-functional teams, and employee engagement, recognizing that successful change requires the collective effort of all stakeholders. By involving employees at all levels, IBM tapped into the diverse expertise and perspectives within the organization, driving innovation, and fostering a customer-centric culture. The transformation led to a cultural shift within IBM, with a renewed focus on innovation, agility, and customer-centricity. The company diversified its offerings, transitioning from a hardware-centric focus to becoming a leading provider of software, services, and consulting. This strategic shift enabled IBM to adapt to the changing market demands, positioning the company for growth and improved competitiveness (Gao, Liu & Ma, 2019)

Overall, IBM's successful transformation showcases the importance of effective change management strategies. By employing Kotter's Eight-Step Model, IBM was able to create a sense of urgency, build a guiding coalition, communicate a clear vision, empower employees, and foster a culture of innovation. The outcome of their transformation was a more agile, customer-focused organization that achieved significant growth and maintained its leadership position in the industry.

- ### Microsoft Corporation

Microsoft Corporation's transformation under CEO Satya Nadella stands as a prominent example of successful change management. Recognizing the need to adapt to the evolving technology landscape, Microsoft embraced a growth mindset and embarked on a transformative journey guided by agile principles. One crucial aspect of Microsoft's approach was the adoption of the Agile Change Management model. This model emphasizes flexibility, collaboration, and iterative processes, aligning well with Microsoft's goal of becoming a more agile and customer-centric organization. By embracing agile practices, Microsoft aimed to enhance its ability to respond to market changes quickly and deliver innovative solutions (Sherer, Kohli & Baron, 2003).

Central to Microsoft's transformation was the empowerment of its employees. Nadella fostered a culture that encouraged experimentation and risk-taking, valuing learning from failures as a means of driving innovation. The company invested in employee development, providing resources and support for continuous learning and skill development. This emphasis on empowering employees contributed to a more engaged and motivated workforce, driving creativity and a sense of ownership in driving the transformation. Microsoft also implemented structural changes to support its transformation efforts. The company restructured teams and departments to promote collaboration, enhance communication channels, and facilitate faster decision-making. These changes aimed to break down silos and foster a more cohesive and agile organizational structure (Gotsch, Lienhard & Schögel, 2019).

As a result of its transformation, Microsoft successfully repositioned itself as a leader in cloud services through its Azure platform. The company's focus on the cloud-first, mobile-first strategy allowed it to capture a significant share of the growing cloud market. This shift contributed to increased revenue, as organizations increasingly adopted Microsoft's cloud solutions. Additionally, the transformation led to improved customer satisfaction, as Microsoft's offerings became more aligned with customer needs and market trends. Beyond financial success, Microsoft's transformation had a profound impact on its organizational culture. The emphasis on agility, innovation, and customer-centricity permeated the company, fostering a more dynamic and adaptive culture. This cultural shift allowed Microsoft to stay at the forefront of technological advancements and maintain its competitiveness in the industry (Sherer, Kohli & Baron, 2003).

In conclusion, Microsoft's transformation under Satya Nadella exemplifies the power of embracing agile principles and empowering employees in driving organizational change. By adopting a growth mindset, restructuring teams, and focusing on the cloud-first strategy, Microsoft successfully repositioned itself as a leader in the cloud services market. The transformation yielded tangible benefits in terms of increased revenue, improved customer satisfaction, and a more innovative and agile organizational culture.

- **General Electric (GE)**

Under the leadership of former CEO Jack Welch, General Electric (GE) implemented the "Work-Out" change management model as a means of driving organizational transformation. Work-Out was designed to break down hierarchical barriers, empower employees, and foster a culture of collaboration and continuous improvement. The Work-Out initiative at GE involved structured workshops where employees from different levels and functions came together to identify and address organizational challenges. These workshops provided a forum for open dialogue, enabling employees to voice their concerns, share ideas, and propose solutions. By engaging employees at all levels, Work-Out aimed to leverage their expertise and insights to drive meaningful change within the organization (Ocasio & Joseph, 2008).

One of the key outcomes of the Work-Out initiative was improved communication. By creating a platform for open dialogue and active participation, GE fostered a culture of transparency and collaboration. Employees felt empowered to express their opinions and contribute to decision-making processes, leading to better communication channels throughout the organization. Moreover, the Work-Out model increased employee engagement by giving them a sense of ownership and involvement in shaping the company's future. By actively participating in problem-solving and decision-making, employees became more invested in the success of the organization. This increased engagement translated into higher levels of motivation, productivity, and commitment to achieving organizational goals (Ocasio & Joseph, 2008).

The Work-Out model also promoted a culture of continuous improvement at GE. By addressing organizational challenges through collaborative workshops, the company encouraged a mindset of seeking innovative solutions and challenging the status quo. This focus on continuous improvement enabled GE to streamline processes, eliminate inefficiencies, and drive operational excellence across its various business units. The implementation of the Work-Out model at GE brought about significant benefits for the organization. The improved communication, increased employee engagement, and culture of continuous improvement fostered by Work-Out contributed to enhanced organizational performance. GE was able to tap into the collective knowledge and expertise of its employees, drive innovation, and adapt to changing market conditions more effectively. The success of the Work-Out initiative at GE highlights the importance of empowering employees and fostering a culture of collaboration in driving organizational change. By breaking down hierarchical barriers and leveraging the insights of employees, GE was able to harness its internal talent and drive positive transformation throughout the organization (Hanley, 2014).

- **Netflix**

Netflix's transformation from a DVD-by-mail rental service to a streaming media provider is a prominent example of successful change management. The company employed a change management model that emphasized agility and customer-centricity to navigate this significant shift in its business model. At the core of Netflix's change management approach was the adoption of Agile and Lean methodologies. These methodologies promote flexibility, adaptability, and a focus on delivering customer value. Netflix embraced rapid iteration and experimentation, allowing them to test and refine their streaming platform based on real-time user feedback and data analysis. This iterative approach enabled the company to make continuous improvements and respond swiftly to changing market demands (Burroughs, 2019).

Another crucial aspect of Netflix's change management strategy was its customer-centric focus. The company recognized the evolving preferences of consumers and the growing demand for on-demand streaming services. By prioritizing the customer experience and leveraging data analytics, Netflix could tailor its content offerings and user interface to provide a personalized and seamless streaming experience. This customer-centric approach allowed Netflix to attract and retain a large subscriber base, ultimately driving its success in the streaming market. Netflix's change management model also emphasized a data-driven decision-making process. The company heavily relied on analytics and data analysis to inform its content acquisition and production strategies. By leveraging viewer data, Netflix could identify emerging trends, preferences, and viewing patterns, enabling them to make strategic decisions about the content they offer. This data-driven approach helped Netflix create a diverse and appealing library of content, catering to a wide range of audience interests (Daidj & Egert, 2018).

The outcomes of Netflix's change management efforts were significant and transformative. The company successfully transitioned from a DVD rental business to a leading streaming service provider, revolutionizing the entertainment industry. Netflix's streaming platform disrupted traditional media distribution models, providing consumers with convenient, on-demand access to a vast library of movies and TV shows. This shift in business model not only propelled Netflix's growth but also reshaped the way people consume and access entertainment worldwide (Burroughs, 2019). The case of Netflix demonstrates the power of embracing agility, customer-centricity, and data-driven decision-making in driving successful change. By employing a change management model that emphasizes these principles, Netflix was able to adapt to the evolving market landscape, innovate rapidly, and create a compelling value proposition for its customers.

- **Procter & Gamble (P&G)**

Procter & Gamble (P&G), a multinational consumer goods company, implemented the "Connect + Develop" change management model to enhance its innovation capabilities and drive growth. The Connect + Develop model focused on the idea that innovation can be accelerated by collaborating with external partners and leveraging their expertise and ideas. P&G recognized that to stay competitive in a rapidly changing market, it needed to tap into a broader network of innovators and sources of innovation. The company established open innovation platforms, such as the P&G's Innovation Portal, to connect with external partners, including startups, universities, and research institutions. Through these platforms, P&G actively sought out innovative ideas, technologies, and solutions that could be incorporated into their product development processes (Andrişan & Modreanu, 2022).

The implementation of Connect + Develop brought about several positive outcomes for P&G. One significant benefit was the increased rate of new product innovations. By opening up to external collaborations, P&G gained access to a diverse range of expertise and ideas that complemented its internal capabilities. This collaboration-driven approach enabled the company to bring new and innovative products to market more efficiently. Additionally, Connect + Develop expanded P&G's market reach. By partnering with external entities, P&G was able to tap into new markets and consumer segments. Collaborations with startups and smaller companies, in particular, provided P&G with opportunities to explore niche markets and introduce products tailored to specific customer needs (Ozkan, 2015).

Moreover, the Connect + Develop model enhanced P&G's competitive advantage. By engaging with external partners and leveraging their expertise, P&G could stay at the forefront of industry trends and advancements. This proactive approach to innovation helped P&G differentiate itself from competitors and maintain its position as a market leader in the consumer goods industry. The implementation of the Connect + Develop change management model at P&G resulted in a more collaborative and innovative culture within the organization. The company embraced external partnerships, leveraged open innovation platforms, and fostered a mindset of collaboration and knowledge sharing. These efforts not only accelerated P&G's innovation capabilities but also contributed to its growth, expanded market presence, and improved competitive advantage in the consumer goods industry (Brown, 2010).

These examples highlight how different organizations have successfully implemented change management models to drive transformation, enhance agility, and achieve positive outcomes. By embracing structured approaches, fostering a culture of collaboration and innovation, and adapting to changing market dynamics, organizations can effectively navigate change and position themselves for long-term success.

CHOOSING THE SUITABLE CHANGE MANAGEMENT APPROACH

Selecting the most appropriate change management approach is crucial for organizations embarking on a transformational journey. With a myriad of change management models and methodologies available, it is essential to choose an approach that aligns with the organization's specific needs, culture, and goals (Arefazar et al., 2022). In this section, the considerations will be explored and guidance for organizations in selecting and implementing the right change management approach will be provided.

- **Assessing Organizational Needs**

The first step in selecting the right approach is to assess the organization's unique needs and challenges. This involves understanding the scope of the change, the desired outcomes, and the readiness of the organization and its employees for change. Conducting a thorough analysis allows organizations to identify the specific areas requiring transformation and determine the level of complexity involved. By understanding their needs, organizations can narrow down the options and focus on approaches that address their specific requirements (Phillips & Klein, 2023).

- **Evaluating Change Management Models**

Once the organizational needs are identified, it is crucial to evaluate different change management models and methodologies available. Each approach has its own principles, frameworks, and tools. Organizations should carefully assess the strengths, limitations, and compatibility of each model with their organizational culture and context. Consider factors such as the level of employee involvement, the emphasis on communication and stakeholder engagement, and the flexibility of the approach. This evaluation process enables organizations to choose a change management model that best suits their unique requirements (Phillips & Klein, 2023).

- **Considering Change Champions and Resources**

Successful implementation of a change management approach relies on having change champions and adequate resources. Change champions are individuals within the organization who are passionate about the change and can drive it forward. Organizations should identify and empower these individuals to lead the change effort effectively. Additionally, organizations need to ensure they have the necessary resources, both in terms of financial investment and human capital, to support the implementation of the chosen change management approach (Supriharyanti & Sukoco, 2023)

- **Building Change Management Capabilities**

Implementing a change management approach requires building the necessary capabilities within the organization. This includes providing training and development opportunities for employees and leaders to enhance their change management skills. Developing a change-ready culture, where employees are open to change and equipped with the necessary tools and knowledge, is vital for successful implementation. Organizations should invest in building change management capabilities to ensure the smooth execution of the chosen approach ((Supriharyanti & Sukoco, 2023)

- **Monitoring and Adjusting**

Implementing a change management approach is an iterative process that requires monitoring, evaluation, and adjustment along the way. Organizations should establish mechanisms to track the progress of the change initiative and gather feedback from stakeholders. Regular assessment allows organizations to identify any challenges or areas that require modification. Being responsive and adaptable to changing circumstances and feedback ensures that the chosen approach remains effective and aligned with the organization's goals (Phillips & Klein, 2023)

Selecting and implementing the right change management approach is essential for organizations seeking successful transformation. By assessing organizational needs, evaluating change management models, considering change champions and resources, building change management capabilities, and monitoring progress, organizations can increase the likelihood of successful implementation. This guidance provides organizations with a structured approach to choosing the most suitable change management approach, enabling them to navigate their transformational journey effectively and achieve their desired outcomes.

OUTCOMES AND BENEFITS OF DYNAMIC CHANGE MANAGEMENT STRATEGIES IN ORGANIZATIONS

Dynamic change management strategies have demonstrated significant outcomes and benefits for organizations that have embraced them. One notable outcome is improved performance. By implementing agile and adaptable approaches to change, organizations can enhance their operational efficiency, productivity, and overall effectiveness. Dynamic change management enables organizations to quickly respond to market shifts, capitalize on emerging opportunities, and address operational inefficiencies, resulting in improved performance metrics and financial outcomes. Another key outcome is increased employee engagement. Dynamic change management strategies prioritize employee involvement and empowerment throughout the change process. By encouraging active participation, soliciting feedback, and fostering a culture of collaboration, organizations can boost employee morale, motivation, and commitment. Engaged employees are more likely to embrace change, contribute innovative ideas, and work towards shared goals, leading to higher levels of productivity, job satisfaction, and talent retention (Arefazar et al., 2022).

Enhanced customer satisfaction is a significant benefit derived from dynamic change management strategies. By adapting swiftly to customer needs and preferences, organizations can deliver products and services that align with evolving market demands. Through continuous improvement and customer-centricity, organizations can build stronger customer relationships, increase customer loyalty, and gain a competitive edge. This, in turn, leads to higher customer satisfaction levels, repeat business, and positive brand reputation (Phillips & Klein, 2023) Effective stakeholder management is another crucial benefit of dynamic change management strategies. By actively engaging and involving stakeholders throughout the change process, organizations can gain their support, mitigate resistance, and build trust. Engaging stakeholders early on helps identify their needs, concerns, and expectations, enabling organizations to tailor change initiatives accordingly. Strong stakeholder relationships foster collaboration, alignment, and shared ownership of the change, increasing the likelihood of successful outcomes (Supriharyanti & Sukoco, 2023).

Streamlined processes and improved efficiency are additional benefits of dynamic change management strategies. By critically evaluating existing processes, identifying bottlenecks, and implementing streamlined workflows, organizations can eliminate waste, reduce costs, and enhance operational efficiency. Dynamic change management encourages continuous improvement and a focus on efficiency, enabling organizations to optimize resource allocation, improve decision-making, and achieve sustainable cost savings. Innovation and competitive advantage are further benefits derived from dynamic change management strategies. By fostering a culture of innovation, organizations can encourage creative thinking, experimentation, and the exploration of new opportunities. Dynamic change management strategies embrace a growth mindset and enable organizations to adapt quickly to disruptive technologies, industry trends, and changing customer expectations. This agility allows organizations to gain a competitive advantage, differentiate themselves in the market, and position themselves as industry leaders (Hanelt et al., 2021).

Furthermore, dynamic change management strategies contribute to organizational resilience. In today's volatile and uncertain business environment, organizations need to be adaptable and resilient to navigate unexpected challenges and disruptions.

By implementing dynamic change management strategies, organizations can build resilience by developing a mindset and culture that embraces change, encourages learning, and fosters agility. This enables organizations to quickly adapt to changing circumstances, mitigate risks, and capitalize on emerging opportunities, ensuring their long-term viability and sustainability (Kok & Siripipatthanakul, 2023). Dynamic change management strategies also promote a culture of continuous improvement. Organizations that embrace these strategies prioritize learning and development, encouraging employees to seek opportunities for growth and enhancement. Through ongoing training, skill-building initiatives, and a focus on personal and professional development, organizations can foster a learning culture that drives innovation, creativity, and adaptability. Continuous improvement allows organizations to stay ahead of the curve, continuously enhancing their capabilities and remaining competitive in a rapidly evolving marketplace (Engida, Alemu & Mulugeta, 2022).

Another benefit of dynamic change management strategies is improved change readiness. By proactively addressing the human element of change, organizations can create a change-ready culture that embraces new ideas, challenges the status quo, and fosters a growth mindset. This readiness to change enables organizations to respond quickly and effectively to external disruptions, market shifts, and strategic initiatives. Employees are more likely to adapt to change, embrace new technologies, and drive transformation when supported by a change-ready culture. Lastly, dynamic change management strategies facilitate better decision-making and risk management. By adopting an iterative and data-driven approach to change, organizations can collect and analyze relevant information, enabling informed decision-making. The continuous monitoring and evaluation of change initiatives help identify potential risks and issues early on, allowing for timely mitigation strategies and course corrections. This proactive approach to decision-making and risk management reduces the likelihood of costly mistakes and maximizes the success of change initiatives (Kok & Siripipatthanakul, 2023).

In summary, dynamic change management strategies offer numerous benefits to organizations. From promoting resilience and a culture of continuous improvement to improving change readiness, decision-making, and risk management, these strategies enable organizations to thrive in a rapidly changing business landscape. By embracing dynamic change management, organizations can position themselves as agile, adaptable, and innovative entities, capable of navigating complexity and driving sustainable success.

CONCLUSION

Change management is of utmost importance in today's fast-paced and dynamic business environment. Organizations face constant external and internal forces that necessitate adaptation and transformation to remain competitive and relevant. Effective change management enables organizations to navigate these changes smoothly, minimizing resistance and maximizing the benefits of transformation. It provides a structured approach to guide individuals, teams, and entire organizations through the process of change, ensuring that goals are achieved, risks are managed, and stakeholders are engaged. Change management helps mitigate the challenges and uncertainties that come with change, fostering a culture of resilience and agility. Moreover, it promotes employee buy-in and commitment, as individuals are more likely to embrace change when they understand its purpose, are involved in the process, and see their concerns addressed. Ultimately, by prioritizing change management, organizations can enhance their ability to adapt, innovate, and thrive in an ever-evolving business landscape.

Dynamic models for organizational transformation are instrumental in helping organizations navigate the complexities of change and achieve successful outcomes. These models provide a framework that goes beyond traditional, linear approaches to change management. They recognize the dynamic nature of today's business environment and the need for flexibility, adaptability, and continuous improvement. Dynamic models, such as Agile Change Management, emphasize iterative processes, collaboration, and rapid response to change. They encourage experimentation, learning from failures, and leveraging emerging opportunities. These models promote a culture of innovation, employee empowerment, and customer-centricity, enabling organizations to stay ahead of the curve and drive meaningful transformation. By embracing dynamic models, organizations can effectively address the challenges of change, seize new opportunities, and create a resilient and future-ready organization.

This study has provided a comprehensive exploration of dynamic change management models for organizational transformation. By examining various models such as Lewin's Three-Step Model, Kotter's Eight-Step Model, ADKAR, and Agile Change Management, we have gained valuable insights into their underlying principles, methodologies, and the benefits they offer to organizations. Through the analysis of real-world examples and case studies, we have seen how these dynamic models have successfully facilitated organizational change and yielded positive outcomes, including increased innovation, improved competitiveness, and enhanced performance.

The objective of this study was to equip organizations with the knowledge and understanding of these dynamic models, empowering them to make informed decisions in their change initiatives. The study has emphasized the importance of change management in today's dynamic business landscape, where organizations must constantly adapt to stay relevant and competitive. What makes this study unique is its focus on dynamic models that embrace agility, continuous improvement, and customer-centricity. While traditional change management models have their merits, dynamic approaches offer a more adaptive and responsive framework that aligns better with the ever-evolving nature of today's business world.

The importance of change management cannot be understated. In a world characterized by rapid technological advancements, globalization, and changing consumer demands, organizations must embrace change to thrive. Successful change initiatives can lead to increased innovation, efficiency, and overall organizational effectiveness. By understanding and implementing dynamic change management models, organizations can navigate the challenges of transformation with confidence and achieve meaningful and sustainable results. This study has shed light on the best practices for implementing these models, including clear communication, stakeholder engagement, and leadership support.

In conclusion, the insights gained from this study will undoubtedly benefit organizations seeking to embark on successful change journeys. By adopting dynamic change management models, organizations can position themselves as agile and adaptive entities, ready to seize new opportunities and overcome challenges in an ever-changing world. Embracing a culture of continuous improvement and innovation, organizations can build a solid foundation for long-term success and growth.

Future studies in the field of change management should focus on several areas to advance our understanding of effective organizational transformation. Firstly, conducting comparative analyses of different change management models in various organizational contexts can provide insights into their strengths and weaknesses, helping identify the most suitable models for specific industries, organizational sizes, and cultural environments. Secondly, investigating the long-term impact of change initiatives and assessing the sustainability of outcomes can shed light on the continued success and adaptability of organizations. Additionally, exploring the role of change leadership, strategies for mitigating resistance and enhancing employee engagement, and the application of dynamic models in digital transformation and global contexts can provide valuable insights for organizations navigating complex change processes. Lastly, studying change in non-profit and public sectors can offer unique perspectives on transformation in these specific contexts. By addressing these areas, future studies can contribute to the knowledge base of change management, enabling organizations to navigate transformation effectively and drive long-term success.

REFERENCES

Adelman-Mullally, T., Nielsen, S., & Chung, S. Y. (2023). Planned change in modern hierarchical organizations: A three-step model. *Journal of Professional Nursing, 46*, 1–6. doi:10.1016/j.profnurs.2023.02.002 PMID:37188397

Alhaderi, S. M. (2021). Kotter's Eight Step Change Model for Employees' Intentional, Cognitive and Emotional Readiness for Change and Developing Regional Economy in Saudi Banking Sector's, Role of Homologous Communication, Learning Demand and Job Involvement. *J. Legal Ethical & Regul. Isses, 24*, 1.

Allegretti, S., Seidenstricker, S., Fischer, H., & Arslan, S. (2021). Executing a business model change: Identifying key characteristics to succeed in volatile markets. Leadership, Education, Personality. *An Interdisciplinary Journal, 3*, 21–33.

Alqudah, I. H., Carballo-Penela, A., & Ruzo-Sanmartín, E. (2022). High-performance human resource management practices and readiness for change: An integrative model including affective commitment, employees' performance, and the moderating role of hierarchy culture. *European Research on Management and Business Economics, 28*(1), 100177. doi:10.1016/j.iedeen.2021.100177

Andrişan, G., & Modreanu, A. (2022). *Achieving Business Success in the Fourth Industrial Revolution: The Case of Procter & Gamble*. Procter & Gamble.

Antoniades, N., Constantinou, C., Allayioti, M., & Biska, A. (2022). Lasting political change performance: Knowledge, awareness, and reinforcement (KARe). *SN Business & Economics, 2*(2), 14. doi:10.100743546-021-00196-w

Arefazar, Y., Nazari, A., Hafezi, M. R., & Maghool, S. A. H. (2022). Prioritizing agile project management strategies as a change management tool in construction projects. *International Journal of Construction Management, 22*(4), 678–689. doi:10.1080/15623599.2019.1644757

Balgobin, R., & Pandit, N. (2001). Stages in the turnaround process: The Case of IBM UK. *European Management Journal, 19*(3), 301–316. doi:10.1016/S0263-2373(01)00027-5

Bridges, W., & Mitchell, S. (2000). Leading transition: A new model for change. *Leader to Leader, 16*(3), 30–36.

Brown, B. (2010). Why innovation matters. *Research Technology Management, 53*(6), 18–23. doi:10.1080/08956308.2010.11657658

Burnes, B. (2020). The origins of Lewin's three-step model of change. *The Journal of Applied Behavioral Science, 56*(1), 32–59. doi:10.1177/0021886319892685

Burroughs, B. (2019). House of Netflix: Streaming media and digital lore. *Popular Communication, 17*(1), 1–17. doi:10.1080/15405702.2017.1343948

Ciampi, F., Demi, S., Magrini, A., Marzi, G., & Papa, A. (2021). Exploring the impact of big data analytics capabilities on business model innovation: The mediating role of entrepreneurial orientation. *Journal of Business Research, 123*, 1–13. doi:10.1016/j.jbusres.2020.09.023

Daidj, N., & Egert, C. (2018). Towards new coopetition-based business models? The case of Netflix on the French market. *Journal of Research in Marketing and Entrepreneurship, 20*(1), 99–120. doi:10.1108/JRME-11-2016-0049

Engida, Z. M., Alemu, A. E., & Mulugeta, M. A. (2022). The effect of change leadership on employees' readiness to change: The mediating role of organizational culture. *Future Business Journal, 8*(1), 1–13. doi:10.118643093-022-00148-2

Errida, A., & Lotfi, B. (2021). The determinants of organizational change management success: Literature review and case study. *International Journal of Engineering Business Management, 13*, 18479790211016273. doi:10.1177/18479790211016273

Franklin, M. (2021). *Agile change management: A practical framework for successful change planning and implementation.* Kogan Page Publishers.

Fusch, G. E., Ness, L. R., Booker, J. M., & Fusch, P. (2020). People and process: Successful change management initiatives. *Journal of Sustainable Social Change, 12*(1), 13.

Gao, Y., Liu, X., & Ma, X. (2019). How do firms meet the challenge of technological change by redesigning innovation ecosystem? A case study of IBM. *International Journal of Technology Management, 80*(3-4), 241–265. doi:10.1504/IJTM.2019.100285

Garrett, M. D. (2022). Applying appreciative inquiry to research in the field of inclusive education. *Canadian Journal for New Scholars in Education/Revue canadienne des jeunes chercheures et chercheurs en éducation, 13*(1).

Ghosh, S., Hughes, M., Hodgkinson, I., & Hughes, P. (2022). Digital transformation of industrial businesses: A dynamic capability approach. *Technovation, 113*, 102414. doi:10.1016/j.technovation.2021.102414

Gotsch, M. L., Lienhard, S. D., & Schögel, M. (2019). *Case Study: Change Management & Leadership at Microsoft.*

Graf, A. C., Jacob, E., Twigg, D., & Nattabi, B. (2020). Contemporary nursing graduates' transition to practice: A critical review of transition models. *Journal of Clinical Nursing*, *29*(15-16), 3097–3107. doi:10.1111/jocn.15234 PMID:32129522

Hanelt, A., Bohnsack, R., Marz, D., & Antunes Marante, C. (2021). A systematic review of the literature on digital transformation: Insights and implications for strategy and organizational change. *Journal of Management Studies*, *58*(5), 1159–1197. doi:10.1111/joms.12639

Hanley, C. (2014). Putting the bias in skill-biased technological change? A relational perspective on white-collar automation at General Electric. *The American Behavioral Scientist*, *58*(3), 400–415. doi:10.1177/0002764213503339

Kang, S. P., Chen, Y., Svihla, V., Gallup, A., Ferris, K., & Datye, A. K. (2022). Guiding change in higher education: An emergent, iterative application of Kotter's change model. *Studies in Higher Education*, *47*(2), 270–289. doi:10.1080/030750 79.2020.1741540

Kang, S. P., Chen, Y., Svihla, V., Gallup, A., Ferris, K., & Datye, A. K. (2022). Guiding change in higher education: An emergent, iterative application of Kotter's change model. *Studies in Higher Education*, *47*(2), 270–289. doi:10.1080/030750 79.2020.1741540

Kok, S. L., & Siripipatthanakul, S. (2023). Change Management Model in Corporate Culture and Values: A Case Study of Intel Cooperation. *Advance Knowledge for Executives*, *2*(1), 1–30.

Lakshman, C. (2005). Top executive knowledge leadership: Managing knowledge to lead change at General Electric. *Journal of Change Management*, *5*(4), 429–446. doi:10.1080/14697010500401540

Marnada, P., Raharjo, T., Hardian, B., & Prasetyo, A. (2022). Agile project management challenge in handling scope and change: A systematic literature review. *Procedia Computer Science*, *197*, 290–300. doi:10.1016/j.procs.2021.12.143

Memon, F. A., Shah, S., & Khoso, I. U. (2020). Role of leadership communication in creating change readiness: Revisiting Kurt Lewin's model in telecommunication sector of Pakistan. *Indian Journal of Science and Technology*, *13*(26), 2625–2632. doi:10.17485/IJST/v13i26.933

Mizrak, K. C. (2020). Agile occupational safety management system model and evaluation of the proposed model in an automotive company. *International Journal of Management and Administration*, *4*(8), 228-244.

Morgan, A. M., Jobe, R. L., Konopa, J. K., & Downs, L. D. (2022). Quality assurance, meet quality appreciation: Using appreciative inquiry to define faculty quality standards. *Higher Learning Research Communications*, *12*(1), 98–111. doi:10.18870/hlrc.v12i1.1301

Naslund, D., & Kale, R. (2020). Is agile the latest management fad? A review of success factors of agile transformations. *International Journal of Quality and Service Sciences*, *12*(4), 489–504. doi:10.1108/IJQSS-12-2019-0142

O'Rourke, T., Higuchi, K. S., & Hogg, W. (2016). Stakeholder participation in system change: A new conceptual model. *Worldviews on Evidence-Based Nursing*, *13*(4), 261–269. doi:10.1111/wvn.12165 PMID:27258681

Ocasio, W., & Joseph, J. (2008). Rise and fall-or transformation?: The evolution of strategic planning at the General Electric Company, 1940–2006. *Long Range Planning*, *41*(3), 248–272. doi:10.1016/j.lrp.2008.02.010

Odiaga, J., Guglielmo, M. J., Catrambone, C., Gierlowski, T., Bruti, C., Richter, L., & Miller, J. (2021). Kotter's Change Model In Higher Education: Transforming Siloed Education To A Culture Of Interprofessionalism. Journal of Organizational Culture, *Communications and Conflict*, *25*(2), 1–7.

Ozkan, N. N. (2015). An example of open innovation: P&G. *Procedia: Social and Behavioral Sciences*, *195*, 1496–1502. doi:10.1016/j.sbspro.2015.06.450

Phillips, J., & Klein, J. D. (2023). Change management: From theory to practice. *TechTrends*, *67*(1), 189–197. doi:10.100711528-022-00775-0 PMID:36105238

Randall, L. M., & Coakley, L. A. (2007). Applying adaptive leadership to successful change initiatives in academia. *Leadership and Organization Development Journal*, *28*(4), 325–335. doi:10.1108/01437730710752201

Samosir, P., & Jayadi, R. (2023). A Change Management for Transformation of Digital Banking In Indonesia. *Jurnal Sistem Cerdas*, *6*(1), 29–43.

Sherer, S. A., Kohli, R., & Baron, A. (2003). Complementary investment in change management and IT investment payoff. *Information Systems Frontiers*, *5*(3), 321–333. doi:10.1023/A:1025609613076

Sittrop, D., & Crosthwaite, C. (2021). Minimising risk—the application of kotter's change management model on customer relationship management systems: A case study. *Journal of Risk and Financial Management*, *14*(10), 496. doi:10.3390/jrfm14100496

Supriharyanti, E., & Sukoco, B. M. (2023). Organizational change capability: A systematic review and future research directions. *Management Research Review*, *46*(1), 46–81. doi:10.1108/MRR-01-2021-0039

Venter, K., & Moolman, A. (2022). An Appreciative Inquiry Approach to Community-Based Research for Development of a Social Enterprise. *Community-based Research with Vulnerable Populations: Ethical, Inclusive and Sustainable Frameworks for Knowledge Generation*, 169-186. Taylor & Francis.

Chapter 10

Assessing Disruptive Innovation Through Analysing Sustainability Financing and Capital Structure Performance of Nifty 50 Companies in India

Rohit Sood

iD https://orcid.org/0000-0002-4127-7781
Lovely Professional University, India

ABSTRACT

This research represents the impact of sustainability financing and capital structure performance measured using the Nifty companies gearing ratios having an impact on enhanced efficiency of the firm. The sustainability of the debt is being considered relevant for the company if the company is able to honour all of the current liabilities and non-current liabilities without jeopardizing with the ultimate goal for enhanced financial performance and can make itself prone to the defaults in the turbulent times. This research attempts analyse the relationship between the sustainable finance and the debt ratio of Nifty 50 companies with an objective to test the risk reward ration with respect to leverage financing.

DOI: 10.4018/978-1-6684-9814-9.ch010

INTRODUCTION

The company's performance can be attributed to the optimal financial ratios for analysing the daily sustainable operations for efficient future performance of the company in terms of enhanced operational cash flows. The ability of a country to expand its economy and capital markets is determined by its effectiveness (Hutagalung, 2020). The flexibility and low cost for the sources like equity and debt as well as the internal sources cost risk and reward analysis should be considered for assessing the sustainability of the operations for the company. The operational earning are a type of risky equity that varies with company's future cash flow projections and the external shocks and need to be managed with utmost care for the sustainable operations and long term earnings feasibility of the company.

Capital structure is a combination of debt and equity securities used to finance real investments. In 1958, Modigliani and Miller proposed the concept of capital structure analysis (Peter Brusov, 2018). Since Modigliani and Miller, several studies have been conducted to examine capital structure and refute their theorem. As a result, several theories about capital structure have emerged have been created, such as the trade-off theory proposed by Myers in 1984 (Myers, 1984), the resource based theory proposed by Myers and Majluf in 1984, which recommended that managers preferred using internal funds, the agency theory proposed by Jensen and Meckling in 1976 (Michael C. Jensen, n.d.), which proposed that increasing debt levels could mitigate the principle-agent problem, and so on.

The greatest likely returns of a stock, the national economy's average risk-free rate of return, and the market risk premium are frequently used to determine equity valuation. The financing mix of internal and external sources of finance in a portfolio significantly affects the long-term returns anticipated by stakeholders and financial management. Returns on capital projects are typically defined cash flows from investments expressed as a percentage of the project's cost. Financial analysts typically regard the debt-to-equity ratio as one of the most important capital structure factors for a firm's valuation. A company's financial leverage is determined by several factors, including its debt vs equity performance, debt service, debt coverage and debt-to-asset ratio.

Going to depend on the financial strategy of each company. In one company, debt capital may not exist, whereas in another, it may exceed owned capital. The typical capital structure of a corporation is represented by the ratio between the two. The capital structure of a new company could be one of the four models listed below:

- A capital structure based solely on equity shares.
- A capital Structure, which includes both equity and preferred shares.
- A capital Structure, which includes both equity and debentures.

- A capital Structure, which includes equity shares, preference shares, and debentures

The appearance of the daily operations of the company, the consistency of earnings, the nature of the money market, the investor's attitude, and other factors all influence the choice of an appropriate capital structure. First, understand the fundamental difference between equity and debt. Debt is a liability that must be repaid with interest regardless of the company's profitability. In contrast to equity, which is made up of the money of shareholders or owners and is reliant on the company's profits for dividend payments. A high percentage of leverage in the capital structure raises the risk of financial insolvency for the company in difficult times. However, debt financing is less expensive than obtaining funds through shares. As a result, there are Nifty 50 companies that rely on how their asset allocation is carried out and how much of their debt to ratio—if it is greater than one—is contributed, as well as how their return on assets and return on equity—with both debt and equity contributions—operate.

Literature Review

- Lisdawati (2023): Dividend is considered as a moderating variable and different ratios are being considered along with dividend to see the impact on stock prices and in turn on the financial performance of the companies of an Indonesian stock exchange. The impact on financial performance for the said moderating variable is being analysed in term of operational and financial performance of the company and it is found that the dividend outlay has been been able to moderate the debt equity ratio effect on the financial performance as well as share price of the company.
- Yuwen Dai, (2020): During the last decade, ESG investing has been a key criterion for Chinese economic operations, particularly the capital market. He investigated the case of ESG investing in China in this work by analysing the performance of equities indexes selected using an ESG screening method. Overall, we show that investing in ESG stock indexes can increase portfolio diversification while also increasing risk-adjusted returns.
- Mansi Jain, Gagandeep Sharma, Mrinalini Srivastava (2019): They discovered that "sustainable investment" refers to a variety of asset classes chosen with environmental, social, and governance (ESG) issues in mind. The foreign capital is being attracted by the performance of these indices, which made the firm global in the G-local environment for efficient capital markets. As per the analysis, the sustainable indices and traditional indices are considered to be having no statistical significant difference in financial performance.

- Yusni Nuryani, Denok Surnasi (2020): intends to investigate how the leverage impact through debt-to-equity ratio and current ratio affect dividend changes. A statistical analysis explanatory research analysis technique is used, resulted in a significance level of 0.045 0.05, indicating that the debt-to-equity ratio has a significant impact on the predicted dividend of 34.2%. And thus the considered variables can be seen as relevant for having an impact on efficient operational performance of the firm.

- Matthew W, Sherwood and Julia L. Pollard, (2017): According to the study's findings, ESG integration leads to significant outperformance. The study's findings suggest that including ESG emerging market stocks in institutional portfolios may increase returns while decreasing negative risk.

- Lyle, (2017): evaluates historical data to determine how the market views debt and possible locations for the ideal ratio. To look for potential patterns in risk adjusted expected returns, CAPM and the Fama-French three and four factor models will be used. The market efficient debt/equity ratio is calculated by combining two variables: the book to market ratio and market capitalization. The findings of this study show that having too much and too little leverage will result in lower returns.

- RG Eccles, SJ Potter, MD Kastrapeli, (2017): They consider social and governance issues when making investment decisions. The authors claim that the barriers to ESG integration are not as severe as previously thought. The main impediment is a lack of high-quality data on how businesses perform in relation to important ESG characteristics.

- M Limkriangkrai, SzeKee Koh, RB Durand, (2017): They discovered that firms with high composite ESG scores have more leverage. High ratings and low ratings in G rating category have less cash in hand, and have lower dividend pay-outs respectively. The business is getting less impacted through S ratings lending decisions. The impact of no discernible difference ESG based returns through different ESG ratings can lead higher risk and no cost benefit with regard investing in ESG.

- LT Stark, Parth Venket, Qifei Zhu, (2017): They discovered that Environmental, Social, and Governance (ESG) investing theories assume groups of investors with different ESG preferences or ideas. They discovered that companies with strong ESG reputations are preferred by long-term investors. This corresponds to the implications of the investor horizon.

- NC Ashwin Kumar, Camile Smith, Leila Badis and Nan Wang (2016): Reduced risk, according to conventional financial thinking, equals lower profits. A recent mathematical study found that organisations that combine ESG considerations have lower stock volatility. The study examined 157 Dow Jones Index companies over a two-year period.

- Oliveira, Ana Rita Camilo De,(2016): The dividend policy structure and corporate governance is being studied for examining the cultural dimensions in dividend policy and its impact on the financial performance of the company. The both of the above stated variables are working in sync to mitigate the dividend policy and agency related issues of the company. The three cultural dimensions developed by Geert Hofstede serve as proxies for culture and corporate governance practices are being studied to attain the enhanced operational performance.

- Bhandari, (1988): While controlling for business size, beta, demonstrates a positive relationship between projected common stock returns and the debt-to-equity ratio. This connection is unaffected by changes to the estimation method, market proxy, and so on. According to the available data, the "premium" of the debt-to-equity ratio is unlikely to be a simple "risk premium."

Objective

To examine the impact of a Debt Equity (D/E) Ratio of greater than one on NIFTY 50 company returns i.e. Return on Equity (ROE), Return on Assets (ROA) and Return on Capital Employed (ROCE).

To determine the moderating effect of Environmental Social Governance (ESG) concerns on returns i.e. Return on Equity (ROE), Return on Assets (ROA) and Return on Capital Employed (ROCE) of companies with debt-equity ratios greater than one.

Research Methodology

The current study examines the relationship between the Debt-to-Equity Ratio and Sustainable Financing and the Return on Assets, Return on Equity, and Return on Capital Employed, as well as how the Debt-to-Equity Ratio and Sustainable Financing evolve and how the Return on Assets, Return on Equity, and Return on Capital Employed respond to it. The scale used in previous studies will be used as the instrument in this study.

To achieve the aforementioned goal, the study employed correlation and regression analysis on the companies under consideration. The secondary data was obtained from the official NSE website and the Trading Fuel websites. The ten-year research period, from March 2010 to March 2021, was considered. If the debt-to-equity ratio is greater than one, 58 companies from the Nifty 50 index are considered for additional data analysis. Three ratios are used to assess capital structure, one of which is the debt-equity ratio.

Data Collection- Secondary data is gathered from the official sites of the NSE and Trading Fuel. The twelve-year research period, from March 2010 to March 2021, was considered. If the debt-to-equity ratio is greater than one, 58 companies from the Nifty 50 index are considered for additional data analysis.

The data is based on the names of NIFTY 50 companies with a debt-to-equity ratio greater than one, as well as the debt-to-equity ratio, return on assets, return on capital employed, and return on equity of the companies mentioned above.

OPERATIONAL DEFINITION OF VARIABLES

- **Dependent Variables in the research:** the research is Return on Assets, Return on Equity, Return on Capital Employed.

Return on assets (ROA) measures net income using total assets.

$$ROA = \frac{Net\ Income}{Total\ Assets}$$

Return on equity (ROE) is a ratio to measure a company's ability to use its resources to generate return on equity.

$$ROE = \frac{Net\ Income}{Shareholder's\ Equity}$$

Return on Capital Employed (ROCE) Return on capital employed (ROCE) is a financial ratio used to assess an organization's profitability and capital efficiency.

$$ROCE = \frac{EBIT}{Capital\ Employed}$$

- **Independent Variable in the research:** The independent variable in this study is the Debt-to-Equity Ratio and Sustainable Financing.

Debt to Equity Ratio (DER) is the ratio between the total debt against the total equity.

$$Debt\ to\ Equity\ ratio = \frac{Total\ Debt}{Total\ Shareholder'sequity}$$

Sustainable Financing is the concept that investing requires taking into account environmental, social, and governance issues in addition to financial returns.

Causal Research- It is classified as conclusive research because it seeks to establish a link between two or more variables. The goal of causal research, also known as explanatory research, is to determine whether two different events have a cause-and-effect relationship. Because many different factors can contribute to cause-and-effect, researchers design experiments to obtain statistical proof of the relationship between the circumstances. The quantitative sampling technique is used to develop mathematical models, ideas, and hypotheses related to the research topic.

EMPIRICAL ANALYSIS: METHODOLOGY

Correlation Analysis

Table 1 POWER GRID CORP OF INDIA NIFTY 50 (January 2011- March 2021)

Table 1. Source output: SPSS

Particular (Pair)	Correlation Coefficient	Sig value
Return on Equity to Debt/ Equity	-0.70	0.849
Return on Equity to Return on Capital Employed	0.75	0.012
Return on Equity to Return on assets	0.676	0.32
Debt / Equity Ratio to Return on Capital Employed	-0.646	0.044
Debt/ Equity Ratio to Return on Assets	-0.532	0.114
Return on Capital Employed to Return on Assets	0.867	0.001

After advocating above calculated field it can be advocated that the debt to equity is having inverse relation with the return of capital employed and which further signifies that there is significant difference between these two ratios by accepting the alternative hypothesis.

Correlation Analysis

Table 2 ADANI PORTS & SPECIAL ECONOMIC ZONENIFTY 50 (January 2011- March 2021)

Table 2. Source output: SPSS

Particular (Pair)	Correlation Coefficient	Sig value
Return on Equity to Debt/ Equity	-0.06	0.884
Return on Equity to Return on Capital Employed	0.789	0.02
Return on Equity to Return on assets	-0.378	0.356
Debt / Equity Ratio to Return on Capital Employed	-0.051	0.905
Debt/ Equity Ratio to Return on Assets	0.346	0.401
Return on Capital Employed to Return on Assets	-0.56	0.148

The weakest correlation has been shown between debt-to-equity ratio and return on equity is -0.06 which signifies that within a rise in the debt-to-equity ratio of ADANI PORTS the return on the equity has been diminishing with the use of more debt for their assets.

Correlation Analysis

Table 3 JSW STEELS NIFTY 50 (January 2011- March 2021)

Table 3. Source output: SPSS

Particular (Pair)	Correlation Coefficient	Sig value
Return on Equity to Debt/ Equity	0.11	0.808
Return on Equity to Return on Capital Employed	0.937	0.002
Return on Equity to Return on assets	0.92	0.003
Debt / Equity Ratio to Return on Capital Employed	-0.084	0.858
Debt/ Equity Ratio to Return on Assets	0.029	0.951
Return on Capital Employed to Return on Assets	0.964	0

After analysing, it can be depicted that a strong correlation has been maintain between return on the equity and return on the capital employed by having 0.93

correlation, which means that with increase in return on the equity the dependent variable return on the capital employed will be increased by 0.93 and it has also showed a significant relation between two variables.

Correlation Analysis

Table 4 NTPC NIFTY 50 (January 2011- March 2021)

Table 4. Source output: SPSS

Particular (Pair)	Correlation Coefficient	Sig value
Return on Equity to Debt/ Equity	-0.04	0.968
Return on Equity to Return on Capital Employed	0.395	0.605
Return on Equity to Return on assets	0.416	0.584
Debt / Equity Ratio to Return on Capital Employed	-0.038	0.962
Debt/ Equity Ratio to Return on Assets	-0.457	0.543
Return on Capital Employed to Return on Assets	0.996	0.004

In this case, debt to equity has a negative correlation with in all the three dependent variables, which are ROE, ROA, and ROCE, demonstrating that increasing debt to equity would result in a negative rise in these NTPC independent variables.

Correlation Analysis

Table 5 TATA MOTORS NIFTY 50 (January 2011- March 2021)

Table 5. Source output SPSS

Particular (Pair)	Correlation Coefficient	Sig value
Return on Equity to Debt/ Equity	-0.742	0.258
Return on Equity to Return on Capital Employed	0.437	0.563
Return on Equity to Return on assets	0.96	0.037
Debt / Equity Ratio to Return on Capital Employed	0.103	0.897
Debt/ Equity Ratio to Return on Assets	-0.892	0.108
Return on Capital Employed to Return on Assets	0.286	0.714

Here, in this company analysis of correlation the debt-to-equity is most negatively affected with the association of return on assets which means that as longer as the firm is having more returns from assets which are totally levered one and financed through the debt funding and is negatively correlated with the return on assets which shows that there is significant relation between the return on the equity and return on assets passing alternative hypothesis.

Correlation Analysis

Table 6 HDFC LTD NIFTY 50 (January 2011 - March 2021)

Table 6. Source output: SPSS

Particular (Pair)	Correlation Coefficient	Sig value
Return on Equity to Debt/ Equity	0.939	0.006
Return on Equity to Return on Capital Employed	0.076	0.885
Return on Equity to Return on assets	0.803	0.054
Debt / Equity Ratio to Return on Capital Employed	0.106	0.849
Debt/ Equity Ratio to Return on Assets	0.561	0.247
Return on Capital Employed to Return on Assets	-0.097	0.855

The above calculation signifies that only significant relation between return on equity and debt to equity which means as an development sector under nifty 50 companies from last many years the company is having more return from its shareholders or equity as by having more debt in its activities.

Correlation Analysis

Table 7 UPL NIFTY 50 (January 2011- March 2021)

Table 7. Source output: SPSS

Particular (Pair)	Correlation Coefficient	Sig value
Return on Equity to Debt/ Equity	-0.563	0.245
Return on Equity to Return on Capital Employed	0.745	0.089
Return on Equity to Return on assets	-0.845	0.245
Debt / Equity Ratio to Return on Capital Employed	-0.651	0.162
Debt/ Equity Ratio to Return on Assets	-0.753	0.084
Return on Capital Employed to Return on Assets	0.967	0.002

The company is having more ratio of debt and its more assets are financed through debts and showing high degree of positive correlation with ROCE and ROA. Moreover, it is showing moderate negative degree of correlation of ROCE with respect to Debt-to-equity ratio. Also, it has neglected the alternative hypothesis with respect to all debt-to-equity dependency ratios.

Correlation Analysis

Table 8 INDIAN OIL CORPORATION LTD NIFTY 50 (January 2011- March 2021)

Table 8. Source output: SPSS

Particular (Pair)	Correlation Coefficient	Sig value
Return on Equity to Debt/ Equity	-0.013	0.992
Return on Equity to Return on Capital Employed	0.999	0.028
Return on Equity to Return on assets	-0.582	0.605
Debt / Equity Ratio to Return on Capital Employed	0.031	0.98
Debt/ Equity Ratio to Return on Assets	0.821	0.387
Return on Capital Employed to Return on Assets	-0.546	0.605

After visualizing the above interpretation, the debt-to-equity ratio has showed highest association with the ROA. Though, it has only passed its alternative hypothesis between the return on the equity and return on the capital employed. Hence, therefore, this company also showed that there is no such relevance impact of Debt-to-equity to other financial performances.

Hypothesis Findings: Methodology

H0 = Debt to Equity Ratio (Independent variable has been affected adversely and shows no significant relation while impacting on other comparable variables)

H1 = There is significant Relation and difference between return on equity and Debt to equity

H2 = There is significant Relation and difference between return on the equity & the capital employed

H3 = There is significant Relation and difference between return on equity and return on assets

H4 = There is significant Relation and difference between ROCE and Debt to equity

H5 = There is significant Relation and difference between ROCE and Return on assets

Financial Sustainability (ESG)

To assess the sustainable financing, the another factor environmental (E), social (S), corporate governance (G) is considered to look at the independent effects as well as composite effects of the ESG ratings on Nifty 50 stock returns and company feasible operational and financing decisions. Firms with high aggregate ESG ratings have more leverage. Individual ratings lead to different conclusions: firms with low E and high G ratings are more inclined to raise debt. Companies with high G ratings retain less money, and companies with low G ratings pay out fewer dividends. S ratings have minimal impact on company loan decisions. There does not appear to be a significant variation in risk-adjusted returns for portfolios based on ESG evaluations, meaning that ESG investing is free.

The risk reward relationship is assessed through the calculated ESG scores and it has been observed that a firm with good ESG rating are doing better in terms of risk management perspective a firm with negative ESG rating. Financial analysis along with ESG ratings for firms can complement each other to provide investors with a more complete view of a strategic and long potential.

Few Points that can't be ignored:

- According to prior research, low performance is described as a grade of less than 50, while excellent play is defined as a grade of further than 70.
- Why A company with an exceptional ESG score will have fewer to no external or internal difficulties and will adhere to best practises in all ESG areas.

- A company with a high ESG score adheres to best practises in all ESG classes and has no negative environmental or social impacts.

The average ESG score of a firm indicates if it is on track to meet ESG requirement is actively pursuing major ESG objectives. A poor rating shows that no best practices are being used, which indicates that the business is having a harmful influence on the environment and is harming its staff.

Proceedings

The objective is to evaluate the effect of Environmental Social Governance scores on the financial performance through financial ratios such as Return on Investment, return on Capital Employed and the Return on Equity over the NIFTY 50 companies with the Debt- Equity Ratio greater than 1 for the year 2021. Where, we have correlated the ESG scores with different ratios such as ROA, ROE and ROCE to find if there is any existence of any relation between ESG and these ratios considering one at a time.

Where, the environmental factors such as Resource use, Emissions, Innovation, Workforce effects on the ROA, ROE, ROCE of the companies or not same relation between the Social Factors such as Workforce, Human Rights, Community, Product responsibility effects the ROA, ROE, ROCE of the companies or not, including the governance factors such as Management, Shareholders, CSR Activity effects the ROA, ROE, ROCE of the companies described above or not.

ESG Allusion Proportion

Figure 1. Shows the investment amount by the NTPC Ltd. for respective ESG variables

NTPC LIMITED			
Corporate Social Responsibility Expenses	356.72	(in crore)	Environmental
Total no. of female employees	1,633		Workforce
Total no. of male employees	19,138		Workforce
Dividend per share	7		Shareholders
EPS	15.66		Shareholders
Promoters	51.11%		Management
Pledge	0%		Management
Revenue	1,32,669	(in crore)	Management
Total no of training and awareness programs held	5,897		Human Rights
Employee Training cost	21	(in crore)	Human Rights
Marketing Cost	1,717.47	(in crore)	Product Responsibility

Figure 2. Shows the investment amount by the Powergrid CorporationLtd. for respective ESG variables

Powergrid			
Corporate Social Responsibility Expenses	346.21	(in crore)	Environmental
Total no. of female employees	672		Workforce
Total no. of male employees	7864		Workforce
Dividend per share	4		Shareholders
EPS	21.36		Shareholders
Promoters	51.34%		Management
Pledge	0%		Management
Revenue	11,350.44	(in crore)	Management
Total no of training and awareness programs held	6114		Human Rights
Employee Training cost	20	(in crore)	Human Rights
Marketing Cost	103.14	(in crore)	Product Responsibility

Figure 3. Shows the investment amount by the IOC Ltd. for respective ESG variables

Corporate Social Responsibility Expenses	460.37 Crore	Enviromental
Total No of Female Employees	2,776 In Total	Workforce
Total No of Female Employees	31,254 In Total	Workforce
Dividend Per Share	2.10 Rs	Shareholders
EPS	26.34 Rs	Shareholders
Promoter	51.5% Total Holding	Management
Pledge	0%	Management
Revenue	589335 Crore	Management
Total No of Training and Awareness Program Held	19 Training Centers, Not able to find No. of programmes held	Human Rights
Employee Training Cost	92.92 Crore	Human Rights
Marketing Cost	Not Able To Find	Product Responsibility
	Indian Oil Corporation	

Figure 4. Shows the investment amount by the UPL. for respective ESG variables

	UPL		
Corporate Social Responsibility Expenses	100	(in crore)	Environmental
Total no. of female employees	3916		Workforce
Total no. of male employees	9138		Workforce
Dividend per share	2.49RS		Shareholders
EPS	15.39		Shareholders
Promoters	26.42%		Management
Pledge	0%		Management
Revenue	38,694.00	(in crore)	Management
Total no of training and awareness programs held			Human Rights
Employee Training cost		(in crore)	Human Rights
Marketing Cost		(in crore)	Product Responsibility

Figure 5. Shows the investment amount by the HDFC Ltd. for respective ESG variables

	HDFC LTD.		
Corporate Social Responsibility Expenses	763	(in crore)	Environmental
Total no. of female employees	36810		Workforce
Total no. of male employees	104769		Workforce
Dividend per share	7.53RS		Shareholders
EPS	76.01		Shareholders
Promoters	20.97%		Management
Pledge	0%		Management
Revenue	1.36 lakh	(in crore)	Management
Total no of training and awareness programs held	more than 2000 program held didn't find the exact value		Human Rights
Employee Training cost	1262	(in lakh)	Human Rights
Marketing Cost		(in crore)	Product Responsibility

Figure 6. Shows the investment amount by the Tata Motors Ltd. for respective ESG variables

	TaTa Motors		
Corporate Social Responsibility Expenses	23.69	(in crore)	Environmental
Total no. of female employees	3426		Workforce
Total no. of male employees	48925		Workforce
Dividend per share	do dividend from last 5 years		Shareholders
EPS	-3.63		Shareholders
Promoters	7.67%		Management
Pledge	0%		Management
Revenue	46,880.97	(in crore)	Management
Total no of training and awareness programs held	5000		Human Rights
Employee Training cost	3601	(in crore)	Human Rights
Marketing Cost	321..49	(in crore)	Product Responsibility

Figure 7. Shows the investment amount by the JSW Steel Ltd. for respective ESG variables

JSW Steel			
Absolute Emissions (Scope 1 & Scope 2)	million tC	44.21	Environmental
CO_2 Emission Intensity	tCO_2/tcs	2.5	Environmental
Specific Dust Emission Intensity (PM)	kg/tcs	0.488	Environmental
Specific NOx Emission Intensity	kg/tcs	1.26	Environmental
Specific SOx Emission Intensity	kg/tcs	1.895	Environmental
Total Employees [1]	number	12398	Social
Management	number	5466	Social
Non-Management	number	6932	Social
Permanent Women Employees	number	666	Social
Differently Abled Employees	number	28	Social
Contractual Employees	number	30227	Social
Total Members (Directors)	Nos	6	Governance
Independent Directors	Nos	2	Governance
Number of meetings	Nos	2	Governance
Total CSR expenditure	Rs crore	200.34	Governance

Figure 8. Shows the investment amount by the Adani Ports SEZ Ltd. for respective ESG variables

Adani Ports & Special Economic Zone			
Corporate Social Responsibility Expenses	72.99	(in crore)	Environmental
Total no. of female employees	2,809		Workforce
Total no. of male employees	42		Workforce
Dividend per share	5		Shareholders
EPS	24.58		Shareholders
Promoters	63.83%		Management
Pledge	13%		Management
Revenue	12,550	(in crore)	Management
Training hours per Worker	40	(in Hours)	Human Rights
Sales and Marketing Satisfaction Score	4.19	(Out of 5)	Product Responsibility

Figure 9. Shows the composite ESG and individual correlation of 'E', 'S', 'G' with Variables like ROE, ROCE, ROA and D/E ratio

Correlations

		ESG	E	S	G	ROE	ROCE	ROA	DEBT EQUITY RATIO
ESG	Pearson Correlation	1	.935	.978	.795	.056	.127	-.792	-.375
	Sig. (2-tailed)		.020	.004	.108	.928	.839	.110	.534
	N	5	5	5	5	5	5	5	5
E	Pearson Correlation	.935	1	.873	.547	.076	.264	-.539	-.597
	Sig. (2-tailed)	.020		.054	.340	.904	.668	.349	.287
	N	5	5	5	5	5	5	5	5
S	Pearson Correlation	.978	.873	1	.801	.099	.067	-.857	-.187
	Sig. (2-tailed)	.004	.054		.103	.874	.915	.064	.764
	N	5	5	5	5	5	5	5	5
G	Pearson Correlation	.795	.547	.801	1	-.063	-.118	-.927	-.042
	Sig. (2-tailed)	.108	.340	.103		.920	.850	.023	.946
	N	5	5	5	5	5	5	5	5
ROE	Pearson Correlation	.056	.076	.099	-.063	1	.877	-.222	-.135
	Sig. (2-tailed)	.928	.904	.874	.920		.051	.719	.828
	N	5	5	5	5	5	5	5	5
ROCE	Pearson Correlation	.127	.264	.067	-.118	.877	1	-.041	-.583
	Sig. (2-tailed)	.839	.668	.915	.850	.051		.948	.302
	N	5	5	5	5	5	5	5	5
ROA	Pearson Correlation	-.792	-.539	-.857	-.927	-.222	-.041	1	-.101
	Sig. (2-tailed)	.110	.349	.064	.023	.719	.948		.872
	N	5	5	5	5	5	5	5	5
DEBT EQUITY RATIO	Pearson Correlation	-.375	-.597	-.187	-.042	-.135	-.583	-.101	1
	Sig. (2-tailed)	.534	.287	.764	.946	.828	.302	.872	
	N	5	5	5	5	5	5	5	5

*. Correlation is significant at the 0.05 level (2-tailed).

**. Correlation is significant at the 0.01 level (2-tailed).

The above table demonstrate that ESG is highly negative correlated with the ROA, which signifies that when the total ESG score shows inverse relationship with the return on assets when the assets are utilized out of the business activity, obviously the assets will generate no returns over this. However, the "S" factor in the ESG shows the actual association with the ROE. As, there is increase in the social activities the equity returns will be increase because there will be more demand of the equity in the market also there are very renowned companies like TATA are into known for its social activities.

H0= There is not negative influence between the two variables
H1= There is significant negative influence between two variables

Figure 10. ESG influence over ROE

Coefficients[a]

Model		Unstandardized Coefficients		Standardized Coefficients	t	Sig.
		B	Std. Error	Beta		
1	(Constant)	42.751	14.036		3.046	.093
	ROE	-.434	.779	-.366	-.557	.634

a. Dependent Variable: ESG

The above table shows that the ESG here the P value is more than the 0.05 so it shows that the null hypothesis is retained over here which proves that when the company is having more returns on equity the ESG factor score will lead to increase and it rejects the negative influence between the two indicators.

Figure 11. ESG influence over ROCE

Coefficients[a]

Model		Unstandardized Coefficients		Standardized Coefficients	t	Sig.
		B	Std. Error	Beta		
1	(Constant)	41.880	10.358		4.043	.056
	ROCE	-.442	.637	-.441	-.695	.559

a. Dependent Variable: ESG

The above table shows that the P value is almost equal which retains the alternative hypothesis for this type of return showing that there is negatively affecting return between the two variables as more activities of ESG will lead to lesser return for capital employed as more funds are employed over outside the company which can depict the negative influence over the generation of capital returns.

Figure 12. ESG influence over D/E

Coefficients[a]

Model		Unstandardized Coefficients		Standardized Coefficients	t	Sig.
		B	Std. Error	Beta		
1	(Constant)	83.425	92.563		.901	.463
	DEBT EQUITY RATIO	-36.012	69.252	-.345	-.520	.655

a. Dependent Variable: ESG

The above table calculation shows the P value >0.05 here the null hypothesis is retained by stating the calculation that there is not negative influence as if the ESG scores increases/decreases the D/E will also increases/decreases as to move forward for any kind of CSR activities, product responsibility, management, controlling of emissions, a firm requires more funding to have control over these this can be only generated through outside activities.

Figure 13. D/E as well as ESG impact on financial performance (ROCE)

Model Summary

Model	R	R Square	Adjusted R Square	Std. Error of the Estimate
1	.165[a]	.027	.009	4.57759

a. Predictors: (Constant), DEBT EQUITY RATIO

ANOVA[a]

Model		Sum of Squares	df	Mean Square	F	Sig.
1	Regression	32.183	1	32.183	1.536	.220[b]
	Residual	1152.490	55	20.954		
	Total	1184.673	56			

a. Dependent Variable: ROCE

b. Predictors: (Constant), DEBT EQUITY RATIO

Figure 14. D/E as well as ESG impact on financial performance (ROA)

Model Summary

Model	R	R Square	Adjusted R Square	Std. Error of the Estimate
1	.252[a]	.063	.046	1.86981

a. Predictors: (Constant), DEBT EQUITY RATIO

ANOVA[a]

Model		Sum of Squares	df	Mean Square	F	Sig.
1	Regression	13.013	1	13.013	3.722	.059[b]
	Residual	192.291	55	3.496		
	Total	205.304	56			

a. Dependent Variable: ROA

b. Predictors: (Constant), DEBT EQUITY RATIO

As per the computation and analysis done as above, it can be determined that the debt-to-equity ratio of above said companies shows no such significant impact as the hypothesis null are retained over here with a more significance value. Moreover, the R square of return on the capital employed & return over assets shows up to 2.7% to 6.3% that average comes out to be very less in number and even amounted to be worth. The significance value of above author's calculation proven to be worth as here the alternative hypothesis are rejected. Also, the selected sample firms that have received greater equity financing will not have a substantial influence on ROA. It backs Modigliani and Miller's (1958) irrelevance hypothesis. Finally, debt to equity has a considerable negative influence on ROA, but long - term debt and total equity ratio have no substantial effect on ROA. According to descriptive data, the influence of capital structure on return on equity (ROE) is greater in sample firms that use equity funding, with an average equity ratio of 0.836. Additionally, the regression results suggest that total equity ratio has a negative but minor influence on ROA. The selected sample firms that have received greater equity financing will not have a substantial influence on ROA. It backs Modigliani and Miller's (1958) irrelevance hypothesis. In summary, debt equity ratio has a big negative influence on ROE, total debt ratio has a significant positive impact on ROE, and total equity has a negligible impact on ROE.

Further moving towards, ESG part of the respective paper, which shows no such significant impact over the financial sustainability of the companies under nifty 50. However, the companies are influenced negatively or positively somewhat but did not showed as much prominent impact to be proven as the main factor responsible for financial sustainability of the listed proven companies.

LIMITATIONS OF STUDY

To analyse the impact of gearing on financial performance of the companies after financial crisis of 2009 and to reduce the lag as well as to attain the normalcy, data has been collected from the year 2011 to the year 2021, for precise interpretation and analysis. The study belongs to 2011 to (Quarter1, 2021 as the pandemic has started from 2019-2020 and external events will be having an impact on the fundamentals, analyst interpretation and market timing. A separate study can be conducted for the said period to understand the impact of external exigencies and fundamentals on stock returns. Moreover, ESG factors are mainly composed and compared with the debt equity. Conversely, factors other than ESG can be taken for the measuring the influence with debt equity.

REFERENCES

Afanny, A., Ginting, R. R., Tarigan, A. E. B., & Hutagalung, G. (2022). The The Effect of Current Ratio and Debt to Equity Ratio on Company Value with Return on Asset as Intervening Variable in Food and Beverage Companies Listed on the Indonesia Stock Exchange for Period 2017-2020. *International Journal of Social Science Research and Review*, *5*(10), 1–12. doi:10.47814/ijssrr.v5i10.559

Amanda, R. I. (2019). The Impact Of Cash Turnover, Receivable Turnover, Inventory Turnover, Current Ratio And Debt To Equity Ratio On Profitability. *Journal of Reseach in Management*, *2*(2). doi:10.32424/jorim.v2i2.66

Ananda, M., Gulo, F. D., Purba, M. N., & Ginting, W. A. (2023). Analysis of return on asset, net profit margin, debt to equity ratio, on stock prices of financial. *Journal of Research in Business, Economics, and Education*, *5*(3), 61–70. doi:10.55683/jrbee.v5i3.439

Bhandari, L. C. (1988). Debt/Equity ratio and expected common stock returns: Empirical evidence. *The Journal of Finance*, *43*(2), 507–528. doi:10.1111/j.1540-6261.1988.tb03952.x

Bharadwaj, A., Bharadwaj, S. G., & Konsynski, B. R. (1999). Information Technology Effects on Firm Performance as Measured by Tobin's q. *Management Science*, *45*(7), 1008–1024. doi:10.1287/mnsc.45.7.1008

Cheng, B., Ioannou, I., & Serafeim, G. (2013). Corporate social responsibility and access to finance. *Strategic Management Journal*, *35*(1), 1–23. doi:10.1002mj.2131

Kim, S., & Li, Z. (2021). Understanding the impact of ESG practices in corporate finance. *Sustainability (Basel)*, *13*(7), 3746. doi:10.3390u13073746

Lins, K. V., Servaes, H., & Tamayo, A. (2017). Social Capital, Trust, and Firm Performance: The Value of Corporate Social Responsibility during the Financial Crisis. *The Journal of Finance*, *72*(4), 1785–1824. doi:10.1111/jofi.12505

Lisdawati, L. (2023). The Effect of Financial Performance and Company Size on Stock Price with Dividend Policy as A Moderating Variable. Interna*tional Journal of Educational Administration, Management, and Leadership,* 57–64. doi:10.51629/ijeamal.v4i1.121

Lisdawati, L. (2023b). The Effect of Financial Performance and Company Size on Stock Price with Dividend Policy as A Moderating Variable. *International Journal of Educational Administration, Management, and Leadership*, 57–64. doi:10.51629/ijeamal.v4i1.121

Loughran, T., & Ritter, J. R. (1997). The operating performance of firms conducting seasoned equity offerings. *The Journal of Finance*, *52*(5), 1823–1850. doi:10.1111/j.1540-6261.1997.tb02743.x

Nukala, V. B., & Rao, S. S. P. (2021). Role of debt-to-equity ratio in project investment valuation, assessing risk and return in capital markets. *Future Business Journal*, *7*(1), 13. Advance online publication. doi:10.118643093-021-00058-9

Said, H. B. (2013). Impact of ownership structure on debt equity Ratio: A static and a dynamic analytical framework. *International Business Research*, *6*(6). doi:10.5539/ibr.v6n6p162

Thakur-Wernz, P., Cantwell, J., & Samant, S. (2019). Impact of international entry choices on the nature and type of innovation: Evidence from emerging economy firms from the Indian bio-pharmaceutical industry. *International Business Review*, *28*(6), 101601. doi:10.1016/j.ibusrev.2019.101601

Vale, P. M., Gibbs, H. K., Vale, R., Christie, M., Florence, E., Munger, J., & Sabaini, D. (2019). The expansion of intensive beef farming to the Brazilian Amazon. *Global Environmental Change*, *57*, 101922. doi:10.1016/j.gloenvcha.2019.05.006

Chapter 11
AI (Artifical Intelligence):
Romance or Science Fiction?
The Origins and Trajectory

Fabian A. Salum
iD https://orcid.org/0000-0002-3871-0855
Fundação Dom Cabral, Brazil

Paulo Vicente Santos Alves
iD https://orcid.org/0000-0003-2418-1873
Fundação Dom Cabral, Brazil

Karina Garcia Coleta
Fundação Dom Cabral, Brazil

ABSTRACT

From where and when did the interest of humanity in the future arise? Initially, the answer is in the records of ideas and imagination of several futuristic writers who anticipated the transition the world is going on. Among the futuristic works, the book Brave New World by Aldous Huxley is a classic. Although Huxley wrote it more than 90 years ago, the book approaches questions and aspects of the future challenges of humanity. The hypothetical universe of Huxley makes comparisons with the "transformations" that the world has gone through for decades. Artificial pregnancy - "in vitro fertilization" - was a provocative and extraordinary work during that period, considering that the first test tube baby was born 40 years after it. That is the reason for the questioning: Romance or science fiction? Are we experiencing the prophecies made by Huxley and his precursors? What will be the limits and challenges with the advances of artificial intelligence (AI)? The intelligent use of AI is a way to create development opportunities.

DOI: 10.4018/978-1-6684-9814-9.ch011

THE TRAJECTORY

In the last decades, technological advances in computing have accelerated a lot due, mainly, to the increase in speed of processing. Technologies that were only very limited, or imagined, began to become possible. That is the case of AI, which just began to reach a new degree of usability and practicability.

Science fiction can imagine the world that will result from technological advances and their social and political impacts decades in advance. Issac Asimov (1920-1992) was one of the first to deal with the subject of artificial intelligence in his series of Robots.

George Orwell (1903-1950)[1] imagined a world in which technology would allow almost total control over the lives of individuals. Technology would become a dictatorship tool with cameras spread everywhere. Aldous Huxley (1894-1963)[2] went in a different direction and imagined a world in which access to pleasure and information would make society more easily controlled and absentminded by a dominant elite.

Artur C. Clark (1917-2008)[3] wrote about the possible use of artificial satellites[4] (Clark, 1945), breaking the frontier between science and fiction. In a more distant future, he imagined space elevators, modern cities spread throughout the galaxy, and flying cars.

Their visions converge to our present world, full of electronic equipment at the service of humans, and screens spread everywhere. Technology is part of the daily life of the XXIst Century. Dreamed of in the past, AI materializes in the present as increasingly user-friendly tools.

In the imagination, in science fiction films, AI has to take a form to help the viewer visualize them as a plot character. This formed in the popular imagination an idea of what artificial intelligence and its effects could be. Many became blockbusters in theaters. They are stuffed with robotic figures, humanoid or not, that steal the attention of the spectators. They often appear as villains, such as HAL 9000[5] and VIKI[6], but also as beings fighting for their identity, such as Ava[7], Data[8], and Andrew[9]. But Star Wars androids are possibly the best-known scene. Who doesn't like the adorable duo R2-D2 and C-3PO, from the Star Wars saga?!

Figure 1. C-3PO and R2-D2, characters that enchanted the Star Wars saga

Although we do not find robots strolling in the streets, AI is part of our daily lives. Just with a cell phone we can connect to every part of the world, order a particular car, watch films, order meals, monitor vital activities in real-time, read books (e-books), and many other things not previously imagined.

Due to the COVID-19 pandemic, in 2020, several technologies became protagonists in people's daily lives. Video conferencing apps such as Zoom, Skype, and Google Meet, distance education platforms, which were already present in our lives, have gained more space, as well as team and class management tools such as Microsoft Teams.

With social isolation, our homes have become offices. The home office has become a common expression and a benefit of the companies' HRs to employees. In addition, the space of physical learning has become a new channel of teaching as well as the EAD mode (distance learning), which is here to stay!

In this context, we can not fail to mention that, mainly to professionals of technology companies and startup entrepreneurs, it meant the agile promotion of solutions and the development of new functional tools that could meet society's new needs.

Now, in 2023, we have a new *buzzword – Artificial Intelligence* – AI.

And how will it materialize in the actual and practical organizational context?

To the computing scientist John McCarty (1927-2011)[10], AI is the Science and the engineering to make smart machines and computers capable of tasks, understanding human intelligence but not limited to purely biological aspects (McCarty, 2007).

To Professor McCarty, AI are computer program capable of executing human tasks through the development of proper programming and engineering.

With the evolution of technology, a new area within AI has drawn the attention of researchers and developers from around the world: *Machine Learning*. If AI is a wide field that encompasses systems and machines that mimic human intelligence, *Machine Learning* comprises the AI field, which focuses on the construction of systems that learn or improve performance through the data that they consume. Compreende o campo da AI que foca a construção de sistemas que aprendem ou melhoram o desempenho, através dos dados que consomem (Oracle, 2023).

AI is the mechanism responsible for the algorithms of social networks, behind online shopping sites, banking applications, and internet search sites. Therefore, we are surrounded by systems that use this technology.

An increasingly frequent example in our daily lives is access ordinances in commercial buildings and smart homes and offices. In these places we are invited to interact with electronic devices of facial recognition, biometrics, and lighting control interconnected, connected by an app on the mobile or by voice command, through, for example, Alexa[11] and Apple Home[12]. They are all equipped with programs developed by machine learning concepts.

However, since the 2000s, the use of AI and Machine Learning has been limited due to not so user-friendly tools. It was necessary to learn to program in computer languages such as R. Python and Arduino. Thus, the use of these tools was hidden within applications, proprietary software, and devices used in everyday life. Only now, we are witnessing more open and user-friendly tools that can be more broadly integrated.

In a way, this is equivalent to what happened about 40 years ago, when the first computer applications to make spreadsheets (Lotus 1, 2, and 3), text editors (Carta Certa, Wordstar, and Chi-Writer), databases (Clipper) and presentations (Harvard Graphics) appeared. Though outdated nowadays, they were a leap forward in usability compared to the hardships of programming in languages such as BASIC, FORTRAN, and COBOL.

This **reduces the time of training and use** of AI and machine learning for the average user, allowing such technologies to be accessible to more people and in a more integrated way. The new AI tools of strategic use allow us to offer answers much faster and more effectively. Directly, very coherent answers are obtained to questions or demands that we address to AI. However, if we compare the time spent to perform exploratory navigation on sites and social networks consulted to find an answer to the same demanded theme, it certainly consumes more time.

However, not everything is a competitive advantage when it involves AI, at least until now. After all, everything evolves very quickly in this field of research. One of the recurring problems of these systems can be proven when we ask the mechanisms for probabilistic analysis.

Probabilistic or logical reasoning analysis excludes other potential sources of information or response support from the AI tools' radar. That ends up creating informational bubbles limited to biases. A practical example is fake news, widespread in social media environments and spreads six times faster than truth, informed information of collective interest (Luísa, 2019).

It is up to the query agents to know how to ask the question concisely and then filter the information of the answers. In this way, move forward and make decisions consistent with the interpretive reality of the facts.

Another example is the result of some tests we did in our environment. It is important to emphasize that, as we work in a business school and as teachers of the Fundação Dom Cabral, the tests carried out took into account the use of simple and other more complex questions. We ran tests that included part of the answer within the question. This materializes when we practice interpretive analysis or when we analyze an enigma. Only the human brain can look for correlations in riddles placed in question formats as - used by the human being.

ChatGTP / Plus: The great AI Frenzy in the World

In November 2022, OpenAI (the research and development company in artificial intelligence) made available free public access to the impressive new program Generative Pre-Trained Transformer 3, or GPT-3, also called ChatGPT. It attracted huge attention from the media and university students around the world. The tool based on artificial intelligence enables the writing of text sequences and dialogues with an impressive similarity to human writing. It offers coherent answers in sequences of sentences based on the most diverse topics.

In the process of certifying the authenticity of articles and publications, OpenAI launched on January 31, 2023 "the classifier", whose function is to analyze and identify the differences between texts produced by humans or by AI. This product is not yet fully reliable, but it is an answer to the questions of educators in business schools and universities about the impacts of texts generated by artificial intelligence in classrooms.

On February 10, 2023, the company announced the **"Plus" version of ChatGPT** in Brazil. OpenAI provided the subscription version. The service has been available in the USA since the beginning of February and is offered in that country at US$20, about R$105 per month at the current exchange rate. Besides Brazil, the European Union and the UK also received the paid version (the premium version of the chatbot).

The advantage of the paid service is that you have priority access to ChatGPT. That ensures faster responses and preferential access to new features and software improvements. In recent weeks, free users have often found the service unavailable because it reached its capacity limit (at capacity) due to its success.

In the ChatGPT layout, we have a small and straightforward framework guiding the user to lead their questions to the platform to maximize their answers.

Figure 2. ChatGPT layout developed by OpenAI

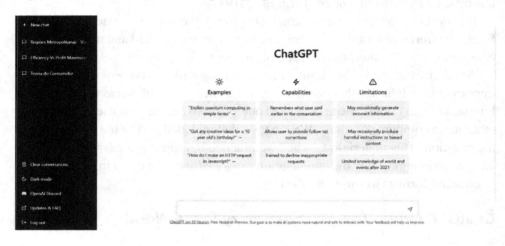

When entering a query term or phrase in ChatGPT, it will search for information available on the web, at ultra-speed. If a statistical, mathematical, or programming logic question is presented, it will make assimilations and calculate based on the information provided in the questions. See the following example, Figure 3:

Figure 3. Interpretive and non-consultation testing using ChatGPT on February 14, 2023

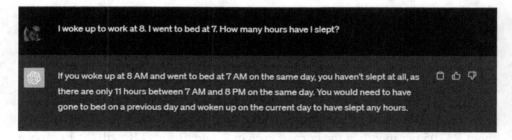

190

At another time, we consulted the meaning of the expression "Consumer Theory", and ChatGPT brought the following definition:

Consumer theory is a part of economics that studies how people make purchasing decisions, taking into account their income, preferences, and other factors. She considers that consumers seek to maximize their well-being, that is, the value they perceive in exchange for the money spent on goods and services. Consumer theory also considers that prices and income influence consumers' purchasing decisions. (OpenAI, 2023)

If we look into the texts and manuals of introduction to economics, this definition is correct. An interesting fact is that, in the body of the answer essay, there is no citation of the main sources of information present in the quick search on Google, such as Wikipedia (2023) or Brasil Escola (2023).

After a week, we searched again the same term: "Consumer Theory" (OpenAI, 2023). The answer presented, despite having similarities with the previous week, was a text with different wording (see Figure 4). Next, we clicked on the option Regenerate Response (Redo the answer), a command that generates a new text with the same question or term. Again, a new answer was presented. (Figure 5).

Figure 4 . ChatGPT's second answer to consumer theory on February 10, 2023

CHATGPT

The theory of consumer is an economic concept that examines how individuals make choices regarding the allocation of their resources to maximize their utility or satisfaction. It analyzes factors like preferences, budget constraints, and consumer behavior to understand how people decide what to buy and in what quantities.

Figure 5. ChatGPT's first answer to consumer theory on February 10, 2023

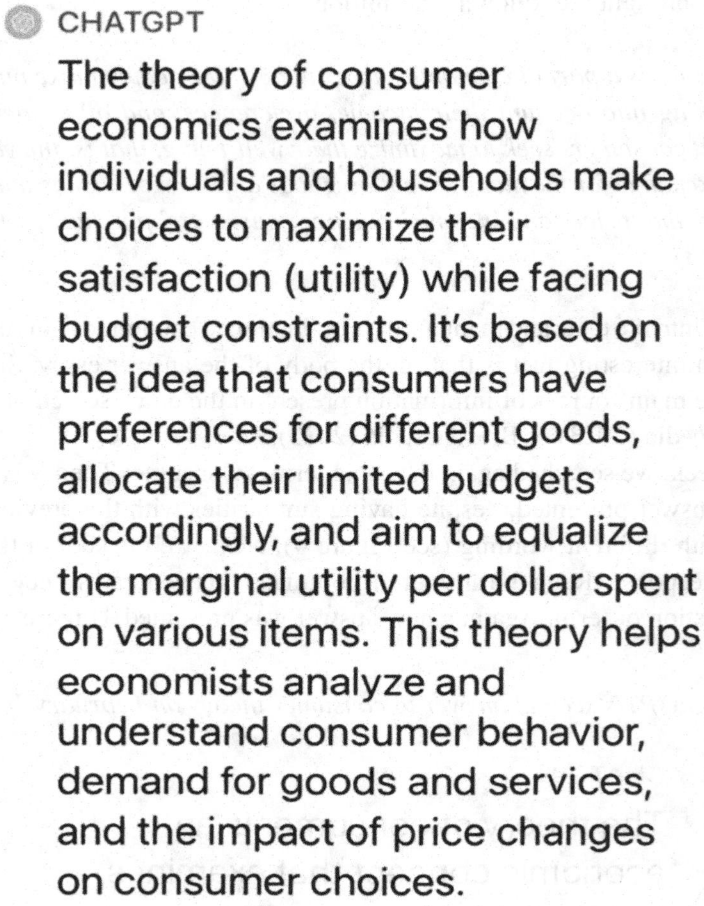

CHATGPT

The theory of consumer economics examines how individuals and households make choices to maximize their satisfaction (utility) while facing budget constraints. It's based on the idea that consumers have preferences for different goods, allocate their limited budgets accordingly, and aim to equalize the marginal utility per dollar spent on various items. This theory helps economists analyze and understand consumer behavior, demand for goods and services, and the impact of price changes on consumer choices.

Another interesting aspect of ChatGPT is the possibility of asking him to write a certain text in a specific style, such as in the form of a poem or as a formal text like sales text, or even as a child with limited vocabulary.

Among the analyses and reflections present in this article, we cannot fail to highlight the delivery potential of this AI tool. However, there are potential impacts on the ability to develop logical reasoning, given that for any situation of consultation, research, or even curiosity, just click on ChatGPT and ask what you want to know.

Something similar we have experienced for some time. It is worth remembering the unprecedented experience of using search engines like Google and Yahoo, among others. They have become known in the same process of popularization and internet access worldwide. The difference is that Google provides several links to sites that may or may not present the information you want. You have the prerogative of query and choice in organic query results and/or sponsored links. However, ChatGPT will provide a unique and well-cohesive answer, as if it were written by a human. That is, "it answers everything!".

However, it is important to note that the systems that became popular at the beginning of the year, like all AI and Machine Learning technology, are not infallible. On the contrary, it also makes crass errors, considering that a search for verification in the web environment can bring disqualified sources or even lies. A BBC News (2023) report points to a survey conducted on the platform with the question: "When did Brazil win an Oscar?". The tool answered that Brazil won on three occasions, which is incorrect information. After all, Brazil never won an Oscar, despite having been nominated on several occasions. It serves as one of the examples that we can associate with this need for the continuous evolution of the software, which does not deteriorate or denigrate its innovative capacity.

How Can AI Impact the Business Environment?

New digital technologies directly impact people's lives, whether in personal, academic, health, or business affairs. Today companies are highly influenced by technological solutions, using various tools, apps, and programs to manage their business, in the most diverse scopes.

A constant question we face:

- Is it possible for AI to replace human leaders, managers, and executives in organizations?

The answer is: No! Executives and leaders within organizations must continue their journey of evolution and promote interpretative and decision-making capacity based on the evaluation of processes and decision-making. In this regard, only the human mind can analytically raise a series of scenarios, probabilities, correlations, trends, and local empirical aspects. For the more advanced equipment, both AI and Machine Learning, it is impossible (so far) to develop the ability to make decisions, as humans do by measuring their potential consequences, impacts, and derived effects, especially in assignments assigned to leaders in sport, politics, business management, medical prescription, etc. Our lives are guided by choices and consequences.

Amid so much technological immersion in organizations, more and more processes are managed with software and interconnected solutions. This reality demands managers and executives, as well as the body of employees, to know the potential of the tools and their applications, besides being aware of the innovations developed and launched at all times.

Kara McWilliams, head of the ETS company[14], which supports all students and educators by developing research-based and AI-based solutions that enable personalized learning paths, states that these new tools will not replace people, on the contrary, will select the professionals of the future, as the fittest, those who best use the tools of artificial intelligence. " I believe that AI will not replace people, but people who use AI will replace people" (Jack, 2023), McWilliams says. However, the researcher points out that ChatGPT can help teachers in their routine activities, such as creating presentations, developing notes for lectures, and planning classes.

Artificial intelligence, when well analyzed, developed, and targeted, can accelerate the process of discoveries and new possibilities. The speed that AI has to process information and make probabilistic analyses is a relevant tool that will help executives in decision-making with some accuracy and agility.

Amid the meteoric success of ChatGPT, Microsoft announced a $10 billion investment in the OpenAI company, creator of the tool (O Globo, 2023). It is not the first time the billionaire Bill Gates' company has funded OpenAI. In 2019, Microsoft had already invested 1 billion dollars in the company. In 2021, the company repeated the feat in search of internal advantages of its products compared to its competitors, such as Google (Alphabet), Amazon, and Meta. The company also ended its investment in the Metaverso project in the same week, a promise that has not become popular.

Considered one of Today's technology giants, Google announced on February 6, 2023, the creation of a chatbot (Bard) to compete directly with the OpenAI ChatGPT (G1, 2023). The new tool from Google will use the *Language Model for Dialogue Applications* (Lamda), a sophisticated system for creating dialogs based on Machine Learning, superior to other artificial intelligence such as Alexa, Google Assistant, and Siri.

Optimistic or not, Artificial Intelligence tools have gained more and more space in our society, as well as in academic environments and even in the art world (DW Brasil, 2023). Our task is to know these tools and their potential, having on the horizon several skills that only the human brain can perform.

Will Leapfrogging be Able to Accelerate AI in Organizations?

Leapfrogging is a term used in economics in the study of growth theories. Also known as technology leapfrogging, this phenomenon is characterized by the application of more current technological practices without necessarily going through previous stages.

While developing countries represent more fertile ground for leapfrogging, incremental changes are rapidly absorbed by countries and companies with established experience.

Leapfrogging does not have a standard, step-by-step model or framework but the ability to connect four major disciplines: **management, entrepreneurship, innovation, and technology. Technology is the means** that allows companies, startups, or projects within organizations to reach and overcome barriers, deficiencies, and obstacles, transforming them into opportunities.

Fintechs such as Nubank (Brazil) and M-Pesa (Africa) offer a mobile financial service that allows users to transfer and borrow a loan, buy credit, and pay mobile bills. EVC Plus (Somalia) differentiates itself from M-Pesa by using US dollars as currency in the platform's operations. The opportunities detected connect to the needs of users and ecosystems with the technologies that drive solutions (Leapfrogging). These leaps resulted from the provision of free-of-charge banking services to products that are also offered by other banks (Nubank), migration of the population to the city from a limited banking system (M-Pesa); civil war and terrorism; and political and economic instability (EVC Plus).

Mapping other segments, we chose the area of Health. The AutoBed platform by GE(NY) reduced to up to four hours the waiting time of patients in the emergency rooms of the hospital, monitoring beds (sensors in the beds). Using IoT, the hospital nursing staff knows when a bed is released and where it is. Another example is Happiest Baby's (CA) SNOO cradle, one of the most differentiated IoT examples. The featured belly swing helps a safe sleep for the baby, while the crying sensor with an automatic adjustment of sound and movement prevents it from rolling. That improves the sleep quality of the parents.

And How Can Artificial Intelligence (AI) Accelerate This Leap?

The large gaps in infrastructure, technology, and incentive policies for innovation and entrepreneurship demand disruptive solutions to leverage value and contribute to economic and social progress.

AI has the potential to transform how industries operate, making them more efficient and productive so that the leap gains even more speed and agility.

At the same time that AI accelerates processes, it requires qualified human capital, with technical knowledge and critical analysis capacity, to promote the acceleration of the leap. That is the big leap, as the value proposition is to use minimal effort to achieve the maximum, saving time for more relevant activities.

In this sense, it is worth highlighting a competitive advantage for companies that aim to accelerate the execution of their processes. However, they should be able to choose the appropriate tools, work on the organization's culture, prepare leadership, and select skills to add value to the business and generate sustainable results. In addition, the absence of any ethical and/or regulatory guidelines deliberated by the top management may weaken the integration of technologies into processes. In the short term, that represents a risk of legitimacy in the use of AI which can set precedents and harm society.

Therefore, one of the challenges that companies have faced is the preparation of leaders to promote Leapfrogging through management and the intelligent use of new AI tools (Salum; Coleta, 2023).

The Future of Work and the Technological Revolution

The recent advances in robotization and artificial intelligence have raised eyebrows concerning a creative disruption wave in the job market. But, the evidence and the theory point out that we are entering a new wave of technological development as the fifth Kondratieff cycle ends and the forecasted sixth cycle begins.

To understand the future of work and its relationship with Human Resources and the role of education as a preparation for work life, we must beforehand try to forecast all those impacts separately on the categories that will allow you to form a general view of our research.

Kondratieff Cycles is an excellent historiographic model for understanding what we live in the 2020s. It was devised nearly one hundred years ago by a Russian mathematician who realized that there were technological and economic cycles every 50-60 years (Alves, 2018; Freeman & Perez, 1988; Kondratieff, 1935). All those cycles ended in a crisis, forcing capitalism to reinvent itself through technological development.

Table 1. Below shows the author's interpretation of those cycles: Kondratieff cycles

Cycle	Period	Description
1st Cycle	1770-1820	Initial mechanization
2nd Cycle	1820-1870	Steam, telegraph, and railroads
3rd Cycle	1870-1930	Electricity, internal combustion, and heavy engineering
4th Cycle	1930-1980	Mass production, Fordism, nuclear power, and television
5th Cycle	1980-2030	Telecommunications and Informatics
6th Cycle	2030-2080?	?

Source: Elaborated by the authors.

The current cycle is also ending a crisis with the pandemic (2020-22), the war in Ukraine, the USA-China decoupling, and climate change. That again forces capitalism to find solutions through technology, and a new set of technologies is coming.

Significant is the fact that the USA is trying to bring back manufacturing to its territory or geographically close allies. To do this "reshoring" and "nearshoring", the technologies developed have five objectives, shown in Table 2.

Table 2. Objectives of the five technological revolution

Number	Objective	Technological axis
1	Reduce the need for an unskilled labor force	Robotization
2	Create new jobs through creative destruction	Robotization and Digital transformation
3	Increase longevity of skilled workforce	Human enhancement
4	Allow for greater dispersion of workforce	Digital transformation
5	Find new resource pools	New Energy Sources and Space Economy

Source: Elabored by the authors.

Those five objectives indicate at least six axes of technological development, and they will affect how we work and live.

What we see nowadays is just the beginning of the process of change. The apex will be in the 2040s, according to the Kondratieff model. We will present our analyze of the changes in the work environment. It will summarize those effects along three lines of reasoning: extreme robotization, new business models, and future competencies.

Extreme Robotization

Advanced Robots and artificial intelligence are a new wave in a long history of automatization that goes back to the first industrial revolution or even before, depending on how one considers this evolution. They will substitute repetitive, dangerous, and low-intellectual capital jobs. However, they will generate new jobs in robotics knowledge, programming, design, and fine mechanics. These jobs will be more sophisticated in intellectual capital, forcing an increase in educational level in general.

Some developments point to houses and small buildings built by robots, or even 3D printed, in a few years. Artificial intelligence will substitute drivers in taxis, buses, and trucks in areas where the logistic infrastructure is good enough for them, with smooth roads and good geolocation. Robots will also replace services and factory workers. Artificial intelligence will replace several repetitive intellectual jobs.

So, the demand for human labor will only decrease in those jobs that robots cannot do better than human beings. According to our perception, three types of jobs can be reduced: dealing with other humans, solving problems, and creating (or creativity). And even in those areas, the robot will penetrate only to some extent.

That will generate more jobs than destroy it due to the "creative destruction". Schumpeter (1962) created this concept, which may be more intuitive. When there is a technological improvement in a product or service production, it reduces the number of workers needed. However, production cost decreases even further because other expenses, like energy, materials, water, and workspace, are also reduced. Therefore, that means more people can afford the same product or service, and the demand increases proportionally more than the loss of jobs. That creates a net increase in employment, but only if demand elasticity means a lower price will increase demand.

Also, in each technological revolution, new markets are created from scratch. That happens when an enabling technology allows for entirely new products. Good past examples are electricity, oil, and electronics. For example, the household white-line appliances did not destroy an old market but created entirely new ones.

The problem will not be a lack of jobs but the skill to use those machines. Much like in previous revolutions, it takes 20-30 years to create a critical mass of workers apt to deal with those technologies, and, again, that is compatible with the Kondratieff cycles model. We will see a bottleneck of skill during the 2020s and 2030s, which will be solved in the 2040s, allowing for more remarkable economic growth.

New Business Models

Gradual changes and traditional business (business as usual) aren't enough to adapt to those changes brought by this technological revolution. We are going through a period of several crises, but also of a new technological revolution. Existing companies must create new business models to survive and grow in this new environment.

Some actions can be suggested based on recent evidence of adaptation during and after the pandemic.

- The organization must develop appropriate mobility policies, standards, and travel protocols, revisit travel policies, and face-to-face meetings. Cost reduction must be balanced with efficacy.
- There's a need to offer medical and psychological support to employees who have been isolated for months and will now work remotely or in hybrid mode.

- Leaders should be predisposed to understand the needs and demands of the employees concerning the challenges and learning of the new post-pandemic reality and work modalities.
- A recovery and business continuity plan applicable to different scenarios and moments should be created since new crises will inevitably occur.
- The organization must develop a new long-range strategic plan focused on adapting the operations to the new post-pandemic environment considering the latest emerging technologies.
- Risk management must be prioritized by organizations again.

According to a WEF (2023) survey, the key driver to business transformation is technology adaption. That supports the hypothesis that this technology revolution is the way to evolve from the current crisis into a new Kondratieff cycle. Technology will not only alter the operating procedures but create new business models.

Another important aspect is that organizations must build resilience into their business models (Salum, Coleta & Tadeu, 2021). The final phase of the Fifth Kondratieff cycle will bring new challenges, some of which can be perceived and forecasted, like a new pandemic, the continuation of the war in Ukraine, and the USA-China growing competition, but others can't be predicted. Building resilience is the only way to prepare for those future problems.

Finally, entirely new industries will appear, potentially new business models with them or adaptations of old proven ones. That isn't limited to digital transformation but also new logistics, new manufacturing, a new health system, new educational systems, a space-based economy, and new energy and raw material sources.

New Competencies of the Future

It's now possible to make a tentative list of future competencies. The table 3 shows our perception of which will be those and organized those competencies according to each of the four trends discussed, plus another group for "decision" in which the decision cycle of analysis, decision, and implementation is included. This final group applies mainly (but not exclusively) to managers, directors, board members, and shareholders.

The list isn't exhaustive but tries to capture the most relevant competencies in each of the five groups.

Table 3. The critical competencies of the future

Decision Cycle		
Analyze in complexity	Decide under uncertainty and risk	Implement under scarcity

Robotization	Longevity	Dispersion	Business Models
Dealing with people	Self-taught	Dealing with different cultures	Experimental
Problem Solving	Emotional control	Teamwork	Systems thinking
Creatitivity	Self Determination	Argumentative Logic	Persuasive

Source: Source: Elabored by the authors.

This list isn't definitive, as there are several unknowns in the future, but it's an initial proposition for debate.

The decision cycle will be improved by the technological revolution in itself due to a better gathering of data, processing this data into information, and supporting decisions with this information.

However, the excess of information will lead to the competence being capable of analyzing in this complex environment, and therefore sensemaking of all this information become critical.

Decisions will never be with zero risk, as this will lead to "analysis paralysis." Decision-makers must tolerate a certain level of risk and be capable of managing this risk. This is a journey of understanding oneself and its organization.

Finally, any decision must be implemented in time, money, political power, and human resources scarcity. Most "ideal decisions" won't be realistic, and understanding what is achievable is critical.

A final provocation is for the reader to ask him or herself in which of those competencies you are best, in which you are worse, and which is the more important for your current task. There's obviously no" correct" answer, it's just a provocation, and the answers will vary from person to person and from job to job.

REFERENCES

G1. (2023). *ChatGPT ganha rival criado pelo Google, o Bard.* G1. https://g1.globo.com/tecnologia/noticia/2023/02/06/google-anuncia-bard-robo-conversador-rival-do-chatgpt.ghtml

Alves, P. V. S. (2018). *Um século em quatro atos.* Alta Books.

BBC News. (2023). *O que é ChatGPT e por que alguns o veem como ameaça.* BBC News. https://www.bbc.com/portuguese/geral-64297796

Brasil D. W. (2023) *Will we be replaced by robots?* [Vídeo]. Youtube. https://www.youtube.com/watch?v=A7kCeat4LF4

Clarke, A. C. (1945). Extra-Terrestrial Relays – Can Rocket Stations Give World-wide Radio Coverage? *Wireless World.*, *51*(10), 305–308.

Escola, B. (2023). *Microeconomia.* Brasil Escola. https://brasilescola.uol.com.br/economia/microeconomia.htm

Freeman, C., & Perez, C. (1988). Structural crises of adjustment, business cycles and investment behavior. In G. Dosi (ed.) Technical Change and Economic Theory. Pinter publisher's limited.

Globo. (2023). *Microsoft anuncia investimento de 10 bilhões na criadora do ChatGPT.* Bloomberg. https://oglobo.globo.com/economia/tecnologia/noticia/2023/01/microsoft-anuncia-investimento-de-us-10-bilhoes-na-criadora-do-chatgpt.ghtml

Jack, A. (2023). AI chatbot's MBA exam pass poses test for business schools. *Financial Times.* https://www.ft.com/content/7229ba86-142a-49f6-9821-f55c07536b7c

Kondratieff, N. D., & Stolper, W. F. (1935, November). The Long waves in Economic Life. *The Review of Economics and Statistics*, *XVII*(6), 105–115. doi:10.2307/1928486

Luísa, I. (2019). *No Twitter, fake news se espalham 6 vezes mais rápido que notícias verdadeiras.* Super Interessante. https://super.abril.com.br/tecnologia/no-twitter-fake-news-se-espalham-6-vezes-mais-rapido-que-noticias-verdadeiras/

McCarthy, J. (2007). *What is artificial intelligence?* Computer Science Department Stanford University. https://www-formal.stanford.edu/jmc/whatisai.pdf

Open A. I. (2023). *ChatGPT (Jan 30 version)* [Large language model]. https://chat.openai.com/

Oracle. (2023). *What is machine learning.* Oracle. https://www.oracle.com/br/artificial-intelligence/machine-learning/what-is-machine-learning/

Salum, F., & Coleta, K. (2023). *Leapfrogging será capaz de acelerar a IA nas organizações?* São Paulo: MITSloan Management Review Brasil. https://mitsloanreview.com.br/post/leapfrogging-sera-capaz-de-acelerar-a-ia-nas-organizacoes

Salum, F.; Coleta, K.; Tadeu, H. (2021). *Business Resilience: Essential competence Lessons for 2021.* São Paulo: FDC and Grant Thornton.

Schumpeter, J. A. (1962). *Capitalism, Socialism, and Democracy.* Harper & Row.

WEF. (2023). The future of jobs Report 2023. *Insight Report.* WEF. https://www.weforum.org/reports/the-future-of-jobs-report-2023/

Wikipedia. (2023). *Teoria do consumidor.* Wikipedia. https://pt.wikipedia.org/wiki/Teoria_do_consumidor

ENDNOTES

[1] British writer and essayist, author of several works, among them, 1984 (1949) a dystopian novel.

[2] British writer, author of several novels, among them - Brave New World (1932).

[3] British science fiction writer, author of works such as The City and the Stars (1956), A Space Odyssey (1968), and the tale The Sentinel (1951), which gave rise to the award-winning in the Rama Encounter film 2001: A Space Odyssey.

[4] Clarke, Arthur C. (October 1945). *"Extra-Terrestrial Relays – Can Rocket Stations Give World-wide Radio Coverage?". Wireless World. Vol. 51, n. 10. pp. 305–308.*

[5] *2001: A Space Odyssey* (1968).

[6] *The Robot* (2004).

[7] *Ex-Machina* (2015).

[8] *Star Trek: The Next Generation* (1987-1994).

[9] *Bicentennial Man.*

[10] Researcher and Professor of the Coputing Science Departament of the Stanford University.

[11] Electronic equipment that plays the role of virtual assistant, ALEXA, developed by Amazon. (Explanatory note of the authors).

[12] Electronic equipment that plays the role of virtual assistant, SIRI, developed by Apple. (Explanatory note of the authors).

Compilation of References

Abbink, D. A. (2022). Artificial Intelligence for Automated Vehicle Control and Traffic Operations: Challenges and Opportunities. In G. Meyer & S. Beiker (Eds.), *Road Vehicle Automation 8. AVS 2020 2020. Lecture Notes in Mobility.* Springer. doi:10.1007/978-3-030-80063-5_6

Adelman-Mullally, T., Nielsen, S., & Chung, S. Y. (2023). Planned change in modern hierarchical organizations: A three-step model. *Journal of Professional Nursing, 46,* 1–6. doi:10.1016/j.profnurs.2023.02.002 PMID:37188397

Afanny, A., Ginting, R. R., Tarigan, A. E. B., & Hutagalung, G. (2022). The The Effect of Current Ratio and Debt to Equity Ratio on Company Value with Return on Asset as Intervening Variable in Food and Beverage Companies Listed on the Indonesia Stock Exchange for Period 2017-2020. *International Journal of Social Science Research and Review, 5*(10), 1–12. doi:10.47814/ijssrr.v5i10.559

Agencia Brasil. (2023). Papa Francisco alerta para potenciais perigos da inteligência artificial. Agencia Brasil. https://agenciabrasil.ebc.com.br/internacional/noticia/2023-08/papa-alerta-contra-potenciais-perigos-da-inteligencia-artificial, accessed on August, 2023.

Alcaraz, C., Najera, P., & Roman, R. (2016). AI for industrial control systems security: A survey. *Computers & Security, 56,* 1–12. doi:10.1016/j.cose.2015.10.010

Alhaderi, S. M. (2021). Kotter's Eight Step Change Model for Employees' Intentional, Cognitive and Emotional Readiness for Change and Developing Regional Economy in Saudi Banking Sector's, Role of Homologous Communication, Learning Demand and Job Involvement. *J. Legal Ethical & Regul. Isses, 24,* 1.

Allegretti, S., Seidenstricker, S., Fischer, H., & Arslan, S. (2021). Executing a business model change: Identifying key characteristics to succeed in volatile markets. Leadership, Education, Personality. *An Interdisciplinary Journal, 3,* 21–33.

Aloe, L. (2004). Rita Levi-Montalcini: The discovery of nerve growth factor and modern neurobiology. *Trends in Cell Biology, 14*(7), 395–399. doi:10.1016/j.tcb.2004.05.011 PMID:15246433

Alqudah, I. H., Carballo-Penela, A., & Ruzo-Sanmartín, E. (2022). High-performance human resource management practices and readiness for change: An integrative model including affective commitment, employees' performance, and the moderating role of hierarchy culture. *European Research on Management and Business Economics*, *28*(1), 100177. doi:10.1016/j. iedeen.2021.100177

Alturkistani, H. A., Tashkandi, F. M., & Mohammedsaleh, Z. M. (2016). Histological stains: A literature review and case study. *Global Journal of Health Science*, *8*(3), 72. doi:10.5539/gjhs. v8n3p72 PMID:26493433

Alvarez-Napagao, S. (2021). *knowlEdge Project – Concept, Methodology and Innovations for Artificial Intelligence in Industry 4.0*. In IEEE 19th International Conference on Industrial Informatics (INDIN), Palma de Mallorca, Spain.

Alves, P. V. S. (2018). *Um século em quatro atos*. Alta Books.

Amanda, R. I. (2019). The Impact Of Cash Turnover, Receivable Turnover, Inventory Turnover, Current Ratio And Debt To Equity Ratio On Profitability. *Journal of Reseach in Management*, *2*(2). doi:10.32424/jorim.v2i2.66

Ananda, M., Gulo, F. D., Purba, M. N., & Ginting, W. A. (2023). Analysis of return on asset, net profit margin, debt to equity ratio, on stock prices of financial. *Journal of Research in Business, Economics, and Education*, *5*(3), 61–70. doi:10.55683/jrbee.v5i3.439

Andrişan, G., & Modreanu, A. (2022). *Achieving Business Success in the Fourth Industrial Revolution: The Case of Procter & Gamble*. Procter & Gamble.

Angwin, J., Larson, J., Mattu, S., & Kirchner, L. (2016). *Machine Bias*. ProPublica. https://www. propublica.org/article/machine-bias-risk-assessments-in-criminal-sentencing

Antoniades, N., Constantinou, C., Allayioti, M., & Biska, A. (2022). Lasting political change performance: Knowledge, awareness, and reinforcement (KARe). *SN Business & Economics*, *2*(2), 14. doi:10.100743546-021-00196-w

Archana, U. (2016). *Causality relationship between interest rate and stock returns in India–An Analytical Study*. Sage.

Arefazar, Y., Nazari, A., Hafezi, M. R., & Maghool, S. A. H. (2022). Prioritizing agile project management strategies as a change management tool in construction projects. *International Journal of Construction Management*, *22*(4), 678–689. doi:10.1080/15623599.2019.1644757

Arjovsky, M., Chintala, S., & Bottou, L. (2017). *Wasserstein gan*. arXiv preprint arXiv:1701.07875.

Asai, E. (2014). The "Lotus Sutra" as the Core of Japanese Buddhism: Shifts in Representations of its Fundamental Principle. *Japanese Journal of Religious Studies*, *41*(1), 45–64. doi:10.18874/jjrs.41.1.2014.45-64

Aslan, L. (2021). The evolving competencies of the public auditor and the future of public sector auditing. In Contemporary Studies in Economic and Financial Analysis, 105, 113-129. doi:10.1108/S1569-375920200000105008

Awoleye, O., Okolie, S., Akinwunmi, A., Adebiyi, A., & Misra, S. (2020). A survey of artificial intelligence-based cybersecurity for industrial control systems. *Computers & Security*, *90*, 101708.

Azure Microsoft. (2023). *Machine Learning Algorithms*. Microsoft. https://azure.microsoft.com/en-us/resources/cloud-computing-dictionary/what-are-machine-learning-algorithms

Balasubramanian, N., Yang, Y. E., & Mingtao, X. U. (2022). Substituting Human Decision-Making with Machine Learning: Implications for Organizational Learning. *Academy of Management Review*, *47*(3), 448–465. doi:10.5465/amr.2019.0470

Balgobin, R., & Pandit, N. (2001). Stages in the turnaround process: The Case of IBM UK. *European Management Journal*, *19*(3), 301–316. doi:10.1016/S0263-2373(01)00027-5

Banerji, S., & Mitra, S. (2022). Deep learning in histopathology: A review. *Wiley Interdisciplinary Reviews. Data Mining and Knowledge Discovery*, *12*(1), e1439. doi:10.1002/widm.1439

Barsky, R., & DeLong, B. (1991). Forecasting pre-World War I inflation: The Fisher effect and the gold Standard. *The Quarterly Journal of Economics*, *CVI*(3), 3, 815–836. doi:10.2307/2937928

Baxi, V., Edwards, R., Montalto, M., & Saha, S. (2022). Digital pathology and artificial intelligence in translational medicine and clinical practice. *Modern Pathology*, *35*(1), 23–32. doi:10.103841379-021-00919-2 PMID:34611303

BBC News. (2023). *O que é ChatGPT e por que alguns o veem como ameaça*. BBC News. https://www.bbc.com/portuguese/geral-64297796

Beam, A. L., & Kohane, I. S. (2018). Big data and machine learning in health care. *Journal of the American Medical Association*, *319*(13), 1317–1318. doi:10.1001/jama.2017.18391 PMID:29532063

Beethoven X. A. I. Project (2023). *Beethoven 10th symphony hypothetical creation*. BeethovenX. https://www.beethovenx-ai.com/, accessed on January, 2023.

Bernanke, B., & Gertler, M. (1999). Monetary policy and asset price volatility. *Federal Reserve Bank of Kansas City Economic Review*, *84*, 17–50.

Bhandari, L. C. (1988). Debt/Equity ratio and expected common stock returns: Empirical evidence. *The Journal of Finance*, *43*(2), 507–528. doi:10.1111/j.1540-6261.1988.tb03952.x

Bharadwaj, A., Bharadwaj, S. G., & Konsynski, B. R. (1999). Information Technology Effects on Firm Performance as Measured by Tobin's q. *Management Science*, *45*(7), 1008–1024. doi:10.1287/mnsc.45.7.1008

Bhattacharyya, B. (1979). The concept of existence and Nagarjuna's Doctrine of Sunyata. *Journal of Indian Philosophy*, *7*(4), 335–344. doi:10.1007/BF02346781

Bickmore, T. W., Schulman, D., Sidner, C., & Sidner, C. L. (2010). A reusable framework for health counseling dialogue systems based on a behavioral medicine ontology. *Journal of Biomedical Informatics*, *43*(2), 183–197. doi:10.1016/j.jbi.2010.12.006 PMID:21220044

Blackburn-Grenon, F., Abran, A., Rioux, M., & Wong, T. (2021). A Team-Based Workshop to Capture Organizational Knowledge for Identifying AI Proof-of-Value Projects. *IEEE Engineering Management Review*, *49*(2), 181–195. doi:10.1109/EMR.2021.3063688

Blasco, J., Esteve, M., Gonzalez, J. J., & Rifà-Pous, H. (2018). Sentiment Analysis for Cybersecurity Threat Detection. *13th International Conference on Availability, Reliability and Security (ARES)*, (pp. 1-6). MIT.

Bleaney, M., & Fielding, D. (2002). Exchange rate regimes, inflation and output volatility in developing countries. *Journal of Development Economics*, *68*(1), 233–245. doi:10.1016/S0304-3878(02)00002-0

Bostrom, N. (2014). *Superintelligence: Paths, dangers, strategies*. Oxford University Press.

Branson, W. H. (1979). *Macroeconomic Theory and Policy*. Princeton University.

Brasil D. W. (2023) *Will we be replaced by robots?* [Vídeo]. Youtube. https://www.youtube.com/watch?v=A7kCeat4LF4

Brauckmann, S. (2012). Karl Ernst von Baer (1792-1876) and evolution. *The International Journal of Developmental Biology*, *56*(9), 653–660. doi:10.1387/ijdb.120018sb PMID:23319342

Bridges, W., & Mitchell, S. (2000). Leading transition: A new model for change. *Leader to Leader*, *16*(3), 30–36.

Broom, D. (2019). Sentience. In J. C. Chloe (Ed.), *Encyclopedia of Animal Behavior* (2nd ed., Vol. 1, pp. 131–133). Elsevier: Academic Press. doi:10.1016/B978-0-12-809633-8.90147-X

Brown, O. (2023 The Story of ChatGPT and OpenAI: The Evolution of GPT Models. *Medium*. https://medium.com/illumination/the-story-of-chatgpt-and-openai-the-evolution-of-gpt-models-abf201316a9.

Brown, S. (2021). What is machine learning. MIT Sloan Ideas to Matter, April 2021. Available at https://mitsloan.mit.edu/ideas-made-to-matter/machine-learning-explained, accessed on March, 2023.

Brown, B. (2010). Why innovation matters. *Research Technology Management*, *53*(6), 18–23. doi:10.1080/08956308.2010.11657658

Bryan, J., & Moriano, P. (2023). Graph-based machine learning improves just-in-time defect prediction. *PLoS One*, *18*(4), e0284077. doi:10.1371/journal.pone.0284077 PMID:37053155

Buduma, N., Buduma, N., & Papa, J. (2022). *Fundamentals of Deep Learning* (2nd ed.). O'Reilly Media, Inc.

Burnes, B. (2020). The origins of Lewin's three-step model of change. *The Journal of Applied Behavioral Science*, *56*(1), 32–59. doi:10.1177/0021886319892685

Burroughs, B. (2019). House of Netflix: Streaming media and digital lore. *Popular Communication*, *17*(1), 1–17. doi:10.1080/15405702.2017.1343948

Byrne, M. (2023). The Disruptive Impacts of Next Generation Generative Artificial Intelligence. *Computers, Informatics. Computers, Informatics, Nursing*, *41*(7), 479–481. doi:10.1097/CIN.0000000000001044 PMID:37417716

Cabeças, A., & Da Silva, M. M. (2020). Project management in the fourth industrial revolution. Revista Internacional de Tecnologia. *Ciencia y Sociedad*, *9*(2), 79–96.

Cakmakci, M. (2019). Interaction in project management approach within industry 4.0. In Lecture Notes in Mechanical Engineering (pp. 176-189).

Calvo, R. A., Deterding, S., Ryan, R. M., & Rigby, C. S. (2022). The impact of virtual agents on people's privacy attitudes and behaviors. *Human-Computer Interaction*, *37*(3), 285–353.

Cervený, L., Sloup, R., Cervená, T., Riedl, M., & Palátová, P. (2022). Industry 4.0 as an Opportunity and Challenge for the Furniture Industry—A Case Study. *Sustainability (Basel)*, *14*(20), 13325. doi:10.3390u142013325

Cheng, B., Ioannou, I., & Serafeim, G. (2013). Corporate social responsibility and access to finance. *Strategic Management Journal*, *35*(1), 1–23. doi:10.1002mj.2131

Chen, J., Wu, L., & Xu, X. (2020). Employee training and awareness in phishing resistance: Evidence from a field experiment. *Journal of Management Information Systems*, *37*(1), 201–235. doi:10.1080/07421222.2019.1703634

Chhabra, A. (2017). Derivation of human induced pluripotent stem cell (iPSC) lines and mechanism of pluripotency: Historical perspective and recent advances. *Stem Cell Reviews and Reports*, *13*(6), 757–773. doi:10.100712015-017-9766-9 PMID:28918520

Chung, K., & Deisseroth, K. (2013). CLARITY for mapping the nervous system. *Nature Methods*, *10*(6), 508–513. doi:10.1038/nmeth.2481 PMID:23722210

Churchland, P. M. (1988). Perceptual Plasticity and Theoretical Neutrality: A Reply to Jerry Fodor. *Philosophy of Science*, *55*(2), 167–187. doi:10.1086/289425

Ciampi, F., Demi, S., Magrini, A., Marzi, G., & Papa, A. (2021). Exploring the impact of big data analytics capabilities on business model innovation: The mediating role of entrepreneurial orientation. *Journal of Business Research*, *123*, 1–13. doi:10.1016/j.jbusres.2020.09.023

Clarke, A. C. (1945). Extra-Terrestrial Relays – Can Rocket Stations Give World-wide Radio Coverage? *Wireless World.*, *51*(10), 305–308.

Cobb, M. (2000). Reading and writing the book of nature: Jan Swammerdam (1637–1680). *Endeavour*, *24*(3), 122–128. doi:10.1016/S0160-9327(00)01306-5

Cummings, M. L., & Li, S. (2021). Subjectivity in the Creation of Machine Learning Models. *ACM Journal of Data and Information Quality*, *13*(2), 1–19. doi:10.1145/3418034

Daidj, N., & Egert, C. (2018). Towards new coopetition-based business models? The case of Netflix on the French market. *Journal of Research in Marketing and Entrepreneurship*, *20*(1), 99–120. doi:10.1108/JRME-11-2016-0049

Darko, A., Chan, A. P. C., Adabre, M. A., Edwards, D. J., Hosseini, M. R., & Ameyaw, E. E. (2020). Artificial intelligence in the AEC industry: Scientometric analysis and visualization of research activities. *Automation in Construction*, *112*, 103081. doi:10.1016/j.autcon.2020.103081

Databricks. (2023). 2023 state of the art of Data + AI. *Databricks*. https://www.databricks.com/resources/ebook/state-of-data-ai/thank-you,

Davenport, T. H., & Kalakota, R. (2019). The potential for artificial intelligence in healthcare. *Future Healthcare Journal*, *6*(2), 94–98. doi:10.7861/futurehosp.6-2-94 PMID:31363513

David, H. (1988). Rudolf Virchow and modern aspects of tumor pathology. *Pathology, Research and Practice*, *183*(3), 356–364. doi:10.1016/S0344-0338(88)80138-9 PMID:3047716

Davidson, D. (1970). Mental Events. In L. Foster & J. W. Swanson (Eds.), *Experience and Theory*. Humanities Press.

De Falco, S. (2012). The discovery of placenta growth factor and its biological activity. *Experimental & Molecular Medicine*, *44*(1), 1–9. doi:10.3858/emm.2012.44.1.025 PMID:22228176

DeMott, J., Koscher, K., & Sherry, C. (2019). Towards effective security information and event management (SIEM) system management. In *Proceedings of the 2019 ACM SIGSAC Conference on Computer and Communications Security* (pp. 2187-2189). ACM. doi: 10.1145/3319535.3363239

Devereux, M. B., & Yetman, J. (2002). Price setting and exchange rate passthrough: Theory and evidence. In Price Adjustment and Monetary Policy. Ottawa: Bank of Canada.

Dolezel, M., Hinton, G. E., Eisner, J., & Popov, M. (2022). Mitigating labor displacement due to artificial intelligence: Evidence from a random assignment field experiment. *The American Economic Review*, *112*(2), 356–379.

Durkee, M. S., Abraham, R., Clark, M. R., & Giger, M. L. (2021). Artificial intelligence and cellular segmentation in tissue microscopy images. *American Journal of Pathology*, *191*(10), 1693–1701. doi:10.1016/j.ajpath.2021.05.022 PMID:34129842

Eita, J. H. (2011). *Determinants of Stock Market Prices in Namibia*. (Working Paper 209). Monash University.

Engida, Z. M., Alemu, A. E., & Mulugeta, M. A. (2022). The effect of change leadership on employees' readiness to change: The mediating role of organizational culture. *Future Business Journal*, *8*(1), 1–13. doi:10.118643093-022-00148-2

Erickson, B. J. (2021). Basic Artificial Intelligence Techniques: Machine Learning and Deep Learning. *Radiologic Clinics of North America*, 59(6), 933–940. doi:10.1016/j.rcl.2021.06.004 PMID:34689878

Errida, A., & Lotfi, B. (2021). The determinants of organizational change management success: Literature review and case study. *International Journal of Engineering Business Management*, 13, 18479790211016273. doi:10.1177/18479790211016273

Ertürk, A., Becker, K., Jährling, N., Mauch, C. P., Hojer, C. D., Egen, J. G., Hellal, F., Bradke, F., Sheng, M., & Dodt, H. U. (2012). Three-dimensional imaging of solvent-cleared organs using 3DISCO. *Nature Protocols*, 7(11), 1983–1995. doi:10.1038/nprot.2012.119 PMID:23060243

Escola, B. (2023). *Microeconomia*. Brasil Escola. https://brasilescola.uol.com.br/economia/microeconomia.htm

Esoso, A. A., Omolayo, M. I., Tien-Chien, J., & Akinlabi, E. T. (2023). Exploring Machine Learning Tools for Enhancing Additive Manufacturing: A Comparative Study. *Ingénierie Des Systèmes d'Information*, 28(3), 535–544. doi:10.18280/isi.280301

Esteva, A., Robicquet, A., Ramsundar, B., Kuleshov, V., DePristo, M., Chou, K., Cui, C., Corrado, G., Thrun, S., & Dean, J. (2019). A guide to deep learning in healthcare. *Nature Medicine*, 25(1), 24–29. doi:10.103841591-018-0316-z PMID:30617335

Foote, K. D. (2022) A brief history of deep learning. *Dataversity*. https://www.dataversity.net/brief-history-deep-learning/ .

Forte, G. C., Altmayer, S., Silva, R. F., Stefani, M. T., Libermann, L. L., Cavion, C. C., Youssef, A., Forghani, R., King, J., Mohamed, T.-L., Andrade, R. G. F., & Hochhegger, B. (2022). Deep learning algorithms for diagnosis of lung cancer: A systematic review and meta-analysis. *Cancers (Basel)*, 14(16), 3856. doi:10.3390/cancers14163856 PMID:36010850

Fradkov, A. L. (2020). Early History of Machine Learning. *IFAC*, 53(2), 1385-1390. doi:10.1016/j.ifacol.2020.12.1888

Franklin, M. (2021). *Agile change management: A practical framework for successful change planning and implementation*. Kogan Page Publishers.

Free Code Camp. (2020). *Machine Learning Principles*. Free Code Camp. https://www.freecodecamp.org/news/machine-learning-principles-explained/.

Freeman, C., & Perez, C. (1988). Structural crises of adjustment, business cycles and investment behavior. In G. Dosi (ed.) Technical Change and Economic Theory. Pinter publisher's limited.

Fusch, G. E., Ness, L. R., Booker, J. M., & Fusch, P. (2020). People and process: Successful change management initiatives. *Journal of Sustainable Social Change*, 12(1), 13.

G1. (2023). *ChatGPT ganha rival criado pelo Google, o Bard*. G1. https://g1.globo.com/tecnologia/noticia/2023/02/06/google-anuncia-bard-robo-conversador-rival-do-chatgpt.ghtml

Gagnon, J. E., & Ihrig, J. (2004). Monetary policy and exchange rate pass through‖. *International Journal of Finance & Economics*, *9*(4), 315–338. doi:10.1002/ijfe.253

Gandomi, A., & Haider, M. (2015). Beyond the hype: Big data concepts, methods, and analytics. *International Journal of Information Management*, *35*(2), 137–144. doi:10.1016/j.ijinfomgt.2014.10.007

Gao, Y., Liu, X., & Ma, X. (2019). How do firms meet the challenge of technological change by redesigning innovation ecosystem? A case study of IBM. *International Journal of Technology Management*, *80*(3-4), 241–265. doi:10.1504/IJTM.2019.100285

Garfield, D. A., & Wray, G. A. (2009). Comparative embryology without a microscope: Using genomic approaches to understand the evolution of development. *Journal of Biology*, *8*(7), 1–4. doi:10.1186/jbiol161 PMID:19664180

Garrett, M. D. (2022). Applying appreciative inquiry to research in the field of inclusive education. *Canadian Journal for New Scholars in Education/Revue canadienne des jeunes chercheures et chercheurs en éducation, 13*(1).

Gartner. (2018). *Gartner Top 10 Strategic Technology Trends for 2018*. Gartner. https://www.gartner.com/smarterwithgartner/gartner-top-10-strategic-technology-trends-for-2018/

Garvalov, B. K., & Ertürk, A. (2017). Seeing whole-tumour heterogeneity. *Nature Biomedical Engineering*, *1*(10), 772–774. doi:10.103841551-017-0150-5 PMID:31015596

Gerlach, S. (2000). *MCIs and monetary policy, 44*(9), 1677-1700.

Ghosh, S., Hughes, M., Hodgkinson, I., & Hughes, P. (2022). Digital transformation of industrial businesses: A dynamic capability approach. *Technovation*, *113*, 102414. doi:10.1016/j.technovation.2021.102414

Globo. (2023). *Microsoft anuncia investimento de 10 bilhões na criadora do ChatGPT*. Bloomberg. https://oglobo.globo.com/economia/tecnologia/noticia/2023/01/microsoft-anuncia-investimento-de-us-10-bilhoes-na-criadora-do-chatgpt.ghtml

Goodfellow, I., Bengio, Y., & Courville, A. (2016). *Deep learning*. MIT press.

Gordon, R. (2023). *Using AI to protect against AI image manipulation*. MIT Campus. https://news.mit.edu/2023/using-ai-protect-against-ai-image-manipulation-0731,

Gotsch, M. L., Lienhard, S. D., & Schögel, M. (2019). *Case Study: Change Management & Leadership at Microsoft*.

Graf, A. C., Jacob, E., Twigg, D., & Nattabi, B. (2020). Contemporary nursing graduates' transition to practice: A critical review of transition models. *Journal of Clinical Nursing*, *29*(15-16), 3097–3107. doi:10.1111/jocn.15234 PMID:32129522

Groner, P. (1995). A Medieval Japanese Reading of the Mo-ho chin-kuan. *Japanese Journal of Religious Studies*, *22*(1/2), 49–81.

Haenssle, H. A., Fink, C., Schneiderbauer, R., Toberer, F., Buhl, T., Blum, A., & Stolz, W. (2018). Man against machine: Diagnostic performance of a deep learning convolutional neural network for dermoscopic melanoma recognition in comparison to 58 dermatologists. *Annals of Oncology : Official Journal of the European Society for Medical Oncology, 29*(8), 1836–1842. doi:10.1093/annonc/mdy166 PMID:29846502

Hambling, D. (2023). Drones with AI targeting system ´better than human´. In *New Scientist.* https://www.newscientist.com/article/2380971-drones-with-ai-targeting-system-claimed-to-be-better-than-human/

Hamburger, V. (1984). Hilde Mangold, co-discoverer of the organizer. *Journal of the History of Biology, 17*(1), 1–11. doi:10.1007/BF00397500 PMID:11611449

Hamdan, A. (2014). Impact of interest rate on stock market; evidence from Pakistani market, e- ISSN: 2278-487X, p-ISSN: 2319-7668. Volume 16, Issue 1. Ver. VII, PP 64-6.

Hanelt, A., Bohnsack, R., Marz, D., & Antunes Marante, C. (2021). A systematic review of the literature on digital transformation: Insights and implications for strategy and organizational change. *Journal of Management Studies, 58*(5), 1159–1197. doi:10.1111/joms.12639

Hanley, C. (2014). Putting the bias in skill-biased technological change? A relational perspective on white-collar automation at General Electric. *The American Behavioral Scientist, 58*(3), 400–415. doi:10.1177/0002764213503339

Heaton, J. (2017). *Deep learning with Python.* Packt Publishing.

He, K., Zhang, X., Ren, S., & Sun, J. (2016). Deep residual learning for image recognition. In *Proceedings of the IEEE conference on computer vision and pattern recognition* (pp. 770-778). IEEE.

Henry Mk Mok, Causality of interest rate, exchange rate and stock prices at stock market open and close in Hong Kong, October 1993, Volume 10, Issue 2, pp 123–143.

Hilde, C. (2008). Monetary Policy and Exchange Rate Interactions in a Small Open Economy. Ime T. Akpan, *Impact of Interest Rates on Stock Prices: An Analysis of the All Share Index, 3*(2), 96-101.

Hildebrand, L. A., Pierce, C. J., Dennis, M., Paracha, M., & Maoz, A. (2021). Artificial intelligence for histology-based detection of microsatellite instability and prediction of response to immunotherapy in colorectal cancer. *Cancers (Basel), 13*(3), 391. doi:10.3390/cancers13030391 PMID:33494280

Huang, Y. (2006). *The effect of Fed monetary policy regimes on the US interest rate swap spreads.* Research Gate.

Huang, G., Liu, Z., Van Der Maaten, L., & Weinberger, K. Q. (2017). Densely connected convolutional networks. In *Proceedings of the IEEE conference on computer vision and pattern recognition* (pp. 4700-4708). IEEE.

Hughes, T. B., Yilmaz, L., & Son, Y. J. (2020). Artificial intelligence in drug discovery: Promises and challenges. *Drug Discovery Today*, 25(4), 784–795.

Hussein, I., Raad, M., Safa, R., Jurjus, R. A., & Jurjus, A. (2015). Once upon a microscopic slide: The story of histology. *Journal of Cytology & Histology*, 06(06), 6. doi:10.4172/2157-7099.1000377

IBM. (2023). *What is deep learning?* IBM. https://www.ibm.com/topics/deep-learning,

IDC. (2022). *White Paper: Scaling AI/ML Initiatives: The critical role of data.* Snowflake. https://www.snowflake.com/thankyou/scaling-ai-ml-initiatives-the-critical-role-of-data/

IEEE. (2023). AI in Virtual Reality. *Digital Reality*. https://digitalreality.ieee.org/publications/ai-in-virtual-reality

Institute for Ethical AI and Machine Learning. (2023). The responsible Machine Learning principles. IEAIML..

Inveritas (2023). How we used ChatGPT to speed up software development. *Medium*. https://medium.com/@inverita/how-we-used-chat-gpt-to-speed-up-the-software-development-process,

Islam, M. R., Islam, S. M. R., Asraf, A., & Khandakar, A. (2020). Artificial Intelligence in Finance: A Comprehensive Review. *IEEE Access : Practical Innovations, Open Solutions*, 8, 89961–89988.

Jack, A. (2023). AI chatbot's MBA exam pass poses test for business schools. *Financial Times*. https://www.ft.com/content/7229ba86-142a-49f6-9821-f55c07536b7c

Jain, A., Kant, K., & Singh, Y. (2020). A review on insider threats: Classification, models and mitigation techniques. *Journal of Information Security and Applications*, 53, 102466. doi:10.1016/j.jisa.2020.102466

Jallow, H., Renukappa, S., & Suresh, S. (2020). Knowledge Management and Artificial Intelligence (AI). *Proceedings of the European Conference on Knowledge Management, ECKM*. European Commission.

Jamil, G. L., & Silva, A. R. (2021). Emerging technologies in a modern competitive scenario: Understanding the panorama for security and privacy requirements. In P. F. Anunciação (Ed.), *Pessoa, C. R. M. and Jamil, G. L. (2021) Digital Transformation and challenges for data security and privacy* (pp. 1–16). IGI Global. doi:10.4018/978-1-7998-4201-9.ch001

Justin, D., Weisz, M., Jessica, H., & Houde, S. (2023). Toward General Design Principles for Generative AI Applications. ACM.

Kaelbling, L. P., Littman, M. L., & Moore, A. W. (1996). Reinforcement learning: A survey. *Journal of Artificial Intelligence Research*, 4, 237–285. doi:10.1613/jair.301

Kandil, M. (2005). Money, interest, and prices: Some international evidence. *International Review of Economics & Finance*, 14(2), 129–147. doi:10.1016/j.iref.2003.11.013

Kang, S. P., Chen, Y., Svihla, V., Gallup, A., Ferris, K., & Datye, A. K. (2022). Guiding change in higher education: An emergent, iterative application of Kotter's change model. *Studies in Higher Education*, *47*(2), 270–289. doi:10.1080/03075079.2020.1741540

Karras, T., Aila, T., Laine, S., & Lehtinen, J. (2017). Progressive growing of GANs for improved quality, stability, and variation. arXiv preprint arXiv:1710.10196.

Khodabakhshian, A., Puolitaival, T., & Kestle, L. (2023). Deterministic and Probabilistic Risk Management Approaches in Construction Projects: A Systematic Literature Review and Comparative Analysis. *Buildings*, *13*(5), 1312. doi:10.3390/buildings13051312

Kim, S., Jang, J., & Lee, S. (2020). Applications of artificial intelligence in transportation: A review. *Transportation Research Part C, Emerging Technologies*, *112*, 631–654.

Kim, S., & Li, Z. (2021). Understanding the impact of ESG practices in corporate finance. *Sustainability (Basel)*, *13*(7), 3746. doi:10.3390u13073746

King, R. (1999). *Indian Philosophy*. Edinburgh University Press.

Kober, J., Bagnell, J. A., & Peters, J. (2013). Reinforcement learning in robotics: A survey. *The International Journal of Robotics Research*, *32*(11), 1238–1274. doi:10.1177/0278364913495721

Kocaballi, A. B., Berkovsky, S., Quiroz, J. C. G., & Kitson, N. (2021). The need for cybersecurity in healthcare: An editorial overview. *Journal of Biomedical Informatics*, *113*, 103649.

Kok, S. L., & Siripipatthanakul, S. (2023). Change Management Model in Corporate Culture and Values: A Case Study of Intel Cooperation. *Advance Knowledge for Executives*, *2*(1), 1–30.

Kondratieff, N. D., & Stolper, W. F. (1935, November). The Long waves in Economic Life. *The Review of Economics and Statistics*, *XVII*(6), 105–115. doi:10.2307/1928486

Korzynski, P., Mazurek, G., Altmann, A., Ejdys, J., Kazlauskaite, R., Paliszkiewicz, J., Wach, K., & Ziemba, E. (2023). Generative artificial intelligence as a new context for management theories: Analysis of ChatGPT. *Central European Management Journal*, *31*(1), 3–13. doi:10.1108/CEMJ-02-2023-0091

Kour, R., Singh, G., Singh, P., & Kant, K. (2021). An intelligent security framework for industrial control systems using machine learning techniques. *Journal of Network and Computer Applications*, *178*, 102966.

Kozovska, Z., Rajcaniova, S., Munteanu, P., Dzacovska, S., & Demkova, L. (2021). CRISPR: History and perspectives to the future. *Biomedicine and Pharmacotherapy*, *141*, 111917. doi:10.1016/j.biopha.2021.111917 PMID:34328110

Krittanawong, C., Zhang, H., Wang, Z., & Aydar, M. (2021). The impact of artificial intelligence on the practice of medicine. *Journal of Geriatric Cardiology : JGC*, *18*(3), 179–185.

Krizhevsky, A., Sutskever, I., & Hinton, G. E. (2012). Imagenet classification with deep convolutional neural networks. In Advances in neural information processing systems (pp. 1097-1105).

Lacerda, B., & Jamil, G. L. (2021). Digital Transformation for Businesses: Adapt or Die! Reflections on How to Rethink Your Business in the Digital Transformation Context. In Anunciação, P. A., Pessoa, C. R. M. & Jamil, G. L. Digital Transformation and Challenges for Data security and privacy. IGI Global Publishers.

LaFleur, R. (1973). Saigyō and the Buddhist Value of Nature. Part I. *History of Religions, 13*(2), 93–128. doi:10.1086/462697

LaFleur, R. (1974). Saigyō and the Buddhist Value of Nature. Part II. *History of Religions, 13*(3), 227–248. doi:10.1086/462703

Lakshman, C. (2005). Top executive knowledge leadership: Managing knowledge to lead change at General Electric. *Journal of Change Management, 5*(4), 429–446. doi:10.1080/14697010500401540

Laskurain-Iturbe, I., Arana-Landín, G., Landeta-Manzano, B., & Uriarte-Gallastegi, N. (2021). Exploring the influence of industry 4.0 technologies on the circular economy. *Journal of Cleaner Production, 321*, 128944. doi:10.1016/j.jclepro.2021.128944

LeCun, Y., Bengio, Y., & Hinton, G. (2015). Deep learning. *Nature, 521*(7553), 436–444. doi:10.1038/nature14539 PMID:26017442

Lee, J., Suh, T., Roy, D., & Baucus, M. (2019). Emerging Technology and Business Model Innovation: The Case of Artificial Intelligence. *Journal of Open Innovation, 5*(3), 44. doi:10.3390/joitmc5030044

Lerner, T. N., Shilyansky, C., Davidson, T. J., Evans, K. E., Beier, K. T., Zalocusky, K. A., Crow, A. K., Malenka, R. C., Luo, L., Tomer, R., & Deisseroth, K. (2015). Intact-brain analyses reveal distinct information carried by SNc dopamine subcircuits. *Cell, 162*(3), 635–647. doi:10.1016/j.cell.2015.07.014 PMID:26232229

Lewis, D. (1966). Argument for the identity theory. *The Journal of Philosophy, 63*(1), 17–25. doi:10.2307/2024524

Lewis, D. (1994). Reduction of mind. In S. Guttenplan (Ed.), *Companion to the Philosophy of Mind* (pp. 412–431). Blackwell.

Liao, T. W., & Hsieh, H. P. (2020). Applications of artificial intelligence in retailing: A review. *Journal of Retailing and Consumer Services, 52*, 101926.

Lins, K. V., Servaes, H., & Tamayo, A. (2017). Social Capital, Trust, and Firm Performance: The Value of Corporate Social Responsibility during the Financial Crisis. *The Journal of Finance, 72*(4), 1785–1824. doi:10.1111/jofi.12505

Lisdawati, L. (2023). The Effect of Financial Performance and Company Size on Stock Price with Dividend Policy as A Moderating Variable. *International Journal of Educational Administration, Management, and Leadership,* 57–64. doi:10.51629/ijeamal.v4i1.121

Litjens, G., Kooi, T., Bejnordi, B. E., Setio, A. A. A., Ciompi, F., Ghafoorian, M., van der Laak, J. A., van Ginneken, B., & Sánchez, C. I. (2017). A survey on deep learning in medical image analysis. *Medical Image Analysis, 42,* 60–88. doi:10.1016/j.media.2017.07.005 PMID:28778026

Liu, X., Faes, L., Kale, A. U., Wagner, S. K., Fu, D. J., Bruynseels, A., Mahendiran, T., Moraes, G., Shamdas, M., Kern, C., Ledsam, J. R., Schmid, M. K., Balaskas, K., Topol, E. J., Bachmann, L. M., Keane, P. A., & Denniston, A. K. (2020). A comparison of deep learning performance against health-care professionals in detecting diseases from medical imaging: A systematic review and meta-analysis. *The Lancet. Digital Health, 2*(6), e271–e297. doi:10.1016/S2589-7500(19)30123-2 PMID:33323251

Liu, Y., Li, Q., & Dong, X. (2021). A hybrid intrusion detection system based on clustering analysis and machine learning algorithms for network security. *Wireless Personal Communications, 117*(2), 921–944. doi:10.100711277-021-08307-w

Liu, Y., Li, S., & Huang, L. (2020). Deep learning based intrusion detection for industrial control systems. *IEEE Transactions on Industrial Informatics, 16*(4), 2552–2561. doi:10.1109/TII.2019.2943199

Li, Y., Jiang, J., & Li, G. (2018). Insider Threat Detection Based on Big Data Analytics and Machine Learning. *2018 IEEE International Conference on Information Reuse and Integration (IRI),* (pp. 113-118). IEEE.

Loeffler, C. M. L., Bruechle, N. O., Jung, M., Seillier, L., Rose, M., Laleh, N. G., ... Kather, J. N. (2022). Artificial intelligence–based detection of FGFR3 mutational status directly from routine histology in bladder cancer: A possible preselection for molecular testing? *European Urology Focus, 8*(2), 472–479. doi:10.1016/j.euf.2021.04.007 PMID:33895087

Loughran, T., & Ritter, J. R. (1997). The operating performance of firms conducting seasoned equity offerings. *The Journal of Finance, 52*(5), 1823–1850. doi:10.1111/j.1540-6261.1997.tb02743.x

Luck, M., & Aylett, R. (2000). Applying artificial intelligence to virtual reality: Intelligent virtual environments. *Applied Artificial Intelligence, 14,* 1, 3–32. doi:10.1080/088395100117133

Luger, G., & Chakrabarti, C. (2017). From Alan Turing to modern AI: Practical solutions and an implicit epistemic stance. *AI & Society, 32*(3), 321–338. doi:10.100700146-016-0646-7

Luísa, I. (2019). *No Twitter, fake news se espalham 6 vezes mais rápido que notícias verdadeiras.* Super Interessante. https://super.abril.com.br/tecnologia/no-twitter-fake-news-se-espalham-6-vezes-mais-rapido-que-noticias-verdadeiras/

Lyu, Q., Xu, X., & Lv, J. (2018). Malware Analysis Based on Natural Language Processing. *IEEE Access : Practical Innovations, Open Solutions, 6,* 56914–56922.

Mahmudul, A. (2010), The impacts of interest rate on stock market: Empirical evidence from Dhaka Stock exchange. *Dhaka, 4*(1), 21-30.

Mann, D. M., Chen, J., Chunara, R., Testa, P. A., Nov, O., & Dredze, M. (2020). COVID-19 transforms health care through telemedicine: Evidence from the field. *Journal of the American Medical Informatics Association : JAMIA, 27*(7), 1132–1135. doi:10.1093/jamia/ocaa072 PMID:32324855

Manuti, A., & Monachino, D. (2020). Managing knowledge at the time of artificial intelligence: An explorative study with knowledge workers. *East European Journal of Psycholinguistics, 7*(2), 179–190. doi:10.29038/eejpl.2020.7.2.man

Manyika, J., Chui, M., Brown, B., Bughin, J., Dobbs, R., Roxburgh, C., & Byers, A. H. (2017). *Harnessing automation for a future that works.* McKinsey Global Institute. https://www.mckinsey.com/featured-insights/future-of-work/harnessing-automation-for-a-future-that-works

Manyika, J., Chui, M., Miremadi, M., Bughin, J., George, K., Willmott, P., & Dewhurst, M. (2017). *A future that works: Automation, employment, and productivity.* McKinsey Global Institute.

Marnada, P., Raharjo, T., Hardian, B., & Prasetyo, A. (2022). Agile project management challenge in handling scope and change: A systematic literature review. *Procedia Computer Science, 197,* 290–300. doi:10.1016/j.procs.2021.12.143

Marr, B. (2023). The 12 AI mistakes you must avoid. *Forbes.* https://www.forbes.com/sites/bernardmarr/2023/04/03/the-12-biggest-ai-mistakes-you-must-avoid/?sh=dc199223af7a, accessed on June, 2023.

Mazzarello, P., Garbarino, C., & Calligaro, A. (2009). How Camillo Golgi became "the Golgi". *FEBS Letters, 583*(23), 3732–3737. doi:10.1016/j.febslet.2009.10.018 PMID:19833130

McCallum, S., & Clark, J. (2023). *What is AI, is it dangerous and what jobs are at risk?* In BBC. https://www.bbc.com/news/technology-65855333,

McCarthy, J. (1959). *Programs with common sense.* Stanford University. https://www-formal.stanford.edu/jmc/mcc59/mcc59.html.

McCarthy, J. (2007). *What is artificial intelligence?* Computer Science Department Stanford University. https://www-formal.stanford.edu/jmc/whatisai.pdf

McCarthy, J., & Hayes, P. J. (1969). Some philosophical problems from the standpoint of artificial intelligence. In B. Meltzer & D. Michie (Eds.), *Machine Intelligence* (Vol. 4, pp. 463–502). Edinburgh University Press.

McKinsey. (2023). *What is generative AI?* McKinsey. https://www.mckinsey.com/featured-insights/mckinsey-explainers/what-is-generative-ai

Memon, F. A., Shah, S., & Khoso, I. U. (2020). Role of leadership communication in creating change readiness: Revisiting Kurt Lewin's model in telecommunication sector of Pakistan. *Indian Journal of Science and Technology, 13*(26), 2625–2632. doi:10.17485/IJST/v13i26.933

Michael R. (1975). The Financial and tax effects of monetary policy on interest rates.

Mili, N., & Mukherjee, A. (2018). AI and IoT: New age of threat vectors and security challenges. *International Journal of Computer Science and Information Security, 16*(4), 43–50.

Mitrofanova, Y. S., Burenina, V. I., Tukshumskaya, A. V., Kuznetsov, A. K., & Popova, T. N. (2022). Smart University: Digital Development Projects Based on Big Data. *Smart Innovation, Systems and Technologies, 305*, 230-240.

Mittal, R., & Mathew, R. (2019). Ethics of artificial intelligence: A review of the social and cultural implications. In *Intelligent Systems Design and Applications* (pp. 97–103). Springer.

Mizrak, K. C. (2020). Agile occupational safety management system model and evaluation of the proposed model in an automotive company. *International Journal of Management and Administration, 4*(8), 228-244.

Mnih, V., Kavukcuoglu, K., Silver, D., Graves, A., Antonoglou, I., Wierstra, D., & Riedmiller, M. (2013). Playing Atari with deep reinforcement learning. arXiv preprint arXiv:1312.5602.

Mnih, V., Kavukcuoglu, K., Silver, D., Rusu, A. A., Veness, J., Bellemare, M. G., & Petersen, S. (2015). Human-level control through deep reinforcement learning. *Nature, 518*(7540), 529–533. doi:10.1038/nature14236 PMID:25719670

Modi, S., Glass, B., Prakash, A., Taylor-Weiner, A., Elliott, H., Wapinski, I., Sugihara, M., Saito, K., Kerner, J. K., Phillips, R., Shibutani, T., Honda, K., Khosla, A., Beck, A. H., & Cogswell, J. (2020). 286P Artificial intelligence analysis of advanced breast cancer patients from a phase I trial of trastuzumab deruxtecan (T-DxD): HER2 and histopathology features as predictors of clinical benefit. *Annals of Oncology : Official Journal of the European Society for Medical Oncology, 31*, S355–S356. doi:10.1016/j.annonc.2020.08.388

Morawski, M., Kirilina, E., Scherf, N., Jäger, C., Reimann, K., Trampel, R., Gavriilidis, F., Geyer, S., Biedermann, B., Arendt, T., & Weiskopf, N. (2018). Developing 3D microscopy with CLARITY on human brain tissue: Towards a tool for informing and validating MRI-based histology. *NeuroImage, 182*, 417–428. doi:10.1016/j.neuroimage.2017.11.060 PMID:29196268

Morgan, A. M., Jobe, R. L., Konopa, J. K., & Downs, L. D. (2022). Quality assurance, meet quality appreciation: Using appreciative inquiry to define faculty quality standards. *Higher Learning Research Communications, 12*(1), 98–111. doi:10.18870/hlrc.v12i1.1301

Moss, R. W. (2008). The life and times of John Beard, DSc (1858-1924). *Integrative Cancer Therapies, 7*(4), 229–251. doi:10.1177/1534735408326174 PMID:19116220

Munga, N. (2013). *The Nairobi stock exchange, its history, organization and role in Kenya economy. Unpublished MBA Project.* University of Nairobi.

Mun, H. W., Siong, E. C., & Thing, T. C. (2008). Stock Market and Economic Growth in Malaysia: Causality Test. *Asian Social Science, 4*(4). Advance online publication. doi:10.5539/ass.v4n4p86

Musumeci, G. (2014). Past, present and future: Overview on histology and histopathology. *J Histol Histopathol*, *1*(5), 1–3. doi:10.7243/2055-091X-1-5

Mutheu, E. (2014). *The relationship between interest rates and share prices of commercial banks listed at the Nairobi Securities Exchange.*

NASA. (2021). *Perseverance Mars Rover Landing on Mars*. NASA. https://mars.nasa.gov/mars2020/.

Naslund, D., & Kale, R. (2020). Is agile the latest management fad? A review of success factors of agile transformations. *International Journal of Quality and Service Sciences*, *12*(4), 489–504. doi:10.1108/IJQSS-12-2019-0142

Needham, J., & Hughes, A. (2015). *A history of embryology*. Cambridge University Press.

Niazi, M., Khan, I. U., & Shah, A. (2021). *A study of cyber security vulnerabilities and risk assessment in higher education institutions.*

Nikāya, S. (2003). Setting in motion the Wheel of Dharma. In The Connected Discourses of the Buddha. A new Translation of the Samyutta Nikāya by Bhikku Bodhi. Boston: Wisdom Publications.

Nukala, V. B., & Rao, S. S. P. (2021). Role of debt-to-equity ratio in project investment valuation, assessing risk and return in capital markets. *Future Business Journal*, *7*(1), 13. Advance online publication. doi:10.118643093-021-00058-9

O'Dell, L. M., & Jahankhani, H. (2020). The evolution of AI and the human-machine interface as a manager in Industry 4.0. In Strategy, Leadership, and AI in the Cyber Ecosystem: The Role of Digital Societies in Information Governance and Decision Making (pp. 3-22).

O'Rahilly, R. (1958). Three and one-half centuries of histology. *Irish Journal of Medical Science*, *33*, 288-292.

O'Rourke, T., Higuchi, K. S., & Hogg, W. (2016). Stakeholder participation in system change: A new conceptual model. *Worldviews on Evidence-Based Nursing*, *13*(4), 261–269. doi:10.1111/wvn.12165 PMID:27258681

Oatley, C. W. (1982). The early history of the scanning electron microscope. *Journal of Applied Physics*, *53*(2), R1–R13. doi:10.1063/1.331666

Obermeyer, Z., Powers, B., Vogeli, C., & Mullainathan, S. (2019). Dissecting racial bias in an algorithm used to manage the health of populations. *Science*, *366*(6464), 447–453. doi:10.1126cience.aax2342 PMID:31649194

Ocasio, W., & Joseph, J. (2008). Rise and fall-or transformation?: The evolution of strategic planning at the General Electric Company, 1940–2006. *Long Range Planning*, *41*(3), 248–272. doi:10.1016/j.lrp.2008.02.010

Odiaga, J., Guglielmo, M. J., Catrambone, C., Gierlowski, T., Bruti, C., Richter, L., & Miller, J. (2021). Kotter's Change Model In Higher Education: Transforming Siloed Education To A Culture Of Interprofessionalism. Journal of Organizational Culture, *Communications and Conflict, 25*(2), 1–7.

Omran, M. (1993, October). Time series analysis of the impact of real interest rates on stock market activity and liquidity in Egypt. *Co-Integration and Error Correction Model Approach, 10*(2), 123–143.

Open A. I. (2023). *ChatGPT (Jan 30 version)* [Large language model]. https://chat.openai.com/

Open A. I. (2023). Generative models. *Open AI*. https://openai.com/research/generative-models.

Oracle. (2023). *What is machine learning.* Oracle. https://www.oracle.com/br/artificial-intelligence/machine-learning/what-is-machine-learning/

Osterman, M. (2019, June 26). The Growing Role of AI in Cybersecurity. *Forbes*. https://www.forbes.com/sites/michaelosterman/2019/06/26/the-growing-role-of-ai-in-cybersecurity/?sh=4fa4d0ad5b5d

Ozkan, N. N. (2015). An example of open innovation: P&G. *Procedia: Social and Behavioral Sciences, 195*, 1496–1502. doi:10.1016/j.sbspro.2015.06.450

Ozyoruk, K. B., Can, S., Darbaz, B., Başak, K., Demir, D., Gokceler, G. I., Serin, G., Hacisalihoglu, U. P., Kurtuluş, E., Lu, M. Y., Chen, T. Y., Williamson, D. F. K., Yılmaz, F., Mahmood, F., & Turan, M. (2022). A deep-learning model for transforming the style of tissue images from cryosectioned to formalin-fixed and paraffin-embedded. *Nature Biomedical Engineering, 6*(12), 1–13. doi:10.103841551-022-00952-9 PMID:36564629

Paddock, S. W., & Eliceiri, K. W. (2014). Laser scanning confocal microscopy: history, applications, and related optical sectioning techniques. *Confocal Microscopy: Methods and Protocols*, 9-47.

Pan, C., Cai, R., Quacquarelli, F. P., Ghasemigharagoz, A., Lourbopoulos, A., Matryba, P., Plesnila, N., Dichgans, M., Hellal, F., & Ertürk, A. (2016). Shrinkage-mediated imaging of entire organs and organisms using uDISCO. *Nature Methods, 13*(10), 859–867. doi:10.1038/nmeth.3964 PMID:27548807

Patelis, A. D. (1997). Stock return predictability: The role of monetary policy. *The Journal of Finance, 52*(5), 1951–1972. doi:10.1111/j.1540-6261.1997.tb02747.x

Peña-Fernández, S., Meso-Ayerdi, K., Larrondo-Ureta, A., & Díaz-Noci, J. (2023). Without journalists, there is no journalism: The social dimension of generative artificial intelligence in the media. *El Profesional de la Información, 32*(2), 1–15. doi:10.3145/epi.2023.mar.27

Peres, R., Schreier, M., Schweidel, D., & Sorescu, A. (2023). Editorial: On ChatGPT and beyond: How generative artificial intelligence may affect research, teaching, and practice. *International Journal of Research in Marketing, 40*(2), 269–275. doi:10.1016/j.ijresmar.2023.03.001

Phillips, J., & Klein, J. D. (2023). Change management: From theory to practice. *TechTrends*, *67*(1), 189–197. doi:10.100711528-022-00775-0 PMID:36105238

Pogosyan, M. A. (2020). Development of individual learning paths system in engineering education. In *Proceedings - Frontiers in Education Conference, FIE* (pp. 1-6). IEEE. 10.1109/FIE44824.2020.9274140

Price, W. N. II, & Cohen, I. G. (2019). Privacy in the age of medical big data. *Nature Medicine*, *25*(1), 37–43. doi:10.103841591-018-0272-7 PMID:30617331

Purity, K. M. (2014). *The effect of inflation and interest rates on stock marketreturns of firms listed at the Nairobi Securities Exchange.* Unpublished report University Of Nairobi, School Of Business.

Qazi, S., Jit, B. P., Das, A., Karthikeyan, M., Saxena, A., Ray, M. D., Singh, A. R., Raza, K., Jayaram, B., & Sharma, A. (2022). BESFA: Bioinformatics based evolutionary, structural & functional analysis of Prostate, Placenta, Ovary, Testis, and Embryo (POTE) paralogs. *Heliyon*, *8*(9), e10476. doi:10.1016/j.heliyon.2022.e10476 PMID:36132183

Radford, A., Metz, L., & Chintala, S. (2015). Unsupervised representation learning with deep convolutional generative adversarial networks. arXiv preprint arXiv:1511.06434.

Rajpurkar, P., Irvin, J., Bagul, A., Ding, D., Duan, T., Mehta, H., & Lungren, M. P. (2017). MURA: Large dataset for abnormality detection in musculoskeletal radiographs. arXiv preprint arXiv:1712.06957.

Rana, B., & Rathore, S. S. (2023). Industry 4.0 – Applications, challenges and opportunities in industries and academia: A review. *Materials Today: Proceedings*, *79*, 389–394. doi:10.1016/j.matpr.2022.12.162

Randall, L. M., & Coakley, L. A. (2007). Applying adaptive leadership to successful change initiatives in academia. *Leadership and Organization Development Journal*, *28*(4), 325–335. doi:10.1108/01437730710752201

Redman, M., King, A., Watson, C., & King, D. (2016). What is CRISPR/Cas9? *Archives of Disease in Childhood - Education and Practice*, *101*(4), 213–215. doi:10.1136/archdischild-2016-310459 PMID:27059283

Renier, N., Wu, Z., Simon, D. J., Yang, J., Ariel, P., & Tessier-Lavigne, M. (2014). iDISCO: A simple, rapid method to immunolabel large tissue samples for volume imaging. *Cell*, *159*(4), 896–910. doi:10.1016/j.cell.2014.10.010 PMID:25417164

Reveles Jensen, K. H., & Berg, R. W. (2017). *Advances and perspectives in tissue clearing using CLARITY.* Academic Press.

Ribatti, D., & Annese, T. (2023). Chick embryo in experimental embryology and more. *Pathology, Research and Practice*, *245*, 154478. doi:10.1016/j.prp.2023.154478 PMID:37100021

Roe, S. A. (1979). Rationalism and embryology: Caspar Friedrich Wolff's theory of epigenesis. *Journal of the History of Biology*, *12*(1), 1–43. doi:10.1007/BF00128134 PMID:11615771

Rudin, C., Chen, C., Chen, Z., Huang, H., Semenova, L. & Zhong, C. (2022). Interpretable machine learning: Fundamental principles and 10 grand challenges. *Statistics Surveys, 16*(none) 1-85. . doi:10.1214/21-SS133

Russell, S. J., & Norvig, P. (2010). *Artificial intelligence: A modern approach* (3rd ed.). Pearson.

Russell, S., & Norvig, P. (2010). *Artificial intelligence: a modern approach*. Pearson Education.

Said, H. B. (2013). Impact of ownership structure on debt equity Ratio: A static and a dynamic analytical framework. *International Business Research*, *6*(6). doi:10.5539/ibr.v6n6p162

Salimans, T., Goodfellow, I., Zaremba, W., Cheung, V., Radford, A., & Chen, X. (2016). Improved techniques for training GANs. In Advances in Neural Information Processing Systems (pp. 2234-2242).

Salum, F., & Coleta, K. (2023). *Leapfrogging será capaz de acelerar a IA nas organizações?* São Paulo: MITSloan Management Review Brasil. https://mitsloanreview.com.br/post/leapfrogging-sera-capaz-de-acelerar-a-ia-nas-organizacoes

Salum, F.; Coleta, K.; Tadeu, H. (2021). *Business Resilience: Essential competence Lessons for 2021*. São Paulo: FDC and Grant Thornton.

Samosir, P., & Jayadi, R. (2023). A Change Management for Transformation of Digital Banking In Indonesia. *Jurnal Sistem Cerdas*, *6*(1), 29–43.

Samuel, A. L. (1959, July). Some studies on Machine learning using the game of checkers. *IBM Systems Journal*, 535–554.

Schneider, S. (2019). *Artificial You. A.I. and the Future of your mind*. Princeton University press.

Schumpeter, J. A. (1962). *Capitalism, Socialism, and Democracy*. Harper & Row.

Searle, J. (1980). Minds, Brains and Programs. *Behavioral and Brain Sciences*, *3*(3), 417–457. doi:10.1017/S0140525X00005756

Sergi, C. (2019). EPAS 1, congenital heart disease, and high altitude: Disclosures by genetics, bioinformatics, and experimental embryology. *Bioscience Reports*, *39*(5), BSR20182197. doi:10.1042/BSR20182197 PMID:31015364

Serov, A. (2013). Subjective Reality and Strong Artificial Intelligence. *ArXiv, abs/1301.6359.*

Shang, G., Low, S. P., & Lim, X. Y. V. (2023). Prospects, drivers of and barriers to artificial intelligence adoption in project management. *Built Environment Project and Asset Management*, *13*(5), 629–645. doi:10.1108/BEPAM-12-2022-0195

Sharma, S., Tiwari, S., & Kumar, V. (2018). Big data analytics and machine learning for cybersecurity: A review. *Journal of Big Data*, *5*(1), 1–20.

Sherer, S. A., Kohli, R., & Baron, A. (2003). Complementary investment in change management and IT investment payoff. *Information Systems Frontiers, 5*(3), 321–333. doi:10.1023/A:1025609613076

Shimomura, O. (2009). Discovery of green fluorescent protein (GFP)(Nobel Lecture). *Angewandte Chemie International Edition, 48*(31), 5590–5602. doi:10.1002/anie.200902240 PMID:19579247

Silver, D., Huang, A., Maddison, C. J., Guez, A., Sifre, L., van den Driessche, G., Schrittwieser, J., Antonoglou, I., Panneershelvam, V., Lanctot, M., Dieleman, S., Grewe, D., Nham, J., Kalchbrenner, N., Sutskever, I., Lillicrap, T., Leach, M., Kavukcuoglu, K., Graepel, T., & Hassabis, D. (2016). Mastering the game of Go with deep neural networks and tree search. *Nature, 529*(7587), 484–489. doi:10.1038/nature16961 PMID:26819042

SilverD.SchrittwieserJ.SimonyanK.AntonoglouI.HuangA.GuezA.HubertT.BakerL.LaiM. BoltonA.ChenY.LillicrapT.HuiF.SifreL.van den DriesscheG.GraepelT.HassabisD.

Singer, P. W., & Friedman, A. (2014). *Cybersecurity and Cyberwar: What Everyone Needs to Know*. Oxford University Press. doi:10.1093/wentk/9780199918096.001.0001

Singh, R., & Garg, V. (2021). Human Factors in NDE 4.0 Development Decisions. *Journal of Nondestructive Evaluation, 40*(3), 71. doi:10.100710921-021-00808-3

Sittrop, D., & Crosthwaite, C. (2021). Minimising risk—the application of kotter's change management model on customer relationship management systems: A case study. *Journal of Risk and Financial Management, 14*(10), 496. doi:10.3390/jrfm14100496

Spemann, H., & Mangold, H. (2003). Induction of embryonic primordia by implantation of organizers from a different species. 1923. *The International Journal of Developmental Biology, 45*(1), 13–38. PMID:11291841

Stadtfeld, M., & Hochedlinger, K. (2010). Induced pluripotency: History, mechanisms, and applications. *Genes & Development, 24*(20), 2239–2263. doi:10.1101/gad.1963910 PMID:20952534

Stanford University. (2022). *Human-centered artificial intelligence research center: How AI is making autonomous vehicles safer*. Stanford University. https://hai.stanford.edu/news/how-ai-making-autonomous-vehicles-safer

Supriharyanti, E., & Sukoco, B. M. (2023). Organizational change capability: A systematic review and future research directions. *Management Research Review, 46*(1), 46–81. doi:10.1108/MRR-01-2021-0039

Suresh Babu, C. V. (2022). *Artificial Intelligence and Expert Systems*. Anniyappa Publications.

Suresh Babu, C. V., & Praveen, S. (2023). Swarm Intelligence and Evolutionary Machine Learning Algorithms for COVID-19: Pandemic and Epidemic Review. In A. Suresh Kumar, U. Kose, S. Sharma, & S. Jerald Nirmal Kumar (Eds.), *Dynamics of Swarm Intelligence Health Analysis for the Next Generation* (pp. 83–103). IGI Global. doi:10.4018/978-1-6684-6894-4.ch005

Sutton, R. S., & Barto, A. G. (2018). *Reinforcement learning: An introduction* (2nd ed.). MIT Press.

Szegedy, C., Liu, W., Jia, Y., Sermanet, P., Reed, S., Anguelov, D., & Rabinovich, A. (2015). Going deeper with convolutions. In *Proceedings of the IEEE conference on computer vision and pattern recognition* (pp. 1-9).

Thakur-Wernz, P., Cantwell, J., & Samant, S. (2019). Impact of international entry choices on the nature and type of innovation: Evidence from emerging economy firms from the Indian bio-pharmaceutical industry. *International Business Review*, 28(6), 101601. doi:10.1016/j.ibusrev.2019.101601

Thorbecke, W. (1997). On stock market returns and monetary policy. *The Journal of Finance*, 76(2), 635–654. doi:10.1111/j.1540-6261.1997.tb04816.x

Titford, M. (2006). A short history of histopathology technique. *Journal of Histotechnology*, 29(2), 99–110. doi:10.1179/his.2006.29.2.99

Topol, E. J. (2018). High-performance medicine: The convergence of human and artificial intelligence. *Nature Medicine*, 25(1), 44–56. doi:10.103841591-018-0300-7 PMID:30617339

Tremblay, D.-G., Yagoubi, A., & Psyché, V. (2021). Digital Transformation: An Analysis of the Role of Technology Service Providers in Montreal's Emerging AI Business Ecosystem. In Digitalization and Firm Performance: Examining the Strategic Impact (pp. 17-44).

Turing, A. (1950). Computing machinery and intelligence. MIND: A quarterly review of Psychology and Phylosophy. Vol. *Lix.*, 236, 433–460.

Turing, A. M. (1950). Computing machinery and intelligence. *Mind*, 59(236), 433–460. doi:10.1093/mind/LIX.236.433

U.S. Food and Drug Administration (FDA). (2019). *Proposed Regulatory Framework for Modifications to Artificial Intelligence/Machine Learning-Based Software as a Medical Device.* FDA. https://www.fda.gov/media/122535/download

Vale, P. M., Gibbs, H. K., Vale, R., Christie, M., Florence, E., Munger, J., & Sabaini, D. (2019). The expansion of intensive beef farming to the Brazilian Amazon. *Global Environmental Change*, 57, 101922. doi:10.1016/j.gloenvcha.2019.05.006

Veeraraghavan, P., & Vasudevan, S. (2020). AI-based cybersecurity for industrial control systems: A comprehensive review. *IEEE Access : Practical Innovations, Open Solutions*, 8, 125318–125335.

Venter, K., & Moolman, A. (2022). An Appreciative Inquiry Approach to Community-Based Research for Development of a Social Enterprise. *Community-based Research with Vulnerable Populations: Ethical, Inclusive and Sustainable Frameworks for Knowledge Generation*, 169-186. Taylor & Francis.

Vetter, T. (1988). *The Ideas and Meditative Practices of Early Buddhism*. E.J. Brill.

von Baer, K. E., & Sarton, G. (1931). The discovery of the mammalian egg and the foundation of modern embryology. *Isis*, 16(2), 315–377. doi:10.1086/346613

Von Krogh, G., Roberson, Q., & Gruber, M. (2023). Recognizing and Utilizing Novel Research Opportunities with Artificial Intelligence. *Academy of Management Journal, 66*(2), 367–373. doi:10.5465/amj.2023.4002

Wach, K., Duong, C. D., Ejdys, J., Kazlauskaitė, R., Korzynski, P., Mazurek, G., Paliszkiewicz, J., & Ziemba, E. (2023). The dark side of generative artificial intelligence: A critical analysis of controversies and risks of ChatGPT. *Entrepreneurial Business and Economics Review, 11*(2), 7–30. doi:10.15678/EBER.2023.110201

Wachnik, B. (2022). Analysis of the use of artificial intelligence in the management of Industry 4.0 projects: The perspective of Polish industry. *Production Engineering Archives, 28*(1), 56–63. doi:10.30657/pea.2022.28.07

Wang, L., & Wong, A. (2020). *COVID-Net: A Tailored Deep Convolutional Neural Network Design for Detection of COVID-19 Cases from Chest Radiography Images.* arXiv preprint arXiv:2003.09871.

Wang, N., Issa, R. R. A., & Anumba, C. J. (2021). Query Answering System for Building Information Modeling Using BERT NN Algorithm and NLG. In *Computing in Civil Engineering 2021 - Selected Papers from the ASCE International Conference on Computing in Civil Engineering 2021* (pp. 425-432). ASCE.

Watts, A. (1989). *The Way of Zen.* Vintage Books.

WEF. (2023). The future of jobs Report 2023. *Insight Report.* WEF. https://www.weforum.org/reports/the-future-of-jobs-report-2023/

Weng, S. F., Reps, J., Kai, J., Garibaldi, J. M., & Qureshi, N. (2018). Can machine-learning improve cardiovascular risk prediction using routine clinical data? *PLoS One, 13*(1), e0194025. PMID:28376093

Westerhoff, J. (2007). *Nagarjuna's Madhyamaka.* University of Durham.

West, J. B. (2013). Marcello Malpighi and the discovery of the pulmonary capillaries and alveoli. *American Journal of Physiology. Lung Cellular and Molecular Physiology, 304*(6), L383–L390. doi:10.1152/ajplung.00016.2013 PMID:23377345

Wikipedia. (2023). *Teoria do consumidor.* Wikipedia. https://pt.wikipedia.org/wiki/Teoria_do_consumidor

Wilson, J. W. (1947). Virchow's contribution to the cell theory. *Journal of the History of Medicine and Allied Sciences, 2*(2), 163–178. doi:10.1093/jhmas/II.2.163 PMID:20249916

Wishart, G. C., Campisi, M., Boswell, M., Chapman, D., Shackleton, V., Iddles, S., Hallett, A., & Britton, P. D. (2010). The accuracy of digital infrared imaging for breast cancer detection in women undergoing breast biopsy. *European Journal of Surgical Oncology, 36*(6), 535–540. doi:10.1016/j.ejso.2010.04.003 PMID:20452740

Compilation of References

Wojtczak, S. (2022). Endowing Artificial Intelligence with legal subjectivity. *AI & Society, 37*(1), 1–9. doi:10.100700146-021-01147-7

World Economic Forum. (2023). *Podcast - AI: Why everyone's talking about the promise and risks of this 'powerful wild beast'*. WEF. https://www.weforum.org/podcasts/radio-davos/episodes/artificial-intelligence-ai-episode-1?source=podcast_

About the Contributors

Nuno Geada has a Master's degree in Systems Information Management by Polytechnic Institute of Setúbal - School of Business Sciences and Management -Setúbal, Degree in Industrial Management and Technology by Polytechnic Institute of Setúbal - School of Technology of Setubal. He has written chapters, and papers to journals about topics regarding information technology management and strategic change management. He is from the Editorial Board - Associate Editor from International Journal of Business Strategy and Automation (IJBSA). He is the Editor of the book Reviving Businesses with New Organizational Change Management Strategies. His main research interests in information systems management, strategy, knowledge management, change management, and information technology management adoption in business contexts throw models and frameworks. He works as a Professor and a Researcher.

George Leal Jamil is a professor of several post-graduation courses from Minas Gerais, Brazil. He has two post-doctoral titles (from Universidade do Porto, Portugal - market intelligence and from Univsersidad Politecnica de Cartagena, Spain - Entrepreneurship). Doctorate in Information Science from the Federal University of Minas Gerais (UFMG), Masters degree in Computer Science (UFMG) and undergraduate in Electric Engineering (UFMG). More than thirty books in the information technology, innovation, project management, information science, marketing and strategic management areas, as author, co-author and Editor. He works also as a business consultant and as an active ecosystem agent in business innovation and startups front in several countries. His main research interests are information systems management, strategy, knowledge management, software engineering, marketing and IT adoption in business contexts. As a lemma: To take scientific knowledge to the people, to the market, improving society.

***

Paulo Alves holds a Ph.D. in Business Administration from FGV, an M.Sc. in Public Administration from FGV, and a B.Sc. in Mechanical Engineering from IME. Currently, he works as a full professor at Fundação Dom Cabral (FDC). He was Under-secretary of Planning to the Secretariat of Planning and Management of the Rio de Janeiro State (SEPLAG-RJ) from 2007 to 2009. His professional experience includes the sectors of government, defense, aerospace, education and energy. He was a Brazilian Army Captain serving from 1990 to 2002. As a professor he has worked at ESPM, FDC, FGV, IBMEC, IME and PUC in Brazil. He has already lectured in Brown University, CKGSB, HULT, INSEAD, ISB, John Hopkins University, Kellogg, NOVA SBE, Saint Gallen, Schulich, Skema, Skolkovo, UT Dallas, and Vlerick in joint programs with FDC. He attended the Global Colloquium in Participant-Centered Learning (GLOCOLL) from Harvard Business School in 2012. He was a consultant to BAT, IADB/BID, Petrobrás, Shell, and the US DoC. Professor Paulo Alves was a Fellow of the Strategic Planning Society (SPS-UK), and is a Founder Member of the Strategic Management Forum. He is the author of the e-book 'Emerging Markets Report published by AVEC, the books 'Jogos de Empresas' (Business Games) published by Pearson/Makron Books, 'Jogos e Simulações de Empresas' (Business Games and Simulations) by Alta Books, 'Gestão Pública Contemporânea' (Contemporary Public Management) by Alta Books, and 'Um século em quatro atos' by Alta books. He won the Best Marketing Strategy prize, given by Publicis, in the L'Oréal Marketing Award 2004 as an advisor professor. He was ranked 29th in the Best Business Professor Award promoted by The Economist Intelligence Unit in 2012-13.

C.V. Suresh Babu is a pioneer in content development. A true entrepreneur, he founded Anniyappa Publications, a company that is highly active in publishing books related to Computer Science and Management. Dr. C.V. Suresh Babu has also ventured into SB Institute, a center for knowledge transfer. He holds a Ph.D. in Engineering Education from the National Institute of Technical Teachers Training & Research in Chennai, along with seven master's degrees in various disciplines such as Engineering, Computer Applications, Management, Commerce, Economics, Psychology, Law, and Education. Additionally, he has UGC-NET/SET qualifications in the fields of Computer Science, Management, Commerce, and Education. Currently, Dr. C.V. Suresh Babu is a Professor in the Department of Information Technology at the School of Computing Science, Hindustan Institute of Technology and Science (Hindustan University) in Padur, Chennai, Tamil Nadu, India. For more information, you can visit his personal blog at .

Karina Coleta is an Associate professor at Fundacao Dom Cabral (FDC) in the areas of Strategy and Business Models since 2017. She also works as a researcher at the FDC Strategy Reference Center. She is the cofounder of the FDC Practical Community in Business Models. She has gathered experience as a researcher since 2001 when she started to work at the Strategy and Marketing Center at the Federal University of Minas Gerais. Since 1999 she has also worked as a technical and literary translator in the fields of Business Administration and Theology. She has papers, book chapters, and teaching cases published in conferences, journals, and databases in Brazil and abroad. Her interest areas are Strategy, Business Models, and Social Impact Businesses. She holds a Ph.D. in Business Administration from Pontifícia Universidade Católica de Minas Gerais. Master's degree in Theology from Faculdade Jesuíta de Teologia e Filosofia. Specialization in Translation Studies from Universidade Gama Filho. Graduation in Economics from Pontifícia Universidade de Minas Gerais.

Joao Manuel Fernandes holds a Bachelor's degree in Portuguese Studies since 2019 and a Master's degree in Philosophy since 2021, with a thesis titled "Errância e Espiritualidade em Matsuo Basho." He is a member of the Centro de Estudos Bocageanos. His research mainly revolves around post-Pombaline Portuguese literature, and Eastern philosophy. He has published articles in national and international Journals, and has attended national and international conferences as a speaker.

Juliana Igarashi has a Master's in Management, Research and Development in the Pharmaceutical Industry by Fundação Oswaldo Cruz (Fiocruz - 2019). She is certified by SAP Global (2015) in MM (Materials Management). Specialization in Production Engineering from Universidade Federal Fluminense (UFF - 2014). Degree in Industrial Pharmacy also from UFF (2009). Worked in the coordination of SAP application projects and New Product Launches in the categories of medicines, cosmetics and health products. From August 2020 to February 2021, he was the technology transfer project leader (technological partner Astrazeneca) for the Final Processing (Drug Product) of the COVID-19 vaccine in Bio-Manguinhos using imported IFA. In March/2021, he took over as technology transfer project leader for the production of the API COVID-19 - Drug Substance. As of March 2022, in addition to acting as project leader in the scale-up of the API COVID-19 produced in Bio-Manguinos, he started to act as Project Manager of the PDP for technology transfer of the monoclonal antibody Adalimuambe

Kubilay Dogan Kilic graduated from Ankara University, Faculty of Science, Department of Biology as valedictorian in the faculty. He works as a Research Assistant Doctor at Ege University Faculty of Medicine, Department of Histology and Embryology. In addition, he is a visiting researcher at the Leibniz Institute Berlin Naturkund Museum. The author has many articles, book chapters, books indexed in national and international indexes, and many national and international presentations.

Jorge Magalhães postgraduated in Competitive Intelligence for Public Health. Doctor and Master in Sciences in Management and Technological Innovation. Has over 20 years of experience in strategic management in the pharmaceutical Industrial Operations and in the last 14 years to act in R, D & I for Public Health area at FIOCRUZ. Published 03 books, 9 book chapters and several articles in journals indexed. Actually work in Technology Innovation Center (NIT-Far) at FIOCRUZ. It is leader of the CNPq Research Group Knowledge Management and Prospecting Health. The emphasis of their research permeate the identification, extraction and analysis of essential information within the "Big data" for Health, regarding the Management and Technological Innovation. The topics covered are inherent in Global Health, in which involves the pharmaceutical industry, pharmochemical and public health. Investigations are carried out through the development of prospective and technological scenarios of information science tools, Competitive Intelligence and Knowledge Management. Included in this context the analysis of BIG DATA, Web 2.0, Health 2.0 Technological Trends, market, Patents and Knowledge Translation.

Filiz Mizrak is an Assistant Professor holding a Doctorate degree in Management and Strategy from Istanbul Medipol University. She was born on May 12, 1986. She completed her undergraduate studies in American Culture and Literature at Istanbul University in 2009. Later, she pursued her Master's degree in Executive MBA at Bahçeşehir University in 2015. Filiz MIZRAK's passion for research and academia led her to obtain her doctoral degree in Management and Strategy from Istanbul Medipol University in 2021. Currently, she is working as an Assistant Professor at Istanbul Medipol University. Her research interests include strategic management, organizational behavior, and business strategy.

Fabian Salum is a professor and leading researcher of competitive strategies, emphasizing Business Models and Innovation Management at FDC. Considered one of the most influential Professors and Researchers in second place in the ranking of the World Scientist and University Ranking of the year 2023. Fabian holds a PhD in Business Administration from the Pontifical Catholic University of Minas Gerais – Brazil, in the sandwich modality at INSEAD – France. He has a Masters in Business Administration from Fundação Pedro Leopoldo (Brazil) and Mechanical

Engineering from the Pontifical Catholic University of Minas Gerais – Brazil. As an executive, he held technical and management positions, reaching C-level positions in companies such as Telemig, Toshiba, Unilever, Lear Corporation, Fiat, and Votorantim. He was entrepreneurial in creating a start-up in the e-commerce and heavy machinery retail sector. He was a partner owner of a bovine leather treatment industry. His professional experience accumulates in Telecommunications, Education, Automotive, Consumer Goods, Mining, Engineering and Energy. As a professor, he has worked at FGV and IBMEC in Brazil and has taught for Kellogg, CKGSB, and INSEAD in joint programs offered by FDC. Professor Salum teaches postgraduate courses, Executive MBA, open programs, and customized programs for large companies, in addition to working in corporate partnership programs for family businesses in Brazil and Latin America. He was a columnist for EXAME Magazine in Brazil and is the author of some articles, books, and chapters published by Cengage Learning, Alta Books, and Palgrave MacMillan. At FDC, Salum was Director of the Sustainable Growth Partnership (PCS), Coordinator of the Innovation Reference Center (CRI Minas), Coordinator of the Strategy Reference Center and Technical Coordinator of the Partners for Excellence Program (PAEX) and, more recently after his stay for 1 year at INSEAD, he creates the Practical Business Model Community () in partnership with other professors from educational institutions in Brazil, Latin America and Europe. He is an independent advisor to medium and large companies and is a member of the Innovation and Strategic Management committees.

Index

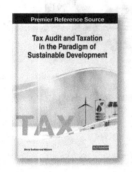  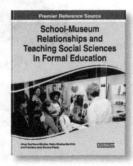 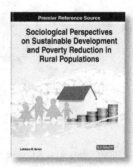

Printed in the United States
by Baker & Taylor Publisher Services